Handbook for Clinical Nutrition Services Management

M. Rosita Schiller, RSM, PhD, RD, LD
Professor and Director, Medical Dietetics Division
The Ohio State University
Columbus, Ohio

Judith A. Gilbride, PhD, RD
Associate Professor, Department of Nutrition,
Food, and Hotel Management
New York University
New York, New York

Julie O'Sullivan Maillet, PhD, RD
Associate Professor and Director, Dietetic Internship
Chairman, Department of Primary Care
University of Medicine and Dentistry of New Jersey
Newark, New Jersey

AN ASPEN PUBLICATION®
Aspen Publishers, Inc.
Gaithersburg, Maryland
1991

Library of Congress Cataloging-in-Publication Data

Schiller, M. Rosita.
Handbook for clinical nutrition services management / M. Rosita Schiller,
Judith A. Gilbride, Julie O'Sullivan Maillet.
p. cm.
Includes bibliographical references.
Includes index.
ISBN: 0-8342-0193-3
1. Dietetics—Practice—Handbooks, manuals, etc. 2. Health facilities—Food
service—Management—Handbooks, manuals, etc. I. Gilbride, Judith A.
II. Maillet, Julie O'Sullivan. III. Title. [DNLM: 1. Dietetics. 2. Food Services,
Hospital—organization & administration. 3. Personnel Management. WX 168
S334h]
RM218.5.S35   1991
362.1'76—dc20
DNLM/DLC
for Library of Congress
90-14539
CIP

Aspen Publishers, Inc., grants permission for photocopying for limited personal or
internal use. This consent does not extend to other kinds of copying, such as copying
for general distribution, for advertising or promotional purposes, for creating new
collective works, or for resale. For information, address Aspen Publishers, Inc.,
Permissions Department, 200 Orchard Ridge Drive, Gaithersburg, Maryland 20878.

Aspen Publishers, Inc., is not affiliated with the American Society
of Parenteral and Enteral Nutrition

The authors have made every effort to ensure the accuracy of the information herein,
particularly with regard to drug selection and dose. However, appropriate information
sources should be consulted, especially for new or unfamiliar drugs or procedures. It
is the responsibility of every practitioner to evaluate the appropriateness of a particular
opinion in the context of actual clinical situations and with due consideration to new
developments. Authors, editors, and the publisher cannot be held responsible for any
typographical or other errors found in this book.

Editorial Services: Lorna Perkins

Library of Congress Catalog Card Number: 90-14539
ISBN: 0-8342-0193-3

Printed in the United States of America

1 2 3 4 5

To the memory of our fathers who
inspired in us high ideals, dedication,
and professionalism.

Table of Contents

Foreword ix

Preface xiii

Acknowledgments xvi

PART I—   FOUNDATIONS OF CLINICAL
             MANAGEMENT   1

Chapter 1—   The Context of Clinical Management   3
             Why Clinical Dietetic Management?   3
             The Scope of Clinical Dietetic Management   4
             Functions of Management   8
             Management Styles 12
             Action Orientation 12

Chapter 2—   Internal and External Influences on Clinical
             Management 17
             Overview 17
             Departmental Milieu 19
             Institutional Characteristics 23
             External Factors Affecting Clinical Management 28
             Guidelines for Analysis 31

Chapter 3—   A Framework for the Clinical Dietetic Manager . . . 35
             Mission and Goals 35
             Establishing Policies and Procedures 36
             Organizational Design 40
             Summary 49

Chapter 4— **Developing Skills for Effective Clinical Management** **51**

Personal Background and Attributes 51
Self-Evaluation 56
Management Skills 56

PART II— **HUMAN DIMENSIONS OF MANAGING DIETETIC PRACTICE** **65**

Chapter 5— **Determining Clinical Nutrition Staffing Needs** **67**

Organizational Plans 67
Systems Identification 68
Process of Patient Care 70
Services Provided to the Patient 77
Cost-Containment Issues 78
Decision-Making Capacity 78
Analyzing Level of Performance 78
Levels of Patient Care 79

Chapter 6— **Staff Recruitment, Selection, and Retention** **85**

Selection of Staff 85
Orientation 89
Performance Appraisal 89
Staff Development 96
Job Satisfaction 97
Retention 97

Chapter 7— **Professional Development** **99**

Patterns of Development 101
Role of the Clinical Dietetic Manager 105
Assessment of Staff Development Needs 105
Continuing Education Alternatives 110
Justifying the Cost of Continuing Education 112

Chapter 8— **Team Building** **119**

Collaboration and Networking 119
Problem Solving 119
Action Plans 120
Incorporating Change and Innovation 122
Delineation of Responsibilities and Rewards 123

Delegation 123
Leadership Styles 124
Mentoring 126

Chapter 9—   **Ethical and Legal Issues** **129**

Concepts in Ethics 129
A Decision-Making Model 132
Clinical Applications 133
Management Applications: Role of the Clinical
    Dietetic Manager 138
Research and Education Applications 143

PART III—   **STRUCTURAL ENVIRONMENT FOR**
    MANAGERIAL DECISION MAKING **147**

Chapter 10—   **Quality Assurance** **149**

Quality Indicators 150
Audits as Research 150
The Quality Assurance Process 152

Chapter 11—   **Productivity and Cost Containment** **161**

Components of Productivity 161
Matching Professional Level and Job Function 162
Time Utilization Review 163
Departmental Productivity 168
Cost Containment 174
Justifying Staffing Needs 175
Costs and Benefits of Clinical Dietetic Services 176
Cost Effectiveness of Nutritional Support 181

Chapter 12—   **Managing Fiscal Affairs** **185**

A Case for Survival 185
Fee-for-Service 187
Cost of Services 190
Budget for Clinical Dietetic Services 190
Budget Reductions 194

Chapter 13—   **Decisions Regarding Equipment and Technology**   **197**

Technology Assessment 198
Establishment of a Formulary 198

Selection of Enteral Equipment 200
Selection of Other Equipment 201

Chapter 14— **Managing Patient Nutrition Education** **209**

Development of a Patient Education Program 210
Preparing Printed Materials 216
Developing Visuals 218

Chapter 15— **Health Promotion and Marketing Plans** **227**

Health Promotion and Disease Prevention 227
Role of the Dietitian in Health Promotion 229
Dietetic Marketing 229

Chapter 16— **Managing Continuity of Care** **237**

Discharge Planning and Referral Systems 237
Ambulatory Care 244
Home Care 248
Developing Continuing Care Programs 252

PART IV— **PROFESSIONAL SKILLS DEVELOPMENT** **259**

Chapter 17— **Communications** **261**

Oral Communications 261
Effective Meeting Management 262
Policy and Procedure Manuals 265
Diet and Nutrition Manuals 266
Short Memos and Letters 267
Reports and Proposals 270
Menu Minders 271
Medical Records 272

Chapter 18— **Research in Clinical Nutrition** **277**

Current Status of Research 277
Importance of Research in the Profession 277
Research Role of the Clinical Dietetic Manager 278
Topics for Clinical Research 286
Research Resources 288
Research Ethics 288

Chapter 19— **Responsibilities in Professional Education** **293**

Components of Professional Education   293
Framework for Clinical Instruction   296
Teaching Responsibilities   297
Assessment of Performance   299
Teaching Other Health Professionals   304

Chapter 20—   Evaluating Clinical Nutrition Services   307

Definitions   307
Essence of Evaluation   308
Evaluation and Planning   310
Evaluation and Quality Assurance   311
Evaluation Process   312

Chapter 21—   Moving toward the Future: Strategic Planning   321

History of Dietetic Practice   321
Evolution of Hospital Dietetics   323
Strategic Planning   325
Issues of the Coming Decades in Dietetics   328
Other Health Care Trends   330
Planning Outcomes   331

Appendix A—   Job Descriptions   335

Appendix B—   Types of Evaluations   339

Appendix C—   Suggested Terminology for Nutrition Services   343

Appendix D—   Nutrition-Related ICD-9-CM Codes   349

Index   353

Foreword

There is little doubt that health care has taken on a business orientation. To function effectively and successfully in this modern, competitive environment, all dietitians need to acquire new skills and knowledge above and beyond their excellent training and preparation in dietetics. They need to develop and hone management, marketing, and sales skills. Dietitians must focus their attention and energies on selling their profession, their services, and themselves. They must be familiar and comfortable with budgeting and reimbursement practices. And, of course, they need to keep pace with technological advances, industry-wide research, and education.

Dietitians also need to acquire and polish the more intangible qualities of leadership and team building.

It is necessary to harness all of these skills to develop strategies and programs to promote the profession, to provide evidence of the cost efficiency of their services, and to compete successfully for funds. Once these formidable professional skills are mastered, they must then be put to use in a highly competitive health care environment.

It is apparent to me that only the strong, well-informed, well-organized, and creative will survive and prosper in this emerging health care environment and helping dietitians acquire those skills is precisely the aim of *Handbook for Clinical Nutrition Services Management* by Drs. Rosita Schiller, Judith Gilbride, and Julie O'Sullivan Maillet. This book offers important insights and practical advice for all those employed in nutrition services and justifiably could be subtitled, "A Guidebook for Survival and Success."

The present status of dietetics—in fact, of the health care profession as a whole—is the result of a veritable revolution, one that continues today and is characterized by explosive changes across a broad spectrum. We see its effects in the diagnosis and treatment of illness in which new technologies, such as lithotripters, arthroscopes, magnetic resonance imagers, and CT scanners, are in wide use. Computers are being applied to x-ray analysis, organ-sharing networks, and diagnostics. Some hospitals are presently using a bedside computer for individual electronic patient records. Noninvasive surgery, including the use of lasers to open blocked arteries, gene therapy, organ implants, artificial organs, biotech wonder drugs, customized cancer treatment, exotic fertility procedures, and even robotics may be common-place before long.

Equally dramatic changes are occurring in nutrition and food. In the not-too-distant future, we may be eating "super foods," and unhealthy ingredients will be missing from our basic four food groups. The American diet may soon include 90 percent fat-free beef and genetically engineered grains, vegetables, and fruits with higher nutritive values. Already, scientists are working on an enzyme that removes cholesterol from ice cream, and researchers are conducting experiments to develop cholesterol-free egg yolks.

There are also changes in modes of health care delivery. Patients are discharged from hospitals "quicker and sicker," and many are treated in their homes or in nursing homes in long-term care, day care, or elderly care programs. Health maintenance organizations (HMOs) and preferred provider organizations (PPOs) are proliferating.

Future health care undoubtedly will be delivered through a combination of solo and group practices, health care conglomerates, megaclinics, and community hospitals. In fact, some predict that, by the year 2000, virtually no physicians will remain in private practice.

Hospitals too are undergoing major changes. Not too long ago the trend was toward national chains. Now it appears that the dominant form may be regional and local alliances between noncompeting institutions that share services—and even staff—to promote effectiveness.

Rising costs and the resultant effort to contain them also are altering American health care. In 1988 health care costs rose by 10 percent, marking another record year in which medical inflation outpaced the consumer price index. By the year 2000, the annual health care bill is expected to exceed 15 percent of the country's gross national product.

At the same time as costs are increasing, reimbursements are declining. For example, a 40 to 50 percent decrease in occupancy rates in hospitals is likely, and the length of stay will decrease further to only 6.3 days in the next few years. Diagnostic-related groups (DRGs) have been instituted in an effort to contain costs.

The health care profession and its practice also are being affected dramatically by external factors, including the state of the national economy and demographic changes, particularly the "graying of America." As the life-span is increasing, the fastest-growing segment in the United States is people older than 80. In fact, by the year 2000, it is estimated that more than five million Americans will be at least 85 years old—ten times the 1950 total. This shift has great economic consequences; it is likely that half of all health care expenditures will be made for this older population segment who are sicker and require more costly care than younger people. For example, more than half of all present-day hospital days are accounted for by those over 65 years old.

Another important trend is the wellness movement and its offshoot, the move toward self-treatment. Being healthy and staying healthy are becoming lifetime pursuits for many Americans, and a number of hospitals have established wellness programs as revenue generators.

All of these changes, developments, and trends spell CHALLENGE—in capital letters—for all health care professionals and for dietitians in particular.

Dietitians may well find themselves working in settings that differ greatly from the traditional ones. Few will be working for independent community hospitals. Those who do may no longer be exclusively in dietetic departments, but rather in geriatric, home care, nursing, and psychology departments and, it is hoped, in top management positions. More will be employed in industry within the intricate organizational structures of corporations. And as hospitals and community services become increasingly involved in alternative health care settings—in nursing homes, PPOs, and HMOs—and even in supermarkets and health clubs, dietitians will find themselves working in these diverse settings as well.

The authors of *Handbook for Clinical Nutrition Services Management,* all experienced and highly knowledgeable professionals, have drawn on their respective professional backgrounds in research, education, and management to create a work that will be an invaluable guide for dietitians no matter where they find themselves working in the present or future. All others employed in or affiliated with nutrition services will find much in this book to assist them in their professional pursuits.

Dr. Rosita Schiller uses her international experience in dietetics to depict accurately the dramatic changes taking place in dietetics, as well as the future of the profession. To this broad-brush perspective, Dr. Judith A. Gilbride, an outstanding teacher, adds her uncommon ability to make theories come alive. Completing this exceptional mix of vision and practical advice are the insights of Dr. Julie O'Sullivan Maillet. A first-class educator, she applies her experience in management to offer a look into the day-to-day workings of the dietitian in clinical practice.

Whether your interest is theoretical or practical or whether your concern is developing management or communications skills, cost-effectiveness guidance, professional development, or marketing—and these are skills for all health care professionals, not only food service managers—you will find the information and guidance you need in *Handbook for Clinical Nutrition Services Management*.

Susan Calvert Finn, PhD, RD
Director, Nutrition Services
Ross Laboratories
Columbus, Ohio

Preface

During the past decade the health care industry has been characterized by dynamism and change. Increased attention has been focused on the importance of nutrition, accountability, cost containment, marketing, productivity, preventive health, and quality assurance. Clinical dietetic managers are central figures in the application of these concepts in nutritional care settings.

Traditionally, the practice of dietetics has been arbitrarily divided into three broad areas of specialization: food service administration, clinical nutrition, and community dietetics. Management components of dietetics have been primarily associated with food service. Only recently have clinical dietitians recognized themselves as managers of nutritional care. With this recognition, dietitians have become aware of the need for management skills to function effectively in the clinical environment.

Dietitians are searching for guidance and resources to help them grapple with management problems confronting them in daily practice. Several newsletters and portions of other books offer fragmented information about the management of nutritional care services. However, this book brings together in one place numerous tools and guidelines often used in clinical management. It is designed both for clinical dietetic managers and clinical dietitians aspiring toward management positions who wish to sharpen their management skills, find fresh approaches to the challenges of daily practice, and gain new insights into clinical management responsibilities. The book can also be used as a textbook for courses in clinical dietetic management in undergraduate, graduate, and dietetic internship programs.

This book illustrates how the principles of management can be applied in patient care settings. Theories, techniques, and tools are drawn from current literature and innovative practice settings and adapted to clinical nutrition management. The holistic approach offered here synthesizes concepts of clinical management into a unified whole.

Foundations of clinical dietetic management are discussed at the outset. Part I provides an overview of management principles and illustrates how mission and goal statements, standards of practice, organizational design, and daily procedures are developed to create the framework for management in the clinical setting. There is a tool for assessing leadership styles, and managers are encouraged to develop a plan for improving areas of weakness that inhibit high-quality managerial performance. Those who use the book are encouraged to ADVANCE practice through embracing some important concepts and activities emphasized by the acronym: *A*ssessment, *D*evelopment, *V*ision, *A*ccounting, *N*utritional care, *C*ommunication, and *E*valuation. Internal and external factors influencing clinical management are then analyzed; readers are encouraged to conduct an individualized analysis of these factors to gain further insight into their own practice settings.

Part II deals with human dimensions of managing dietetic practice. Suggested models are offered for determining staffing needs based on system components, patient services, levels of patient care, levels of performance, and time utilization. The chapter on managing nutritional care personnel covers important aspects of staff selection, orientation, performance appraisal, development, and retention.

Other aspects of human involvement are also addressed. A discussion on professional development offers new insights on patterns of staff development and suggests several alternatives for meeting both inservice and continuing education needs in the department. Team building is an essential task of today's managers. The text offers practical advice on collaboration and networking, problem solving, incorporating change and innovation, delegation, mentoring, and achieving job satisfaction.

Technological advances and diversity of personal value systems contribute to new ethical dilemmas. Ethical dimensions of nutritional care, management, and research and education are discussed, with emphasis on the role of the clinical nutrition manager. Guidelines for practice and a decision-making model are included to encourage ethical behaviors and to facilitate problem identification and sound decision making.

The third part of the book contains strategies for dealing with the technical dimensions of management: quality assurance, productivity, fiscal affairs, equipment and technology, patient education, marketing, and continuity of care. Chapters in this part contain a plethora of data collection forms, analysis sheets, and procedural guidelines. Key elements in this part are directions for time utilization review, costing of services, and a model marketing plan. Step-by-step guidelines are also given for the development of a business plan for extended nutrition services in the community.

The last part addresses professional skills for the clinical nutrition manager. It includes suggestions for improving written communication and providing leadership for research and professional education. A tool is offered for identifying personal development needs and guiding the professional development of staff members.

One important component of this book is an evaluation tool based on criteria for a model nutrition services unit. Clinical nutrition managers can use this instrument to identify departmental strengths and areas needing improvement. The last chapter offers a brief history of clinical dietetics and suggests methods of identifying new trends in the field and steps for preparing a strategic plan to address changes in both health care and dietetic practice.

Major concerns of clinical nutrition managers are addressed in this book. It is designed for those who not only have a strong background in clinical dietetic practice but have also assumed responsibility for the overall management of clinical dietetic services. In this role the clinical manager is responsible for asserting vision, setting goals and plans, motivating others to share in the quest for excellence, communicating details on all facets of the operation, solving problems and introducing innovations, maintaining fiscal accountability in a cost-sensitive environment, and providing opportunities for growth and change of both staff members and the nutrition service unit.

The authors bring both a wealth of experience and creative insights to this project. All have a background in clinical dietetic practice and management. All are currently in academic settings where they continually interact with clinical dietitians who work with their students in all types of dietetic education programs: baccalaureate (Plan IV/V), coordinated, graduate, internship, and approved preprofessional practice (AP4) arrangements. Information presented here is both practical and informed, challenging dietitians to ADVANCE the practice of management in the clinical setting.

Acknowledgments

Writing can be both stimulating and rewarding. It is also hard work and can be accomplished effectively only with the helpful assistance of colleagues and associates who serve as critics, reviewers, supporters, and cheerleaders.

We give special recognition to Linda Toohey, RD; Riva Touger-Decker, RD, MA; Joyce Wolitzer, RD, MA; Nina Rubin, RD, MA; and Doug Maier, RD for reviewing the manuscript. These clinical dietetic managers offered solid criticisms and gave practical suggestions for making the book a down-to-earth guide for dealing with everyday situations in clinical nutrition settings. With their assistance, this book will help dietitians meet the challenges of daily practice, upgrade their managerial skills, and advance the practice of clinical dietetic management.

A note of appreciation goes to Syed Haque, PhD, at the University of Medicine and Dentistry of New Jersey (UMDNJ) for technical assistance on the computer, to Cherlyn Foster for assisting in the design and development of forms, and to the UMDNJ Dietetic Interns class of 1989 for locating current references.

Our gratitude also goes to friends and family members whose understanding and encouragement helped us keep priorities in order even during the rigorous process of manuscript development.

Part I

Foundations of Clinical Management

Chapter 1

The Context of Clinical Management

Competent managers are needed to shape, direct, and control clinical nutrition services. More and more, administrators, physicians, and consumers recognize nutrition as an important dimension of total health care. To achieve maximum effectiveness all nutrition services must be well managed. This chapter provides an introduction to clinical dietetic management, including definitions, justification, scope of practice, functions, styles of management, and a call for action.

Changes in dietetic practice have spawned a new career option: clinical nutrition or clinical dietetic management. This role combines the professional knowledge and skills of dietetics with the administrative and leadership demands of management in a clinical setting.

As manager, the dietitian captures a vision for dietetic services and then applies the principles and functions of management to achieve desired goals through the efforts of subordinates. The clinical dietetic manager comes from the clinical area, but upon promotion, enters into the management arena.

WHY CLINICAL DIETETIC MANAGEMENT?

The growth of the management sector has been dramatic during the last century. Statistics from the U.S. Bureau of the Census indicate that in 1980 more than one-third of workers were classified as "managerial and professional" (Drucker 1988). Management has been instrumental in bringing together people with varied training and skills to achieve common goals. According to Drucker, the fundamental task of management is "to make people capable of joint performance by giving them common goals, common values, the right structure and the ongoing training and development they need to perform and respond to change" (Drucker 1988, 65).

Dietetic staffs are made up of highly educated professionals—what Drucker calls knowledge workers—with diverse knowledge and skills. It is a challenge for managers to raise the productivity of knowledge workers, and therefore they must emphasize the value of human resources and motivation.

More and more, dietetics is described as a service-oriented profession in which job performance focuses on ideas, information, and translation of knowledge and, according to Drucker's viewpoint, in which inputs and outputs are tangible (Drucker 1988).

Major activities of clinical dietetic managers revolve around the nutritional care of patients. Recent changes in health care have had a profound effect on how services are organized and provided. Hospital administrators want to protect "the bottom line" and, at the same time, administer high-quality care.

Fiscal constraints have affected all departments and have caused hospitals to diversify and improve the efficacy and effectiveness of care. Dietitians are often poorly prepared to compete for scarce health care dollars. In fact, a managerial role for the clinical nutritionist arose in 1980 when it became obvious that management of human and material resources was essential to the growth of quality nutrition services. In today's hospital, every dietitian must provide the best quality service in the most time- and cost-effective manner.

A clinical dietetic manager is a dietetic practitioner who manages individuals and resources to accomplish the objectives of a clinical nutrition service. Inherent in this position are a solid base and skills in developing goals and objectives, policies and procedures, and standards of practice for the service; managing staff; increasing productivity and fiscal responsibility; and promoting programs, research, and quality assurance systems. Often, a well-trained clinical manager can assist staff in redefining responsibilities and expanding opportunities for lateral and vertical career changes. Increased visibility results from the promotion of clinical programs and specific services and benefits the profession as a whole. To advance clinical dietetic management, the practitioner needs the right mixture of management tools and techniques, dedication to patient care, and an appreciation of health care structures and organizational policies.

THE SCOPE OF CLINICAL DIETETIC MANAGEMENT

Specific responsibilities of the clinical dietetic manager depend on the nature of the organization, the size of the institution, and the written job description. However, general responsibilities are assumed by all clinical dietetic managers. Exhibit 1-1 provides an overview of clinical dietetic management responsibilities, including managerial functions, components of nutritional care, and various tools or resources used in the system.

Exhibit 1-1 Scope of Clinical Dietetic Management

	Functions Plan Organize Direct Control
Patient Care	*System Tools and Resources*
Screening	Philosophy
Nutritional status assessment	Policies
Nutritional care plans	Procedures
Dietary treatments	Standards of practice
Documentation protocols	Priority scales
Instruction and counseling	Diet manual
Nutrition education	Menu modifications
Patient food services	Specialty products
Specialized nutrition support	Marketing
Monitoring and evaluation	Quality assurance
Team participation	Physical resources
Patient satisfaction	Personnel resources
Discharge planning and referral	Research
Continuity of care	Technology
Productivity and costing	Economic analysis
Financial planning	Budget, accounting

Nutritional Care

Coordinating the management of patient nutritional care is the most obvious and perhaps the most time-consuming facet of the clinical dietetic manager's job. With input from the clinical staff, the manager makes sure that policies and standards of practice are developed and that the work of each staff member is in compliance with these guidelines. Responsibility for nutritional care mandates up-to-date policies, procedures, practices, programs, and resources in every aspect of care delivery.

All hospital nutrition service units are guided by an organizational framework including several elements that are discussed further in the chapters of this book:

- a statement of philosophy putting forth, clearly and succinctly, fundamental beliefs regarding nutrition services
- policies, procedures, and protocols flowing from the statement of philosophy

- standards of practice to guide clinical decision making and delivery of care
- priority scales to determine levels of patient care to be used as a basis for designating the nature of required services (Lutton et al. 1985)
- methods to coordinate patient nutrition services with other institutional units, such as food service, nursing, pharmacy, and rehabilitation therapy
- practices to promote integration of nutrition services with other aspects of health care, such as medical rounds, communication in the medical record, team conferences, and discharge planning meetings
- a program of monitoring, evaluation, and control to assure quality services and care

Responsibility for nutrition education goes beyond ensuring that staff meet minimum requirements for diet and nutrition counseling. Education includes such areas as development and adoption of printed materials; classes for both hospitalized and ambulatory care patients; teaching resources; and outreach programs for the community.

Clinical nutrition managers should promote continuity of care for patients in different settings. This responsibility includes coordination of services provided by various nutrition professionals and referrals for patients who need such services as nutrition counseling, food assistance, classes, or group counseling. Continuity of care requires clearly written discharge summary plans that communicate nutritional care needs to referral agencies and such institutions as long-term care facilities and dialysis units.

Nutrition Service Personnel

In the chain of command, clinical dietetic managers have line authority over their subordinates: clinical dietitians, dietetic technicians, dietetic assistants, patient service supervisors, clerks, and clerical personnel. In this capacity the clinical dietetic manager holds decision-making authority in two key areas. The first includes all personnel management functions: recruitment, screening, interviewing, selection, orientation, training, appraisal, discipline, promotion, and separation. The second area covers daily interactions, such as activities related to assignment, scheduling, communication, motivation, leadership, productivity, and supervision of clinical dietetic personnel.

New Trends in Dietetics

Research in clinical dietetics is gaining new emphasis. Responsibilities in this area may include

- supervision of dietitians engaged in research
- coordination or direction of research projects
- approval of research proposals submitted by individual dietitians
- participation in clinical research studies conducted by others: data collection, consolidation of information, and communication with the principal investigator

In recent years marketing nutrition services has also taken on new importance. Parks and Moody (1986) have suggested that the very survival of dietetics rests on success in marketing both professional services and individual dietitians.

Physical Resources

In most hospitals nutrition services come under the food services department. However, the clinical dietetic manager has authority over certain physical resources, such as

- budget for the nutrition services unit, including salaries, fringe benefits, professional development, teaching materials and supplies, professional travel, reference books and materials, inservice education, subscriptions, equipment, consultation, computers, and software
- equipment, such as mirocomputers, audiovisual equipment, tools for nutritional assessment, programmable calculators, and feeding pumps
- space associated with the delivery of patient nutrition services: dietitian offices for both inpatient and outpatient services, classrooms, and conference rooms

The clinical dietetic manager oversees the organization of nutritional care services, work flow, furnishings, cleanliness, maintenance, and assignment of space. Responsibilities in this area include analysis of space needs, requests for renovations or expansions, and initiatives for relocation as appropriate.

FUNCTIONS OF MANAGEMENT

The clinical dietetic manager generally engages in a standard set of traditional functions or managerial processes. Although these functions are presented as sequential activities for the sake of analysis and discussion, they occur simultaneously during a typical workday. The percentage of time devoted to one or another function of management depends on managerial level and scope of responsibility.

Plan

Planning is simply the predetermination of expected outcomes. A fundamental process critical to the successful delivery of nutrition services, planning includes both long-range goals and short-term objectives. It should occur in every dimension of responsibility: the patient care process, the nutritional care system, continuity of care, personnel, research, marketing, and resource acquisition and utilization.

Some common problems occur in the exercise of the planning function. Adequate time is rarely devoted to strategic or long-range planning. Daily pressures often leave little time for individual or group creative structuring of the future. The planning process is hampered by not taking the time to develop a detailed plan to accomplish innovative ideas. Also, there is a reluctance to take the necessary risks to bring about major changes. Many nutrition service units have no contingency plan for dealing with such changes as decreased patient days, increased use of outpatient and home health care, increased need for long-term residential care, or increased public interest in nutrition and fitness.

Organize

The function of organizing involves the creation and use of formal lines of authority, communication, and staffing. Departmental or unit configuration determines, to some extent, the composition of work groups, work assignments, and division of labor.

Once formal organizational relationships are established, activities related to this function of management include development or revision of a policy and procedure manual, maintenance of formal lines of communication and authority, development and updating of job descriptions, and delegation of authority. Although the formal organization remains somewhat stable, informal relationships often create managerial headaches. Problems arise if the policy and procedure manual and job descriptions are ignored, which can be avoided by their consistent use to guide decision making. The organizing function requires regular attention to assure quality performance.

The staffing function encompasses activities associated with human resources. The personnel department often participates in the recruitment and screening of new staff members. However, it is the responsibility of the clinical dietetic manager to provide job specifications, interview applicants, select candidates, orient employees, and provide necessary training for new hires.

Daily activities of staffing relate principally to recruiting qualified candidates, retaining excellent professionals, evaluating employees, maintaining strong labor relations, and taking disciplinary action when necessary.

Personnel retention and maintenance activities are integral to the smooth operation of nutrition services. It is both time-consuming and expensive to replace employees. Results of a clinical laboratory study revealed that the average cost of replacing one professional worker was $16,010 (Bisonnette 1988, 51). Turnover can be costly.

When employees decide to leave the organization, the impact on the organization should be assessed. Sometimes, job turnover results in departure of "deadwood," thereby offering an opportunity to energize the unit. At other times, the loss of a top-notch dietitian creates a major deficit in expertise, visibility, or productivity in the department. An effective manager will maximize the positive aspects of turnover while limiting its negative impact on nutrition services.

Direct

Directing ensures the realization of goal achievement through the department's daily activities. Because its focus is on managing people to maximize output, the key to effective direction is strong human relations skills. Concepts of importance for this function include supervision, motivation, communication, leadership, discipline, and morale. Many of these topics are considered in detail in Part II, "Human Dimensions of Managing Dietetic Practice." Each is described briefly below.

Supervision is necessary to ensure that workers carry out assigned tasks and that their performance meets established standards. Supervisory style may span the continuum from very close direction to general oversight of activities. Performance improves when employees have at least some autonomy in the discharge of their responsibilities. Tight supervision inhibits creativity and enthusiasm and makes the supervisor, rather than the employee, feel the pressures of employee performance.

Self-motivated employees make management easy. Most dietitians, through their professional commitment, have a wellspring of internal resources: motivation, drive, enthusiasm, and devotion to high ideals. The challenge of any managerial role is to recognize and nurture internal motivation when it exists and to provide external motivation for those subordinates who need it.

Managers devote more time to communication than to any other single activity. Although communication affects all functions of management, it is of particular importance in the function of directing. Skills are needed in both oral and written communication to supervise, motivate, lead, and discipline employees effectively. Three types of communication skills are essential: one-on-one oral communication either face-to-face or on the telephone, oral communication in group settings, and written communications directed toward a single individual or a mass audience.

Many resources on the market can be used to improve either written or oral communication. Chapter 17 describes the preparation of written documents.

Not all managers are leaders, and not all leaders are in managerial positions. Yet, it is the quality of leadership that often distinguishes "adequate" from "effective" managers. This quality is revealed in a variety of situations. First, leaders assert a vision for the unit. They shape ideas and ideals into concrete goals and champion them among subordinates and co-workers. Second, leaders motivate others to share their vision. They have the ability to fire enthusiasm and elicit support from others. Third, leaders have insatiable energy. They never tire of putting forth efforts to capture their vision and make it a reality. Fourth, leaders are not discouraged by problems or setbacks. They find ways to work through and around difficulties, always progressing toward goal achievement. Finally, leaders possess the skill to create a climate in which others can achieve self-fulfillment while contributing to the achievement of organizational goals.

The clinical dietetic manager's leadership style determines how and to what extent workers internalize and support the mission and work of the unit. Strong and effective leaders involve everyone in planning, decision making, goal setting, and job commitment. Leadership success comes from the sustained and concerted efforts of everyone in the department.

The function of directing requires supervisory intervention when employees fail to comply with rules and regulations or when work standards are not maintained. The cause of the noncompliance needs to be evaluated to determine if the system or the individual is the source of the problem.

Disciplinary action may run the gamut from minor to serious, depending on the situation. Imposing disciplinary action requires special skills on the part of the clinical dietetic manager. Of particular importance are problem solving in the early phases of discipline; a firm, serious demeanor; and the ability to communicate clearly in writing the details of employee infractions. Assertiveness and initiative are required to approach individuals whose actions require disciplinary action. Fortitude and courage are necessary qualities if the manager is to take appropriate action, especially when the discipline is unpopular among other employees. Qualities of frankness, justice, equity, impartiality, sincerity, and honesty facilitate the objective handling of employee discipline.

Morale spans a continuum from low to high morale. Low morale can be disruptive to a unit, whereas high morale and positive group attitudes can enhance the quality of nutrition services. High morale is built and maintained primarily through the actions, qualities, and attitudes of supervisors and managers. Other factors, both within and outside the organization, can influence employee sentiments. Managers play a key role in utilizing these factors to heighten employee commitment to departmental programs and activities.

Managers must also coordinate activities, linking one with another in a systematic fashion. Such coordination means abiding by time schedules for sequential activities, especially when several workers are involved. Coordination also implies collaborative relationships with other employees and departments. It requires the management of diverse activities, sometimes in several work locations, to ensure consistency and uniformity of services.

The primary skill needed for coordination is the ability to think conceptually, to see all parts of the whole, and to understand how each dimension relates to the others. Research indicates that conceptual skills are less well developed among young dietitians than either technical or human relations skills (Rinke et al. 1982). Continuing education can be used to enhance skills needed to coordinate nutritional care systems and activities more effectively.

Control

Evaluation and control maintain established standards in every dimension of nutrition services. These processes entail the use of standards, policies, budgets, or other norms established during the planning process both to evaluate performance and take corrective action when there are deviations from expected standards. The concepts of controlling and evaluating may be used interchangeably. In a narrow context, evaluation is sometimes restricted to performance assessment. Controlling, in contrast, includes both a review of performance and a planned approach to correct any observed deficiencies. Both evaluation and control are important functions of the clinical dietetic manager.

MANAGEMENT STYLES

Individuals approach their managerial roles in a variety of ways. The style chosen is greatly influenced by numerous factors, including

- background and upbringing
- personal values
- personality, talents, and qualities
- life experiences, successes, and failures
- administrative values and expectations
- employee attitudes and responses

Management styles are determined by one's emphasis on tasks or on people, as shown in Figure 1-1. Those managers who are primarily focused on getting the job done (task orientation) give top priority to such factors as accountability for goal achievement, rigorous control of the bottom line, strict adherence to standards of practice, and high productivity and quality performance. Alternatively, managers who place greater emphasis on people usually demonstrate

- compassion and understanding for personal needs
- exceptional allowances for human weakness and error
- commitment to group decision making and participative leadership styles
- flexibility in deadlines, standards, and productivity levels to accommodate employee norms and preferences

Effective managers strike a balance between emphasis on the work and on the worker. They demand high standards while at the same time paying attention to employee needs and motivation. They keep focused on organizational goals while helping employees feel personally responsible for the enterprise. They meet productivity and quality standards by creating an environment in which employees are personally committed to high achievement. They channel human energies in the direction where everyone comes out as a winner.

ACTION ORIENTATION

Clinical dietetic management is a complex area of study, involving a wide range of traditional skills in nutritional care and administration as well as newer areas of dietetic practice: marketing, cost-benefit analysis, and re-

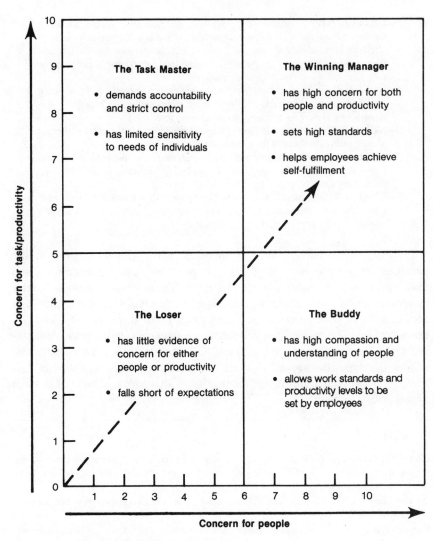

Figure 1-1 Styles of Management

search. One approach to understanding management's interrelated components is to use the acronym ADVANCE. ADVANCE refers to the knowledge and skills required of clinical dietetic practitioners who want to be successful managers.

A—ASSESSMENT is the process of evaluating and examining needs of the patients, the clinical dietetic service, and the organization.

D—DEVELOPMENT entails staff, programs, and self-development, including the professional skills necessary for establishing and initiating a plan of action.

V—VISION is the ability to view the future in technology, nutrition, administration, and health care and create new programs using marketing, strategic planning, and innovative staffing configurations.

A—ACCOUNTING is essential for recording and analyzing productivity, assuring quality controls, conducting and interpreting audits and research projects, formulating budgets, and directing economic analyses.

N—NUTRITION provides the foundation of knowledge for the clinical dietetic service and is the focus of the dietetic team.

C—COMMUNICATION is across the board with the public, patients, administration, and within the department, including education and teaching responsibilities.

E—EVALUATION completes the cycle, having the ability to monitor the environment to achieve the goals and objectives of the clinical dietetic service and the institution with integrity and professionalism.

Clinical dietetic management encompasses the nutritional care process, the management and measurement of the care provided, and the supervision and motivation of those who provide the care. These responsibilities require careful planning, responsive organizational structures, skilled direction and coordination of both processes and personnel, fiscal accountability, and rigorous control. The role of clinical dietetic management is indeed a challenging one. Those who use the ADVANCE approach to management will exhibit the expertise needed to meet this challenge. Later chapters of this book offer detailed information for dealing with various aspects of clinical dietetic management.

REFERENCES

Bisonnette, Catherine. 1988. A study to determine the cost of employee replacement in the clinical laboratories at The Ohio State University Hospitals. Master's thesis, The Ohio State University, Columbus.

Drucker, Peter. 1988. Management and the world's work. *Harvard Bus. Rev.* (September–October): 65–76.

Lutton, Sarah E., Marilyn M. Baker, and Rhonda V. Billman. 1985. Levels of patient nutrition care for use in clinical decision making. *J. Am. Dietet. Assoc.* 85(7):849–51.

Parks, Sara C., and Debra L. Moody. 1986. Marketing: A survival tool for dietetic professionals in the 1990s. *J. Am. Dietet. Assoc.* 86(1):33–39.

Rinke, Wolf J., Beatrice Donaldson David, and Walter T. Bjoraker. 1982. The entry-level generalist dietitian. II. Employers' perceptions of the adequacy of preparation for specific administrative competencies. *J. Am. Dietet. Assoc.* 80(2):139–47.

SUGGESTED READINGS

Bennis, Warren, and Burt Nanus. 1985. *Leaders: Strategies for taking charge.* New York: Harper and Row.

Bezold, Clement. 1989. The future of health care: Implications for the allied health professions. *J. Allied Health* 18(5):437–57.

Carr, Clay. 1989. *The new manager's survival manual.* New York: John Wiley and Sons, Inc.

Fenn, Margaret. 1978. *Making it in management: A behavioral approach for women executives.* Englewood Cliffs, N.J.: Prentice-Hall.

Jacobson, Aileen. 1985. *Women in charge: Dilemmas of women in authority.* New York: Van Nostrand Reinhold Co.

Knox, Thomas. 1984. Hospital manager role demanding more complex skills. *Hosp. Manager* 14(July–August):3–4.

Leibler, Joan G., Ruth E. Levine, and Hyman L. Dervitz. 1984. *Management principles for health professionals.* Gaithersburg, Md.: Aspen Publishers, Inc.

Mason, Marion, Burness G. Wenberg, and P. Kay Welsh. 1982. *The dynamics of clinical dietetics.* 2d ed. New York: John Wiley and Sons, Inc.

McConnell, Charles R. 1988. *Managing the health care professional.* 2d. ed. Gaithersburg, Md.: Aspen Publishers, Inc.

Rinke, Wolf J. 1989. *The winning foodservice manager: Strategies for doing more with less.* Gaithersburg, Md.: Aspen Publishers, Inc.

Thompson, Ann M., and Marcia D. Wood. 1980. *Management strategies for women.* New York: Simon and Schuster.

Chapter 2

Internal and External Influences on Clinical Management

Clinical dietetic managers cannot predetermine everything that happens in and around their sphere of responsibility. Although they can sometimes plan and shape reality to support their goals and desires, managers are controlled by regulations, policies, decisions, programs, and limitations imposed by other individuals, professional organizations, governmental agencies, and society. This chapter explores the influence of these internal and external factors. It also describes how clinical dietetic managers can maximize their effectiveness in the midst of these dominating forces.

OVERVIEW

Figure 2-1 shows internal and external factors that affect decisions and activities within clinical dietetic services. Internal forces include both departmental characteristics and institutional elements. At the departmental level a manager's influence is colored by the qualities of the individual employees, group dynamics, labor relations, employee mix, and organizational structure of the unit. Institutional forces having a major impact on clinical dietetic management are its size, corporate culture, technological advances, financial expectations, resource allocation, responsibility for food service, growth phase, and interdepartmental relations.

External forces also affect managers and their job responsibilities. As described in Chapter 3, the American Dietetic Association and other professional organizations expound written policies that guide management activities on such issues as standards of practice, codes of ethics, credential eligibility, and specialty certification. There are also numerous health care delivery practices, government regulations, and societal forces that sway programming and policy formulation in nutrition service units.

17

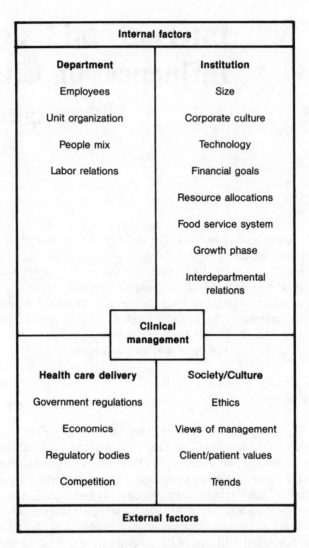

Figure 2-1 Internal and External Influences on Clinical Dietetic Management

DEPARTMENTAL MILIEU

Daily management activities are determined to a great extent by the departmental environment. Factors having particular importance are shown in Figure 2-2, and each is briefly discussed below.

Individual Employees

Individual employees play an important role in determining whether the manager's job is tough, pleasant, or somewhere in between. Each individual has a unique personality that can bring out either the best or the worst in a manager. An effective manager meets the needs of the employees. The larger and more diverse the group of employees, the wider the range of characteristics to be addressed, making need satisfaction a time-consuming and challenging activity.

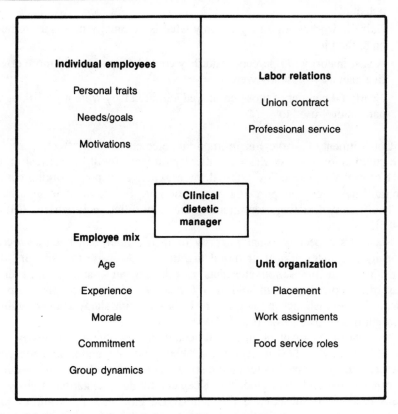

Figure 2-2 Departmental Factors Influencing Managerial Activities

Managerial style is also affected by employee motivation. Some employees shrink from responsibility, take little initiative, and require close supervision. The wise manager takes the initiative to work with these employees to change negative or disruptive behaviors and to foster positive motivation. Other employees are energized by their work. They tend to seek opportunities for advancement, independence, creativity, and growth. When most employees are of this type, the manager is free to spend more time in long-range planning, creative development, coordination, and public relations.

Employee Mix

Bennis and Nanus (1985, 7) have summarized some startling characteristics about today's workforce.

- Less than 25 percent of employees said they were working at full potential.
- Half the workers said they do only what is minimally necessary to hold on to their jobs.
- A vast majority (75 percent) said they could be significantly more effective than they presently were.
- Nearly 60 percent of those employed admitted they were not working as hard as they used to.

Commitment of workers is an important element in their effectiveness. If the group is loyal and dedicated to the department, it will be resilient in the face of problems caused by external forces, change, or poor working conditions. When group support and cooperation are the norm, managers have little difficulty directing, coordinating, and controlling their workers (Munn 1985).

Managers expect personal integrity of their employees, but they occasionally encounter ethical or moral nightmares. A desire to share in "the good life" sometimes motivates dietary workers to get what they can, even if this means pilfering, withholding information, altering records, helping themselves to cash, accepting gifts and bribes, making shady deals, or telling outright lies (Harris 1987, 108–112).

For first-time managers, unethical behaviors may pose a particularly vexing dilemma. It is best to face the problem and take action as necessary. Describe the problem to other administrators, department heads, and security personnel, and seek their guidance. Keep careful documentation of observed transgressions to substantiate the details. Develop new rules and/or procedures addressing the unethical behaviors and rigorously monitor compliance with these new rules. If the problem is serious, report it to the appropriate authorities for referral to the institutional or judicial systems. As in all personnel matters, maintain confidentiality as prescribed by codes of ethical conduct.

A combination of highly qualified employees, low turnover, and longer-term workers having the benefit of regular inservice training helps ensure that employees will meet or exceed job expectations. When turnover is high and workers are inexperienced, daily activities must be focused on meeting minimum standards and handling inevitable crises.

High group morale facilitates management, whereas dealing with disgruntled workers dampens the spirit of even the most optimistic manager. The manager should examine carefully the root of any morale problem and seek to reverse the situation. When low morale is the result of factors outside the control of the clinical dietetic manager, such as job insecurity or labor unrest, the creative manager identifies and reinforces factors within the work unit to boost morale.

Group dynamics has an impact on managerial style. Informal leaders among the employees can promote group cohesion to foster cooperation, or they can influence workers to be disruptive and problematic. Cohesive groups enforce norms for performance and productivity; an effective manager works with informal leaders to ensure that group norms are congruent with managerial expectations.

Labor Relations

Working with a union puts certain constraints on clinical dietetic managers. Union contracts define worker expectations. They influence managerial activities by specifying the limits of supervisory authority. Contracts are helpful, however, in that they provide clear-cut procedures for personnel management and delineate grievance procedures.

Among unionized workers, union stewards often represent employees, placing a third party between managers and their subordinates. Dealing with problems through a steward makes it more difficult to address individual worker transgressions and needs. These issues are discussed further in Chapter 6.

Unit Organization

How the department is organized and nutritional care activities are assigned affect supervision and leadership styles. The relationship of nutrition services to food service operations has the greatest impact in this regard.

However, all types of organization present challenges for the clinical dietetic manager.

When a department includes both food and nutrition services, the clinical dietetic manager is usually subordinate to the department head. There are several advantages to this arrangement. Unification of all nutrition and dietetic services under one umbrella promotes coordination of patient food services and other nutritional care activities. Dietitians can present a strong, unified front, operating from the base of a major department with a large operating budget.

On the other hand, clinical nutrition staff may sacrifice clinical time to meet food service supervisory needs, thus decreasing the emphasis on professional services to patients. If the department head is not a registered dietitian, the clinical dietetic manager must position nutritional care as a high priority in the department and ensure that standards of quality are maintained. Clinical dietitians should be viewed as integral to the medical team even if they are housed in the dietary department. This association will promote a positive image for clinical dietitians among physicians and other health care professionals (Ryan and Foltz 1988).

There are both disadvantages and advantages of independent departmental status for nutrition services. Advantages include an enhanced management position for the clinical dietetic manager, increased opportunity for revenue generation, increased status for clinical dietitians, freedom from food service activities, and greater visibility in the institution. On the negative side of the ledger are administrative pressures to balance income with expenses, less flexibility with fewer resources, complex procedures for coordinating nutrition care with patient food services, and less input into food quality and nutritional products.

Institutional characteristics help determine which organizational structure is best under the circumstances. Many clinical dietitians prefer the autonomy and status of working in a separate department of clinical nutrition services. O'Sullivan Maillet (1989) found that 61 percent of dietitians preferred having clinical dietetic specialists in a department separate from hospital food services.

Departmental structure also influences the nature of work performed by clinical dietetic staff. Within the food service department greater emphasis is placed on patient meals: menu service, diet changes, food ordering, nourishments, tray assembly and delivery, and the like. Departmental meetings often focus on food production, cooking equipment, sanitation, catering, and other topics unrelated to direct patient care and education. An independent department of nutrition can better focus its energies on the nutritional care process, team involvement, patient and staff education, and other activities specifically included in the role delineation for clinical dietitians.

When clinical dietitians are employed by an outside contractor, a key issue is the extent to which clinical dietetic managers are free to influence key decision makers. Being under an outside contract may tend to formalize and constrain interactions with institutional administrators, physicians, nurses, and other department heads.

Alternatively, when one is a member of the same "family" there are more opportunities for direct access to higher administration. Thus, it is somewhat easier to obtain approval for requests, especially if it is clear that such proposals make an important contribution to overall goals of the organization.

INSTITUTIONAL CHARACTERISTICS

The prevailing and anticipated institutional environment has a strong impact on the role and function of clinical dietetic managers. Important factors, shown in Figure 2-3, are institutional size, corporate culture, technological

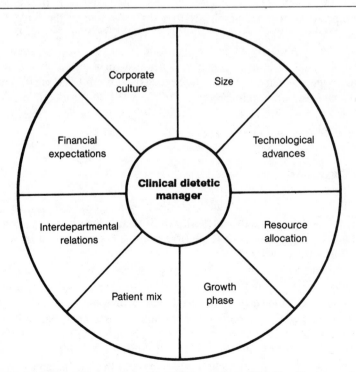

Figure 2-3 Institutional Characteristics That Influence Clinical Nutrition Management

advances, financial expectations, resource allocation, responsibility for patient food services, interdepartmental relations, and the institutional growth curve.

Size

Small institutions are known for their informality and family-like atmosphere. The clinical dietetic manager in a small institution usually is expected to function as a working supervisor with both clinical and management responsibilities. Consequently, more time and attention are given to direct patient care than to managing the unit and directing the work of others. This type of position is excellent preparation for promotion to a more management-oriented job in clinical dietetics.

Corporate Culture

Top management sets a tone for the institution. Work philosophies and leadership styles of chief administrators filter through to the ranks (Nordstrom and Allen 1987), creating an environment that affects the entire organization. When top management insists on no-nonsense, task-oriented toughness, the clinical dietetic manager will need to focus more on productivity than on people. When chief executives focus solely on large profit margins, middle managers are again pressured to deliver high productivity. Institutional views regarding research and revenue generation determine, to some extent, support for initiatives in these areas.

Technological Advances

Institutional technology influences middle-management activities. Many factors, including patient mix, severity of illnesses, length of stay, complexities of service, and professional qualifications, influence the nature and type of nutrition services offered.

Use of a computer decreases the time spent in writing and communicating information. Some departments have computerized systems for nutrient analysis, although many dietitians do these calculations by hand. Others use computers to record and monitor nutritional assessments, care plans, and evaluation criteria. In some cases, dietary personnel spend inordinate amounts of time filling out diet cards and putting names on patient menus. Extensive use of computer technology enhances the sophistication of services, but demands proficiency in information technology.

Financial Expectations

In the past costs associated with clinical nutrition services were always absorbed by the department of dietetics. At that time most clinical dietitian activities related to patient meal service: planning and checking menus, supervising tray service, and filling patients' dietary requests. The role of clinical dietitians has moved toward an emphasis on nutritional status assessment, care planning, quality assurance, and outpatient services. In many instances patients are now screened for level of nutritional risk and charged for nutrition services that exceed basic care. Routine meal service tasks can easily be accomplished by dietetic support personnel.

When emphasis is placed on cost containment and revenue generation, many institutions consider the elimination of positions in clinical nutrition. In those situations, the onus is on the clinical dietetic manager and the clinical staff to

- demonstrate positive patient outcomes resulting from nutrition services
- enhance productivity through delivery of professional services
- demonstrate the cost effectiveness of clinical nutrition services
- recover the costs of these services
- use nutrition services to create revenue for the institution

It should be apparent, however, that the work of clinical dietetic managers is strongly influenced by institutional viewpoints and expectations in this regard.

Patient Mix

Computerized information services make it possible to provide detailed profiles of patient populations. Hospitals can use this database to analyze such variables as patient histories, levels of care required, length of patient stay per diagnosis category, incidence of malnutrition or other comorbidity factors, numbers of patients within each area of specialization, costs of service by disease category, and cost savings realized through various protocols.

The nature and cost of nutrition services vary according to the numbers and types of patients served. If most patients require only menu service or basic diet therapy, a dietetic technician working under the direction of a staff or consultant dietitian can provide many of the necessary functions. However, staff dietitians or credentialed specialists are needed to provide services to patients who require complex diet modifications, specialized nutrition support, or extensive nutrition counseling. The number of patients in each category and the complexity of care required determine to a great extent the organization and delivery of nutrition services.

Resource Allocation

Resources that greatly affect clinical managers include the number of approved positions, the continuing education budget, space, and equipment.

Justification of positions to maintain a dietitian:patient ratio of 1:50–60 (East and Harger 1976) demands both shrewdness and persistence. Unfortunately, in many situations clinical positions are being cut so that each dietitian must serve an average of 100–150 patients, a ratio recommended over 60 years ago when dietetic services were much different than they are today (McEachern 1930). With high dietitian:patient ratios, managers need to devote time to reorganizing the unit to free dietitians from routine and meal-related tasks, updating clinical roles, and justifying clinical nutrition services.

Office space is another valuable resource under the control of top administration. A majority of clinical dietitians have offices near patient units. Many share their offices with diet assistants and dietetic technicians. Ready access to patients and medical personnel is more important than private offices and other status symbols. If clinical dietitians have offices in or near the main kitchen, the clinical dietetic manager should give priority to seeking better locations for the professional staff. Another alternative is to find a second office or shared space with other health care team members in the patient care units.

Administrative decisions determine to some extent the availability of computers and other high-tech equipment for clinical dietitians. Clinical dietetic managers need to facilitate the acquisition of such equipment. However, an even greater challenge is acclimatization of dietitians to the full use of available technology.

Interdepartmental Relationships

Effective nutrition services are fostered through collaboration with numerous departments throughout the hospital. Exhibit 2-1 illustrates some examples of interdepartmental relationships.

Communications between nutrition services and other departments can be enhanced through a variety of interactive groupings, including the following:

- employee recognition committee
- safety committee

- quality assurance committee
- infection control committee
- menu planning committee
- institutional nutrition committee
- discharge planning rounds
- medical rounds
- nutrition support team

Exhibit 2-1 Examples of Interdepartmental Relationships

Accounting	Pays accounts, distributes pay checks
Administration	Monitors performance of the nutrition service unit; accepts reports and proposals
Admitting	Provides census records
Business office	Handles payments for nutrition services
Communications	Pages staff, refers patients to appropriate nutrition services, prints teaching materials
Employee health	Gives physical exams and provides health services to sick or injured employees
Health education	Aids in the development of nutrition education programs
Housekeeping	Keeps offices and other assigned space clean and orderly
Laboratory	Analyzes clinical laboratory data for both hospitalized and ambulatory patients
Laundry	Supplies linens and lab coats as needed
Medical records	Sets policies for documentation of nutritional assessment data, progress notes, and discharge plans
Medical staff	Confers with dietitians regarding patient nutritional assessments, histories, intakes, prescriptions, and evaluations
Nursing service	Communicates daily regarding patient care, supplements and nourishments, tray distribution, menu collection, and nutrition support
Personnel	Maintains employee status changes, recruits new employees, screens applicants, assists with labor relations
Pharmacy	Supplies parenteral formulas for nutrition support
Plant management	Installs, maintains, and repairs equipment
Public relations	Facilitates coverage of news events and nutrition publications
Purchasing	Handles bidding procedures, orders products and services according to specifications
Security	Provides safety, investigates problems and incidents involving security

Source: Adapted from *Policy and Procedure Manual*, Code no. B-2, with permission of the University of Medicine and Dentistry of New Jersey, Newark, NJ.

Organizational Growth Phase

All organizations go through a process of growth, maturation, and decline. The institutional milieu is greatly affected by its phase in the process. Growth is characterized by excitement, change, expanding resources, and new opportunities. Employees do not mind long hours and hard work, because everyone feels a sense of satisfaction at watching the enterprise grow and develop.

During phases of maturation and decline there are often budget cuts, job insecurity, delayed decision making, and an overriding sense of concern and even discouragement. Hospital employees who observe the declining use of hospital facilities and poor attendance at patient education and health programs may feel a sense of hopelessness. Management is difficult, but perhaps even more important during these times of struggle, and managerial performance can be strengthened through contact with other managers, both internally and externally.

EXTERNAL FACTORS AFFECTING CLINICAL MANAGEMENT

Regulatory Factors

Numerous bodies have legislative or regulatory control over activities in hospitals and other health care institutions. Among the most important means of exercising this control are prospective payment systems, hospital accreditation, and state health department regulations.

Prospective Payment Systems

Prospective payment systems—government programs to help control the costs of health care for Medicare patients—have had a dramatic impact on hospitals, nursing homes, and outpatient services. The most important component of prospective payment systems is the diagnostic-related group (DRG), 468 disease categories that provide the basis for patient charges. These systems have contributed to decreased length of stay for hospitalized patients and have been the most effective method for cutting hospital costs (Thompson 1988). Lowered hospital census, diversification of services, health care marketing, increased outpatient care, rigorous review and elimination of nonreimbursable patient care services, and identification of new sources of revenue are primarily the result of rising health care costs and prospective payment systems.

In the aftermath of DRGs, dietitians have become more visible. These regulations have stimulated numerous activities, including

- research showing that nutritional care can decrease the length of hospital stay (Reilly et al. 1988; Robinson et al. 1987; Smith and Smith 1988)
- designation of care levels based on the client's nutritional risk, reflecting the need for different services corresponding to the severity of patient conditions (Blackburn and Hickman 1987)
- studies on cost effectiveness of nutrition support and identification of nutrition-related ICD-9-CM codes that may qualify as a substantial comorbidity or complication
- development of outreach programs, such as innovative diet classes and nutrition counseling services
- initiation of creative revenue generation techniques, such as charging a fee for certain services (Murray et al. 1990), providing hotel-type options for patients and their families, and expanding food services both within and outside the hospital

Efforts to decrease health care costs will continue. Accordingly, clinical dietetic managers must persist in finding ways to curtail costs, increase productivity, and produce revenue to offset expenses incurred in providing nutrition and other patient services.

Hospital Accreditation

The Joint Commission on Accreditation of Healthcare Organizations (Joint Commission) influences many facets of nutrition service. Its *Accreditation Manual for Hospitals: Dietetic Services* stipulates standards related to such factors as organization, staffing, and direction; training and education; food service administration and clinical nutrition services; equipment, sanitation, and safety; orders for and documentation of care; and monitoring and evaluation of dietetic services. Clinical dietetic managers must be thoroughly familiar with these standards. Furthermore, they must develop policies, systems, procedures, methods, and practices that ensure regular compliance at or beyond these standards.

Federal, State, and Local Legislation

Numerous laws govern various aspects of managing nutrition services. Familiarity with these laws is important to ensure a smooth operation. These regulations include

- labor laws covering recruitment, training, compensation, supervision, and maintenance of personnel
- laws related to food quality
- legislation for food safety
- long-term care facility licensure and certification
- sanitation and safety providing for inspection, licensing, and approval of layouts and equipment; food handling permits; cleanliness; and freedom from contamination in food service operations

Societal Factors

Living in an age of dynamism and change, no one can escape the impact of societal issues, trends, and pressures. The most important of these factors are briefly presented here.

Trends in Health Care

The health care market is a volatile one (McManis and Binder 1988). Any dietitian educated before 1980 who has not kept abreast of changes in both health care and dietetic practice is probably unprepared to meet the current challenges of clinical management: rising health care costs, escalating numbers of institutionalized elderly, decreased length of hospital stays, increased biomedical engineering and technology, specialization among health care practitioners, a trend toward outpatient surgery and other medical services, ethical and moral dilemmas, concern for physical fitness, and emphasis on home health care (Bezold 1989; Brown 1988).

Megatrends

Society is beset by overriding changes that affect dietetic practice and management. Owen (1984) summarized major societal changes and their challenges to dietitians. A shift from an industrial to an informational society has promoted use of the computer in management, nutritional care, education, and communication. In a society suffering from high-tech isolation, dietitians bring high touch and warmth through their concern for human life and personal health. With the movement from institutional help to self-help, dietitians can assist employees, colleagues, and the public to take charge of their personal health and nutritional habits. Moving from representation democracy to participatory democracy requires clinical dietetic managers to delegate decision making to the lowest level possible and to facilitate strong group dynamics within the unit. Changing structures from hierarchies to matrices demands that dietitians use networking skills to expand their ideas, information, and resources.

Health Care Consumers

Clients have high expectations of the health care system. Many are dissatisfied with the quality of physicians and medical care, availability of services, and cost of health care (Gibbs 1989). Americans value excellent health, and they expect the system to provide it for them (Barsky 1988).

Diverse cultural and religious attitudes affect public opinion regarding such issues as maternal and child care, prolongation of life, work values, and physical fitness. Representatives of the public want to be part of focus groups and other decision-making bodies for health and nutrition care services.

GUIDELINES FOR ANALYSIS

Although some factors influencing the managerial environment are general, most are specific to a given situation. To obtain a clear picture of one's own milieu, it is helpful to sketch a diagram of unique internal and external factors that affect one's approach to management (Exhibit 2-2). Complete the diagram by identifying strengths and limitations of factors immediately affecting nutrition services. Review the characteristics of the department: people managed, employee mix, labor relations, and organizational factors. Note any professional issues that significantly affect the internal milieu: image, status, legislation, or standards. Define the strengths and limitations of your institution: its corporate culture, access to resources, technology, interdepartmental relations, and general tenor of the organization. Note any external factors that affect your unit in a unique way.

Developing such a diagram will take considerable time, but the product will be well worth the effort. It can become an important management resource for analyzing management problems, setting goals for management or personal development, identifying critical networks, or establishing communication strategies. Moreover, comparisons can be made over time of factors that change, particularly as the twenty-first century advances.

Exhibit 2-2 Assessment of Management Milieu

Influential Factors	Top Two Strengths	Top Two Limitations
Departmental		
Individual employees		
Personalities		
Needs		
Motivations		
Employee mix		
Attitudes		
Age		
Experience		
Morale		
Commitment		
Group dynamics		
Labor relations		
Union contracts		
Labor problems		
Organization		
Line of authority		
Work assignments		
Food service roles		
Professional		
Image		
Status		
Legislation		
Standards		
Institutional		
Size		
Corporate culture		
Technology		
Financial		
expectations		
Resource allocation		
Food service		
Interdepartmental		
relations		
Growth phase		
Patient mix		
External		
Particular		
concerns		

REFERENCES

Barsky, Arthur J. 1988. The paradox of health. *N. Engl. J. Med.* 318(Feb. 18): 414–18.

Bennis, Warren, and Burt Nanus. 1985. *Leaders: Strategies for taking charge.* New York: Harper and Row.

Bezold, Clement. 1989. The future of health care: Implications for the allied health professions. *J. Allied Health* 18(5):437–57.

Blackburn, Sara A., and Susan P. Hickman. 1987. Nutrition care activities and DRGs. *J. Am. Dietet. Assoc.* 87(11):1535–38.

Brown, Montague. 1988. The 1990s: Just around the corner. *Health Care Man. Rev.* 13(2):81–86.

East, Dorothy, and Virginia P. Harger. 1976. Oregon dietitians call for health care planning data. *J. Am. Dietet. Assoc.* 69(10):400–04.

Gibbs, Nancy. 1989. Sick and Tired. *Time* (July 31):48–53.

Harris, Louis. 1987. *Inside America.* New York: Random House, Inc.

MacEachern, Malcolm T. 1930. Factors that influence ratio of personnel to patients. *Modern Hosp.* 35(5):59–61.

McManis, Gerald L., and Clifford Binder. 1988. Health care delivery in the final decade. *Topics Health Rec. Man.* 8(3):1–9.

Munn, Harry E. Jr. 1985. Assessing supervisory leadership behavior. *Health Care Supervisor* 4(1):1–9.

Murray, Nancy, et al. 1990. RDs deserve a piece of $30 billion pie. *Clin. Man.* 6(4):61–64.

Nordstrom, Richard D., and Bruce H. Allen. 1987. Cultural change versus behavioral change. *Health Care Man. Rev.* 12(2):43–49.

O'Sullivan Maillet, Julie. 1989. The services of clinical dietetic specialists in acute care settings as perceived by dietetic practitioners and dietetic educators. Ph.D. diss., New York University, New York.

Owen, Anita L. 1984. Challenges for dietitians in a high tech/high touch society. *J. Am. Dietet. Assoc.* 84(3):285–89.

Reilly, James J., et al. 1988. Economic impact of malnutrition: a model system for hospitalized patients. *JPEN* 12(4):371–76.

Robinson, Georgia, Marjorie Goldstein, and Gary M. Levine. 1987. Impact of nutritional status on DRG length of stay. *JPEN* 11(1):49–51.

Ryan, Alan S., and Mary Beth Foltz. 1988. The role of the clinical dietitian. I. Present professional image and recent image changes. *J. Am. Dietet. Assoc.* 88(6):671–76.

Smith, Alice, and Phillip Smith. 1988. *Superior nutritional care cuts hospital costs.* Chicago: Nutritional Care Management Institute.

Thompson, John D. 1988. DRG prepayment: Its purpose and performance. *Bull. NY Acad. Med.* 64(1):28–51.

SUGGESTED READINGS

Brown, Montague, and Barbara P. McCool. 1987. High-performing managers: Leadership attributes for the 1990s. *Health Care Man. Rev.* 12(2):69–75.

Ross Laboratories. 1985. *The cost effectiveness of nutrition support.* Columbus, Ohio: Ross Laboratories.

Chapter 3

A Framework for the Clinical Dietetic Manager

The unique position of a clinical dietetic manager emphasizes systems management and the maintenance of legal and fiscal controls of a clinical dietetic service in an acute care setting. The clinical manager must put dietetic services in the context of a department and/or institution. This chapter discusses the framework for establishing the services provided by the clinical dietetic staff. It is divided into three sections: the mission, goals, and objectives; procedures based on regulations and standards; and the organizational structure, including job descriptions.

MISSION AND GOALS

The services of clinical dietetics are based on the hospital's mission, purpose, and philosophy. A mission statement spells out the purpose or reason for which the institution exists or serves the public. It generally includes one or more of the following areas: patient care, patient education, education of students and professionals, research, and community services. If one purpose of the institution is the provision of community service, it is easier for the clinical dietetic manager to justify the use of financial resources for a nutrition education program in the local school district.

The mission of a clinical dietetic service should include meeting the nutritional needs of patients through appropriate food/nutrient intake. The unit's mission may also include the education of dietetic students, advanced-level residencies for dietetic practitioners, education of the medical and allied health team, applied dietetic research in collaboration with other departments or alone, community outreach and education, nutrition counseling for ambulatory care, and the feeding of visitors and staff. The unit's mission should be a broad statement of 15 to 30 words, such as "The mission of the clinical dietetic service is to provide nutritious foods and nutrition care to each patient, while educating future dietetic practitioners and contributing to the knowledge base of clinical dietetic practice.''

Once the mission is established by the dietetic staff and approved by appropriate members of the institution, such as administrators and physicians, short- and long-term goals and objectives can be derived from it. Goals are broad statements of direction or interest that provide the meaning for short-range or annual objectives and long-range or strategic planning. The goals for the sample mission statement might be to refine the identification of nutrient needs, to improve the process of food delivery, to educate dietetic practitioners at the technician and dietitian levels, and to participate in ongoing research projects.

The objectives then state how the clinical dietetic manager and the staff are going to achieve the goals. Goals and objectives are derived from the institutional directives and externally accepted standards. They lead to the development of policies to be ratified by the dietetic team members who will implement them. In other words, policies are not set in a vacuum, but are derived from the mission, goals, and objectives.

Figure 3-1 illustrates the relationship between nutritional care and institutional food services. The overall goal of dietetic services is to deliver the right diet and nutrients to the patient. It is generally the clinical dietetic manager's responsibility to ensure this entire process, which starts with identification of nutritional needs through screening and assessment protocols. A diet is then ordered based on physician and dietitian input. Nursing services communicates this information to food services. The food or nutrient mixture is prepared. This step includes menu preparation, menu selection, verification of the appropriate food choice, and forecasting the amount of food to prepare. The next step is the serving of the food. Food-service depends on the purchasing, production, and delivery of foods. Quality control systems—communication techniques to assure the delivery of quality food at the appropriate time and to the appropriate individual—occur in this step. Ingestion of food encompasses tray set-up, meeting needs for feeding assistance, and monitoring techniques to evaluate intake. Finally, evaluation of food intake completes the cycle of meeting patient needs. Are the food/ nutrient needs of the patient being met, and if not, how can better service be provided?

ESTABLISHING POLICIES AND PROCEDURES

Policies, procedures, and protocols are tools essential to achieving the mission, goals, and objectives of the unit. A policy is a wise, expedient, or prudent conduct or management principle, plan, or course of action pursued

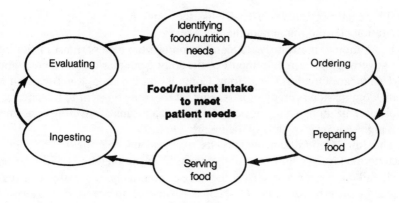

Figure 3-1 The Process of Obtaining the Right Diet

by an organization or individual. A procedure outlines a series of steps to be followed to achieve a particular outcome. A protocol is an original draft or statement of agreement on how to proceed in the case of particular subsets of patients and what criteria are necessary to measure care. Both a procedure and a protocol guide the course of action in a logical sequence. Each component of Figure 3-1 is translated into a series of policies and procedures. An understanding of regulations and standards is fundamental to policy development. Interpretation of these regulations and standards sets the foundation for the establishment of protocols for the clinical dietetic service.

External Regulations

External regulations set minimal levels of performance for the clinical dietetic unit. Local and state codes mandate

- employment of qualified personnel
- fixed organizational standards, such as a policy and procedure manual
- integration with other departments
- equipment standards
- food handling requirements
- systematic methods of recording and serving diets

Copies of these regulations can be obtained from the local or state health department. A meeting or telephone conference can often be arranged with a health department surveyor to discuss the regulations and how the specific institution plans to implement them.

In addition to mandatory standards to protect the patient, most institutions are governed by the requirements of the Joint Commission on Accreditation of Healthcare Organizations (Joint Commission). Although not mandatory, Joint Commission accreditation is required for some types of reimbursement. Most organizations value the accreditation as a means of assuring consumers that high standards of care are being provided.

The Joint Commission updates its requirements each year. The clinical dietetic manager should review the changes in the dietetic services section each fall or winter and check the index thoroughly for indirect changes affecting dietetic services. A detailed review of the recommendations in relation to the specific department should occur annually. The Joint Commission has a toll-free telephone line for questions, and when the manager needs interpretation of a standard, a telephone call is in order. Documentation of the call, responder's name, and decision should be kept on file. In addition, communication with other clinical dietetic managers can help with the appropriate interpretation of Joint Commission regulations.

External Standards

Standards of numerous professional organizations are available to assist in the development of an acceptable level of performance for nutritional care delivery. These standards have evolved over time to guide and shape decisions and practices in dietetics. They help determine what a reasonable level of care is and how ordinary care compares to extraordinary care.

The American Dietetic Association's "Standards of Practice" (1985) are statements that express the dietitian's responsibilities for providing quality nutritional care. The standards of practice (SOP) document is dynamic, flexible, and written for all areas of practice. The "Code of Ethics for the Profession of Dietetics" (1988) defines the moral conduct and professional responsibilities of individuals. Such publications as the position papers of the American Dietetic Association (ADA) provide recommendations for appropriate care. A list of ADA position papers can be obtained by writing to the ADA; a complete set of the position papers is available for purchase. The position of a large professional organization, such as the American Dietetic Association, can add tremendous weight to a convincing argument or justification for initiating a new protocol.

More specific to inpatient quality standards of care are such documents as the American Society of Parenteral and Enteral Nutrition's "Standards for Nutrition Support: Hospitalized Patients" (1984) and "Standards of Practice for Nutrition Support: Dietitians'' (1990). In addition, textbooks and guidelines for care have been written to assist in the development of nutritional care protocols. The American Society of Clinical Nutrition has published "Guidelines for the Establishment of an Institutional Nutrition Committee" (1985) to assist in the establishment of quality services.

Specific Procedures

Figure 3-2 provides an organizational framework for clinical dietetic services. Procedures need to delineate the level and extent of patient services, nutritional care, and nutrition education. Patient services may either be under the direction of clinical dietetics or food services or a joint department and may or may not be the responsibility of the clinical dietetic manager. Patient education has become a limited function of inpatient clinical dietitians because of shorter hospitalizations and increasing numbers of severely ill patients. However, as discharge planning becomes more aggressive, education will be emphasized from day one until discharge.

Continuity of care and referral mechanisms are essential for quality nutritional care. Nutritional care for discharged patients is a major area in which protocols are essential to improve nutrition counseling to outpatients. This topic is discussed in Chapter 16.

The nutritional care structure defines the standards of practice necessary to promote the welfare of hospitalized patients. In the early 1980s there was often one minimal standard for all hospitalized patients, such as one standard

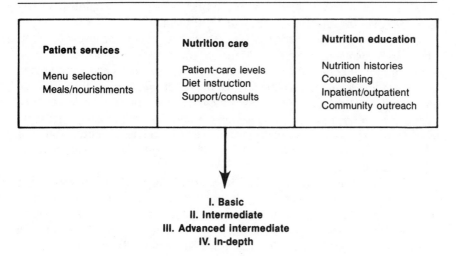

Patient services	Nutrition care	Nutrition education
Menu selection Meals/nourishments	Patient-care levels Diet instruction Support/consults	Nutrition histories Counseling Inpatient/outpatient Community outreach

I. Basic
II. Intermediate
III. Advanced intermediate
IV. In-depth

Figure 3-2 Organization of Clinical Dietetic Services

assessment protocol independent of type of disease or level of nutrition risk. Nutritional care has evolved to where standards of practice need to be delineated for all major categories of patients treated in the institution, as well as having a set of generic guidelines for the institution. Exhibit 3-1 illustrates a nutritional care matrix that defines four levels of care and what is included at each level. Exhibit 3-2 is an example of a policy and detailed procedure for the calculation of energy and protein needs.

After generic protocols are spelled out, specific standards of practice should be delineated for specialty groups, such as liver transplant, dialysis, parenteral or enteral feeding, or pediatric patients. A system of when to review these protocols should be established. A pertinent member of the medical team should collaborate in the development of these standards.

ORGANIZATIONAL DESIGN

In any organization, the structure and tables of organization set the channels of communication and delineate degrees of responsibility and accountability. A commonly used table of organization for clinical dietetic services is shown in Figure 3-3. Although position titles differ among institutions, generally the managerial ladder includes supervisors, managers, and administrators. Supervisors are first-level managers who have direct supervisory responsibility over a group of 5 to 12 employees. For example, in large institutions, there may be a supervisor of the dietetic assistants or a supervisory technician. The administrator holds a top position, ranging from a CEO (chief executive officer) to a department head. The administrator has authority over the total organization or department.

The title of manager may apply to individuals at several levels between supervisors and administrators. Managers have responsibility for a large segment of the operation, including the work of supervisors and a wide range of diverse and complex activities. If the organization has more than 10 to 12 dietitians, the clinical manager may want to designate one or two supervisory dietitian positions to assist in managing the unit. The clinical manager must also decide to whom the dietetic assistants and technicians report, whether a clinical dietetic specialist is needed, and, if so, how this individual relates to the clinical dietitians.

The clinical dietetic manager has the responsibility and authority to design the role of the clinical dietetic team in conjunction with the personnel department and the clinical manager's immediate administrator. Role is defined as a set of expectations or "evaluative standards applied to an incumbent of a particular position" (Gross, Neal, and McEachern 1958). It is important to identify who delineates the team's role because this affects the functioning of

Exhibit 3-1 Patient Nutritional Care Level Activities

	Patient Assessment and Evaluation	Nutritional Care Plan	Patient Counseling, Evaluation and Referral	Medical Record Entries
Basic (level I)	1. Review patient's nursing admission notes for basic data: reason for admission, present height and weight, recent weight change, and special diet at home. 2. Interview patient (meal rounds) for food preferences, allergies, intolerences, eating/feeding problems, and recent weight changes	1. Take action to ensure that patient receives appropriate dietary regimen as planned: check diet roster and patient identification card, write/review menus and nourishments, and follow through on diet changes.	None	1. Enter brief note when patient is seen.
Intermediate (level II)	level I plus: 3. Review patient's medical record for: laboratory data physical exam and history physician's admission notes medications	level I plus: 2. Determine patient's nutrient needs. 3. Confer with other health care team members to discuss nutrition care of patient if appropriate. 4. Prepare formal plan	1. Provide nutrition counseling for single restricted diets for the following patient outcomes: integrate nutrition rationale and food selection principles the ability to plan	level I plus: 2. Enter detailed nutrition care plan, including a summary of patient assessment. 3. Enter recommendation for nutrition intervention. 4. Enter notes about the

Exhibit 3-1 continued

Patient Assessment and Evaluation	Nutritional Care Plan	Patient Counseling, Evaluation and Referral	Medical Record Entries
prognosis other pertinent information 4. Do nutritional evaluation, diet history and evaluation, physical appearance, present knowledge of rationale for and restriction of dietary regimen. 5. Follow-up on initial assessment to include interview of patient to determine acceptance/tolerance of diet and to update initial interview data.	(nutritional needs/education needs, and patient goals) for supporting an in-patient's dietary requirements. 5. Prepare formal plan for providing a patient with needed nutrition education following discharge.	menus knowledge information sources available effect on health status outcomes 2. Evaluate patient's achievements in terms of the outcomes listed above. 3. Refer a patient who needs further nutrition education services after discharge to an appropriate source of such services.	diet counseling provided, including an evaluation of the patient's level of understanding. 5. Enter notes for follow-up referrals. 6. Enter chronological notes that document patient's routine progress.
Advanced intermediate (level III) levels I and II plus: 6. Assess patient needs and prescribe diet and/or recommendations as appropriate.	levels I and II plus: 6. Calculate and develop a menu pattern as appropriate. 7. Monitor patients with increased protein and calorie needs.	level II plus: 4. Provide nutrition counseling for multiple-restricted diets and calculated diets with outcomes as listed in level II.	As in levels I and II

In-depth (level IV)	levels I, II, and III plus: 7. Follow up on the initial assessment to include review of a patient's medical record for updated information. 8. In-depth assessment if appropriate.	levels I, II, and III plus: 8. Present and discuss the nutritional care plan for patient's progress with the health care team. 9. Do daily nutrient intake calculations if appropriate. 10. Monitor tube feedings and hyperalimentation for nutritional adequacy and nutrition-related problems.	As in levels II and III	levels I, II, and III plus: 7. Enter notes documenting significant changes in a patient's nutritional status. 8. Calculate and enter daily nutrient intakes if appropriate.

Source: Adapted from *Journal of the American Dietetic Association,* Vol. 85, No. 7, p. 849, with permission of the American Dietetic Association, © 1985.

Exhibit 3-2 Sample Policy and Procedure

Purpose:	To establish standards of practice in energy and protein needs.
Responsibility:	The Director of Food and Nutrition Services is responsible for the implementation of this policy and is charged with responsibilities for initiating all exceptions and changes.
Policy:	Nutrition assessments will include an evaluation of energy and protein needs and make appropriate recommendations based on this data.
Procedure:	The following formulas will be utilized in calculating energy, protein, and fluid needs. Refer to additional policies for pregnancy, lactation, and pediatric needs.

I. **Energy Needs**

Estimating Desirable Body Weight

Males: 106 pounds (for the first 5 feet in height)
+6 pounds/inch over 5 feet

Females: 100 pounds (for the first 5 feet in height)
+5 pounds/inch over 5 feet

To make adjustments for

small frame:	paraplegia:
subtract 10 percent	subtract 5–10 percent
large frame:	quadraplegia:
add 10 percent	subtract 10–15 percent

obese (over 125 percent DBW):
Actual Body Weight−Desirable Body Weight × .25 DBW

Calculation of Total Daily Energy Requirement (TDE)

TDE = BEE × Activity Factor × Injury Factor

Basal Energy Expenditure (BEE): Harris = Benedict Formula

BEE (males) = 66 + (13.7 × W) + (5 × H) − (6.8 × A)
BEE (females) = 655 + (9.6 × W) + (1.8 × H) − (4.7 × A)
W = body weight in kg
H = body height in cm
A = Age in years

Activity Factor during hospitalization 1.2

Injury Factor surgery 1.1–1.2
trauma 1.1–1.4
infection 1.1–1.5

Exhibit 3-2 continued

II. **Protein Requirements: (refer to renal/liver standards for those patients)**

Method 1: Grams of Protein/kg Desired Body Weight

healthy individual	0.8 gm
maintenance, nonstressed hospitalized patient	1.0 gm
malnourished hospitalized patient	1.2 gm
severe trauma, thermal burns	1.5–2.0 gm
head injury	1.520 gm

Method 2: Calorie: Nitrogen Ratio* (Total Calories/1 gm N)

healthy individual	300:1
maintenance, nonstressed hospitalized patient	200:1
malnourished hopitalized patient	150:1
severe trauma, thermal burns	80–100:1

*6.25 gm N = 1 gm protein

III. **Baseline Fluid Requirements**

Method 1:
Based on desired body weight for height for obese patients and on actual body weight for others:

- Children over 20 kg: 1500 cc + 30 cc/kg above 20 kg
- Previously vigorous young adults with large muscle mass: 40 cc/kg/day
- Adults aged 18 to 55 years: 35 cc/kg/day
- Older patients with no major cardiac or renal disease: 30 cc/kg/day

Source: Adapted from *Policies and Procedures Manual*, Code No. E-30 with permission of the University of Medicine and Dentistry of New Jersey, Newark, New Jersey.

the entire system. A position is defined in relation to others in the organizational system. There are several interrelated roles in health care institutions, and a position cannot be described until other positions to which it is related have been identified. The role relationships of the clinical dietetic manager are illustrated in Figure 3-4. Similar diagrams can be drawn for all members of the clinical dietetic team.

Dietetics is a service-oriented profession in which job performance focuses on ideas, information, and the translation of knowledge. The clinical dietetic manager must design position descriptions that best use the skills of each level of dietetic personnel and meet the diverse needs of the institution. The role delineation studies by the American Dietetic Association in 1989 provide a foundation for the development of position descriptions for the technician and the dietitian (Kane 1990). These studies exemplify where current practice was at a certain point in time, not predicting what should be. Thus,

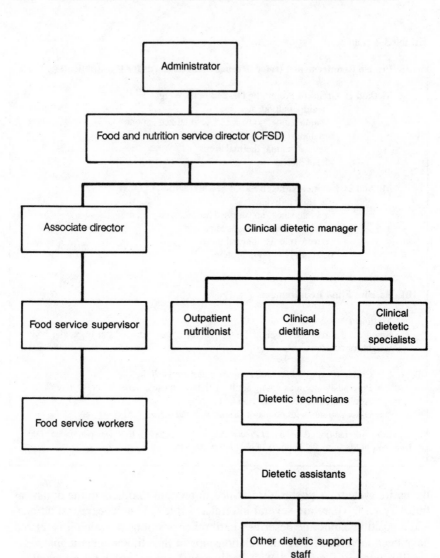

Figure 3-3 Table of Organization of Clinical Dietetic Services

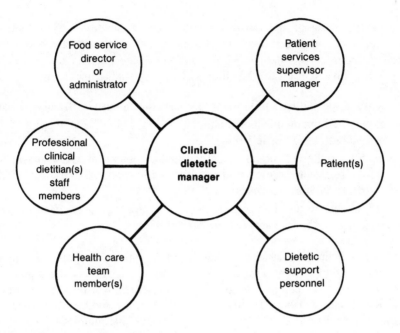

Figure 3-4 Clinical Dietetic Manager Role Relationships

the progressive clinical dietetic manager will go beyond these roles to ad-vance the profession and meet the needs of the specific institution.

Before designing or revising any job descriptions, information should be collected on licensure regulations and reimbursement procedures in the state. Copies of such documents as the *Standard of Practice for Nutrition Support: Dietitians* (1990) from the American Society of Parenteral and Enteral Nutri-tion should be compiled and used in drafting job responsibilities.

The specific job description should be based on the format used within the institution. Appendix A provides a basic position description for a dietetic assistant, technician, and dietitian. Different formats are illustrated; most institutions have a designated format for all positions within the institution. The job description of the clinical dietetic specialist is discussed below because the position is evolving and is thus quite different in each institution.

Responsibilities of the Clinical Specialist

Specialty practice is already a reality in clinical dietetics, although the particulars of what types of specialists are needed and the most economical and effective use of specialists are still open to debate. The question of whether both advanced-level practitioners and narrower specialists are needed underlies this debate. Numerous views are cited in the literature, suggesting diverse roles for the clinical dietetic specialist, including

- work in specialities similar to physician's specialties (Harrington 1976)
- expert in human metabolism and pathophysiology and employed by medical schools (Nestle 1984)
- training in the techniques of enteral and parenteral nutrition and provision of patient assessment and monitoring (Schwartz 1986; *Standards for Nutrition Support: Hospitalized Patients* 1984)
- consultant to the clinical dietitian on complex cases (Baird 1977; Hutchins 1985; *Standards of Practice* 1985)

A 1979 Pennsylvania study asked dietitians about the need for trained generalists as opposed to trained specialists; 46 percent agreed that a generalist was needed, 41 percent disagreed, and 13 percent had no opinion (Parks and Kris-Etherton 1982). Eighty-three percent had responded negatively to narrow specialization. In 1986, nutrition support dietitians were surveyed regarding the need for certification. Dietitians in the narrow area of nutrition support were split: 53 percent favored certification and 47 percent responded negatively (Jones, Bonner, and Stitt 1986). In 1985, Sandrick (1985) queried a random sample of 750 food service directors stratified by hospital size regarding the need for specialists, specifically nutrition support specialists, methods of specialty certification, and the effect of specialization on hospital care. The survey had a 72 percent response rate. The Sandrick study found agreement on the need for specialized practice, that specialization should follow experience and additional education, and that recognition of specialization should come from the ADA (Sandrick 1985).

In 1988, O'Sullivan Maillet conducted a survey on the need and responsibilities of clinical dietetic specialists in the acute care setting. Graduate educators (105) and beyond-entry-level dietetic practitioners (966) were studied. The need for clinical dietetic specialists was indicated by over 75 percent of both groups, with consensus defined as over 60 percent agreement. Practitioners achieved consensus (62 percent) on the need for specialists in narrow categories, including renal, nutrition support, cardiology, pediatrics, and endocrinology. Educators selected the same specialties with 54 percent agreement. There was agreement that specialists would have a positive impact on the profession. Eighty-nine percent of the educators and 69 percent of the practitioners thought the specialist should have responsibility for writing diet orders. Moderate consensus favored the functioning of the specialist in a clinical dietetic department separate from food services. The major distinctions between the clinical dietitian and specialist were the latter's greater knowledge of pathophysiology and the ability to manage complex cases. This study found a trend toward specialists wanting to write diet orders and to provide care to 20 or fewer patients per day. Over 75 percent of the respondents projected a need for between two and nine types of clinical specialists within the next 10 years in clinical dietetic service. Twenty-seven percent of the practitioners and 3 percent of the educators plan to be certified in the next 5 years. One-third of the practitioners already reported that their institutions currently employ specialists, and two-thirds thought their institution needed to use specialists.

SUMMARY

Clinical dietetic managers shape the departmental framework wherein they function. A major responsibility entails the development, evaluation, and revision of documents, tools, and the organizational structure necessary for delivery of services. Mission and goal statements must be formulated to give vision and direction; policies, procedures, and standards are needed for consistency and quality measures. Organizational designs must be established to shape role relationships, scope of responsibility, and lines of authority. Finally, the employment of the clinical dietetic specialist should be considered in light of evolving roles and institutional commitments to in-depth nutritional care for complex medical conditions.

REFERENCES

American Society for Parenteral and Enteral Nutrition. 1984. *Standards for nutrition support: Hospitalized patients. Nutr. Clin. Pract.* 3(1):28–31.

American Society for Parenteral and Enteral Nutrition. 1990. Standards of practice for nutrition support: Dietitians. *Nutr. Clin. Pract.* 5(2):74–78.

Baird, S.C. 1977. Toward development of a theory of the structures underlying the roles of two specialization categories of dietitians: The hospital. Ph.D. diss., University of Houston, Houston.

Code of Ethics for the Profession of Dietetics. 1988. *J. Am. Dietet. Assoc.* 88(12):1592–96.

Gross, Neal, Ward Mason, and Alexander McEachern. 1958. *Explorations in role analysis.* New York: John Wiley and Sons, Inc.

Guidelines for a committee on nutritional care of the hospital medical board. 1985. *Am. J. of Clin. Nutr.* 42(11):906–08.

Harrington, K. 1976. Charging for nutritional services of the hospital dietitian. *J. Am. Dietet. Assoc.* 68(4):344–46.

Hutchins, E. D. 1985. *Training for dietitians working in critical care. Sixth Ross Roundtables on Medical Issues,* Columbus, Ohio.

Joint Commission on the Accreditation of Healthcare Organizations. 1989. *Accreditation manual for hospitals.* Chicago: JCAHO.

Jones, M.G., J.L. Bonner, and K.R. Stitt. 1986. Nutritional support service: Role of the clinical dietitian. *J. Am. Dietet. Assoc.* 86(1):68–71.

Kane, Michael, et al. 1990. Role delineation for dietetic practitioners: Empirical results. *JADA 90(8):1124–31.*

Nestle, Marion. 1984. Leadership in clinical dietetics. Meeting the challenges to roles in nutritional support. *J. Am. Dietet. Assoc.* 84(11):1349–56.

O'Sullivan Maillet, Julie. 1989. The services of clinical dietetic specialists in acute care settings as perceived by dietetic practitioners and dietetic educators. Ph.D. diss., New York University, New York.

Parks, Sara, and Penny Kris-Etherton. 1982. Practitioners view dietetic roles of the 1980s. *J. Am. Dietet. Assoc.* 80(6):574–76.

Sandrick, J.G. 1985. Generalist-specialist issues within the dietetic profession. Ph.D. diss., University of Pittsburgh, Pittsburgh.

Schwartz, Denise. 1986. Critical care patients: What is critical knowledge for dietitians. *Top. Clin. Nutr.* 1(4):1–7.

Standards of Practice for the profession of dietetics. 1985. *J. Am. Dietet. Assoc.* 85(6):723–26.

SUGGESTED READINGS

American Dietetic Association. 1984. *Role delineation and verification for entry-level positions in clinical dietetics.* Chicago: American Dietetic Association.

American Dietetic Association. 1990. *Role delineation for registered dietitians and entry-level dietetic technicians.* Chicago: American Dietetic Association.

D'Costa, Ayres. 1984. *Introducing the dietary manager, Dietary Curr.* Columbus, Ohio: Ross Laboratories.

McClusky, Kathleen, Ligia Fishel, and Rebecca Stover-May. 1987. Nutrition priority system: A model for patient care. *J. Am. Dietet. Assoc.* 87(2):200–03.

Schiller, M.R. 1984. Current hospital practices in clinical dietetics. *J. Am. Dietet. Assoc.* 84(10):1194–97.

Chapter 4

Developing Skills for Effective Clinical Management

Managers are change agents. Their position within the organizational unit ensures the delivery of quality nutrition care. Since the external and internal environment constantly fluctuates and evolves, the clinical manager has a responsibility to keep abreast or get ahead of the changes. This chapter deals with overall skills of the manager and includes a section on self-evaluation.

As shown in the sample job description in Exhibit 4-1, the duties and responsibilities of clinical dietetic managers require a refinement of management skills. The scope of accountability is far-reaching. Many qualities and skills are needed, exceeding the standard expectations for entry-level practice. The goal is to be a good manager, in addition to being a good dietitian. A good manager needs to orchestrate the environment, rather than perform tasks designated for nutritional care practice. The clinical dietetic manager needs also to delegate some managerial tasks and authority to other members of the dietetic team. Conscientious performance of duties requires adroitness in applying the functions of management to the organization and delivery of nutrition services.

PERSONAL BACKGROUND AND ATTRIBUTES

Managerial success is, to a great extent, rooted in one's personal qualities and background. Yet, few clinical dietitians who enter the profession list clinical nutrition management in their long-range goals. The career aspirations of most new graduates focus on the excitement of obtaining a job in the profession and finding satisfaction in direct patient care. Thus, it is rare for a dietitian to prepare systematically for a position in clinical dietetic management.

One of the aims of this book is to provide a framework for the development of both managers and aspiring managers. Many steps can be taken

Exhibit 4-1 Job Description for Clinical Dietetic Manager

Job Title   Clinical Dietetic Manager   Cost Center _____

Department Name   Food and Nutrition Services   Wage Scale _____

Reports to   _____

MAIN FUNCTION

Plans, develops, implements, and maintains optimum nutritional care for patients through the coordination and management of clinical dietetic services.

DUTIES AND RESPONSIBILITIES

- Supervises clinical dietitians, including the Assistant Clinical Dietetic Manager who supervises all Dietary Assistants. Supervision includes recommending actions as to hiring, scheduling, promotions, transfers, salary and merit adjustments, discipline, termination, and annual performance evaluation.
- Establishes, enforces, and evaluates levels of productivity and performance standards for clinical dietetics. This includes standards on recommendations for diet prescriptions, documentation in medical record systems, nutritional assessments, patient follow-up, and patient/family education and counseling.
- Reviews and revises Policies and Procedures and Diet Manuals to reflect Joint Commission and state regulations, as well as current trends in dietetics.
- Identifies, reviews, and evaluates nutrition services through quality assurance and monitoring techniques to improve the quality of nutritional care.
- Serves as a resource person to dietitians, physicians, house staff, nursing services, and food service personnel regarding clinical nutritional practices, developments, and trends.
- Approves nutritional adequacy of selective menus and collaborates with purchasing, production, and patient service areas in the development of patient menus, recipes, and evaluation of new products. Evaluates conformance to quality standards and diet prescriptions.
- Coordinates clinical programs and discharge planning with other departments.
- Develops enteral feeding formulary committee and chairs annual review.
- Collaborates with clinical staff in the selection, development, and adoption of educational materials.
- Establishes and maintains regular, ongoing inservice training programs for clinical dietitians. Topics are based on departmental needs.
- Plans and implements an ongoing inservice training program for residents, staff physicians, and nurses.
- Establishes regular staff meetings within the clinical area to discuss departmental policies and to maintain open communication.

Exhibit 4-1 continued

- Assists in the development of departmental budgets, short- and long-range plans, and programs consistent with departmental and hospital plans.
- Serves as a liaison between nursing, medical personnel, and other allied health personnel in relation to clinical nutrition.
- Participates and contributes to management and professional committees at the hospital, in industry, in professional organizations, and at the community level. Serves as member of hospital committees.
- Plans and coordinates training of dietetic interns and other students from local colleges and universities enrolled in supervised practicums.
- Coordinates and conducts research projects associated with clinical dietetic practice.
- Completes special projects and performs other related duties as assigned.

KNOWLEDGE REQUIRED

Master's Degree in Foods and Nutrition or a related area from an accredited college or university, currently a registered (and licensed) dietitian. A minimum of 3 years administrative or supervisory experience.

during undergraduate education, supervised professional practice, employment in the field, and graduate studies to prepare for a successful career in clinical management. Some personal qualities of aspiring managers are discussed in detail here with suggestions for developing needed skills and qualities for the managerial role.

Self-Perception

Calvert et al. (1982) found that dietitians viewed their own image less positively than other health professionals. Efforts have been devoted to enhancing professional self-image through assertiveness training, marketing oneself, developing media skills and learning political savvy. Two national surveys have documented changes in the field of clinical dietetics. One study revealed that work activities have been upgraded through specialization in the field (Ryan et al. 1988). Another study verified that clinical dietetic practice had changed remarkably during the late 1970s (Schiller 1984). Both professional image and personal self-concepts have improved during the past decade (Ryan et al. 1988). These nationwide results indicate that clinical dietetic managers can achieve similar improvements in self-image within their own institutions.

Equitable compensation is of concern because salaries in women's professions traditionally lag behind salaries in male-dominated fields (Finn and Gussler 1984). One study showed that "small but significant pay inequities exist between hospital jobs held predominantly by men and those held predominantly by women,'' even after taking into account such factors as education and experience (Muller, Vitali, and Brannon 1987). Clinical nutrition managers need to pressure both administrators and legislators to close the gender salary gap by advocating comparable worth surveys and improved salary schedules.

Personal goals can be set that include promotions to management positions. Clinical skills can be used as a basis for career opportunities in such diverse areas as clinical management, departmental administration, coordinating educational programs, marketing, sales, health care administration, or program development.

Experience

Life and work experiences also make a significant contribution to one's personal management style. Exposure to numerous situations, diverse organizations, different departmental operations, varied solutions to problems encountered in daily practice, and unique methods used by others in management positions helps one develop experience and self-confidence. Previous work with a variety of people and sensitivity to their personal needs and motivations help managers cope with personnel and labor relations issues inherent in managerial roles.

Simply being in the field for 5 to 8 years does not prepare one for a management position. Dietitians who engage only in repetitive, unchallenging tasks year after year are not likely to expand their knowledge and experience sufficiently to prepare for a satisfying career in management (Fargen et al. 1982).

One way to set personal career goals as a manager is to answer three key questions:

1. What are the goals (formal and informal) of the institution, and how does my position help me achieve these goals?
2. How does my position help my boss meet his or her goals?
3. What are the outcomes for which I am personally responsible (LeBouef 1984)?

Once you have answered these questions in writing, list several goals for personal accomplishment. LeBouef (1984) recommends the use of index cards to write down three sets of goals, including

1. *routine goals,* which are basic responsibilities that recur or are found in job descriptions

2. *quality goals,* which concern problems that need resolution
3. *innovative goals,* which are new and different while enhancing personal productivity and improving overall clinical services

For example, consider "teaching patients" to be a routine goal. The quality goal would then be "to reduce staff costs by using group teaching methods," and the innovative goal would be "to initiate a library loan system for audio and videotapes with appropriate reimbursable charges."

Once the list is complete, select two quality and two innovative goals and refine them. Refinement means stating them as positive accomplishments, incorporating a challenge, devising deadlines and measurable outcomes, and putting them in perspective. Most important, make them part of a personal long-range plan and review and revise them every 6 months.

Education

The academic preparation required for professional practice is usually insufficient for effective clinical dietetic management. Programs for entry-level practice provide only a foundation in nutritional care and principles of management. Competencies at this level involve primarily technical knowledge and skills, whereas expertise in human relations and conceptual thinking are reserved for advanced training (Rinke 1982).

Clinical dietetic management requires advanced training and often a graduate degree or graduate education for several reasons.

- The baccalaureate degree is designed to support entry-level practice; advanced practice is enhanced by graduate education.
- Graduate degrees help one develop confidence in one's ability to conduct research, provide consultation, manage clinical nutrition, serve as an active member of a health care or management team, and teach physicians or other health care professionals.
- Clinical dietetic management can be considered as an area of specialization. Many leaders in dietetics believe that eligibility for a specialty credential should include both graduate education and several years of successful practice.

Graduate education should provide both content and practice in areas that come under the jurisdiction of the clinical dietetic manager. Appropriate degrees would include, but may not be limited to, medical science, foods and nutrition, clinical nutrition, institutional management, business administration, education, community nutrition, communication, marketing, health care administration, and public health nutrition.

SELF-EVALUATION

Clinical managers need to conduct personal evaluations that are honest and rigorous. A critical look at one's management skills and activities can help improve performance. One method of self-evaluation is completion of a generic tool, such as found in Exhibit 4-2. Generic tools have the advantage of addressing numerous qualities in addition to those specific to dietetics. Many managers vary the tools used from year to year, thereby focusing their attention on a wide variety of skills.

One's managerial success is often assessed through quality monitoring reports and regulatory inspections, but the clinical dietetic manager can also set definitive criteria as a basis for management evaluation. These criteria could include

- percentage of variance from budget
- percentage of staff absenteeism
- percentage of staff turnover
- percentage of successful recruits
- number of employee grievances
- number of positive staff performance reviews
- number of inservice education programs
- levels of staff productivity

Another method of self-evaluation is a rating of performance of job functions. Using the clinical manager's job description, one's performance can be measured against the job description. As with clinical dietitians' evaluations, the manager needs to evaluate success in relation to annual departmental objectives and quality controls.

After completing a self-assessment, write objectives for development based on insights gleaned from this personal assessment. Many managers share results of self-assessment with their mentors for affirmation and support in managerial development.

MANAGEMENT SKILLS

Problem Solving

It is the role of managers to track where and how problems arise, to decide how to improve the situation, and then to proactively work on resolution. If the problem is an employee's lack of understanding or skills, a training program should be established. If the problem stems from employee attitude or morale, human relations efforts are needed. If the problem is environmental, the system needs manipulation.

Exhibit 4-2 Generic Self-Evaluation Tool

Art Bass, the former president of Federal Express and chairman of Midway Airlines, once told me, "Everyone is like a round dowel with a flat side." In other words, everyone has weaknesses. Yet, with all our flaws and flat sides, we can still aspire to any height if we are willing to invest the time and energy.

To improve your performance as a manager, you first need to learn more about yourself—your strengths and weaknesses. After all, as Eric Hoffer said: "To become different from what we are, we must have some awareness of what we are."

You can obtain a comprehensive picture of your leadership capability by honestly answering the following questions. To obtain the maximum benefit from the exercise, reflect on each question. You will then be ready to take the development steps presented at the end of the exercise.

MANAGEMENT INVENTORY

	Always	Usually	Sometimes	Rarely	Ideas or Actions to Improve (Notes)
1. Do you lead from power, not your interpersonal skills?					
2. Do you put the needs of your subordinates above your own?					
3. Do you visualize or identify what is necessary for the long-term success of your department/organization?					
4. Do you communicate a vision of the future to your subordinates?					
5. Do you regularly involve your subordinates in planning for the future?					
6. Do you encourage and inspire everyone to give his or her best?					
7. Do you help employees satisfy their work-related needs?					
8. Do you "go to bat" for your people with upper management?					

	Always	Usually	Sometimes	Rarely	Ideas or Actions to Improve (Notes)
9. Do you hold people accountable for their actions?					
10. Do you treat everyone in a fair but firm manner?					
11. Do you set challenging but realistic performance standards?					
12. Do you expect and insist on excellence?					
13. Do you present a bearing that indicates you are in command?					
14. Do you take disciplinary action against those who fail to measure up?					
15. Do you keep your word?					
16. Do you have the courage to • handle defeat gracefully? • face conflict head-on? • bear your burdens?					
17. Do you give credit to those who make worthwhile suggestions?					

Exhibit 4-2 continued

	Always	Usually	Sometimes	Rarely	Ideas or Actions to Improve (Notes)
18. Do you bring out the best in your employees by showing confidence in them?					
19. Do you maintain a sense of humor?					
20. Do you continually seek new and better ways to reach your department's/ organization's goals?					
21. Do you provide enough performance feedbacks to your subordinates?					
22. Do you keep the confidence of employees who confide in you?					
23. Do you give people the freedom to express opinions that might be different from yours?					
24. Do you recognize the achievements of your subordinates and openly show appreciation for their efforts?					
25. Do you give high priority to resolving employee problems and complaints?					
26. Do you share information openly and willingly?					
27. Do you let your subordinates know what is expected of them?					
28. Do you act on performance violations immediately?					

	Always	Usually	Sometimes	Rarely	Ideas or Actions to Improve (Notes)
29. Do you take the time to explain the reason(s) for changes?					
30. Do you encourage ideas and suggestions, and strive to develop on organizational climate that encourages open and free exchange of information?					
31. Do you put directives in the form of a request rather than a demand?					
32. Do you involve your staff in decision-making?					
33. Do you listen carefully?					
34. Do you encourage subordinates to think on their own?					
35. Do you explain the reason(s) why you have to reject impractical ideas?					
36. Do you assume responsibility for the actions of your employees?					
37. Do you try to instill in your team the desire to be the best?					
38. Do you actively seek promotional opportunities for your outstanding personnel?					
39. Do you regularly spend time with your subordinates?					
40. Do you inform superiors of the favorable things your people do?					

Exhibit 4-2 continued

	Always	Usually	Sometimes	Rarely	Ideas or Actions to Improve (Notes)
41. Do you try to anticipate what could go wrong in your operation?					
42. Do you take action in advance to prevent possible problems?					
43. Do you remain calm during crises?					
44. Do you make difficult decisions without procrastinating?					
45. Do you let people perform in their own style?					
46. Do you concentrate on the areas of your job that have the highest payoff?					
47. Do you delegate as much as possible?					
48. Do you set weekly and daily priorities for what you want to accomplish?					
49. Do you have a positive attitude?					
50. Do you establish deadlines for yourself?					
51. Do you show concern for your workers by ensuring that the workplace is clean, safe and comfortable?					
52. Do you maintain an open mind when a superior questions something about your operation?					

	Always	Usually	Sometimes	Rarely	Ideas or Actions to Improve (Notes)
53. Do you point out to subordinates areas that need improvement?					
54. Do you maintain a sense of urgency for getting important things done promptly and effectively?					
55. Do you keep your mind open to new ideas?					
56. Do you go out of your way to work as a team member?					
57. Do you accept constructive criticism gracefully?					
58. Do you encourage your subordinates to assume greater responsibility for doing their jobs better?					
59. Do you assume the blame when you make a mistake?					
60. Do you treat your subordinates and your peers with courtesy and respect?					
61. Do you work hard at clearing away the obstacles that hinder the performance of your staff?					
62. Do you uniformly enforce important rules and regulations?					
63. Do you demonstrate total commitment to doing the best job possible?					

Exhibit 4-2 continued

	Always	Usually	Sometimes	Rarely	Ideas or Actions to Improve (Notes)
64. Do you make yourself available to everyone—not just those you like or respect?					
65. Do you give people opportunities to develop and to implement their own ideas?					
66. Do you provide opportunities for someone to learn your job?					

	Always	Usually	Sometimes	Rarely	Ideas or Actions to Improve (Notes)
67. Are you tactful when saying "no"?					
68. Do you actively coach your employees?					
69. Do you willingly accept change?					
70. Do you admit when you make a mistake or you don't have an answer?					

ANALYSIS

After answering all the questions, go back over the ones to which you responded "always" and "rarely." Your leadership strengths are identified by your "always" answers. This knowledge is important because successful leaders build on their strengths. They seek positions where they know they can shine.

However, this important strategy can be limiting if you have serious weaknesses that you don't correct or minimize (for example, perhaps you're unable to get along with colleagues or to plan for the future). The people who continually advance in their companies are those who leverage their strengths and never stop trying to overcome their deficiencies.

With this in mind, review the questions you answered "rarely." These areas require work. Use the space marked "notes" to jot down ideas on how to improve. For example, if you infrequently involve your subordinates in planning for the future (question #5), you may decide to hold quarterly planning meetings.

After thinking about all the questions you marked "rarely," rank them according to their importance to your career. Then, adopt the philosophy of taking one step at a time, and develop and

implement a self-improvement program. As you do so, carefully monitor the reactions of your subordinates and peers. Obtain their feedback. If the early results are positive, continue in the direction that you are headed. Evaluate negative feedback to determine where you went wrong.

As you work toward improving your leadership skills, do not expect overnight success. Be patient with yourself: it takes time to turn a new behavior into a comfortable habit. Your subordinates also need time to adjust to changes in your style. At first, they may be suspicious. However, as you demonstrate consistency over time, they will respond favorably.

Your self-development labors will increase your chance of getting a raise and moving up, and you also will gain a sense of accomplishment as you become a more competent leader. Above all, you will improve your capacity to participate in one of life's richest experiences: helping others reach their highest potential.

Source: Reprinted from *Secrets of Effective Leadership* by Fred A. Manske, Jr., Sr. Vice President of Federal Express, with permission of Leadership Education and Development, Inc. © 1988.

Being a Change Agent

Change is constant. It is a process, not an event. A good manager is a good change agent. To succeed, the clinical dietetic manager must be committed to the change; develop the support and resources needed to implement it; provide training before, during, and after the change; and monitor the results of the change.

The process of change has several distinct parts. One way of thinking about change is that it has three distinct parts: initiation, implementation, and incorporation. The initiation phase encompasses a needs assessment, the development of the solution, and the preparation or plan for implementation. Implementing involves putting the program into practice and then reviewing and refining it. Incorporation occurs when the change becomes a part of the system. Maintenance of the change is important in the incorporation phase. Change of a system is unlikely unless all three components are completed (Petroglia 1987).

Leadership in Clinical Management

Leadership is widely discussed, but remains an elusive quality. It is both a process and a property and is defined as follows:

> The process of leadership is the use of noncoercive influence to direct and coordinate the activities of the members of an organized group toward the accomplishment of group objectives. As a property, leadership is a set of qualities attributed to those who are perceived to successfully employ such characteristics (Jago 1982).

The first part of this definition sounds like a definition of participatory management. The set of characteristics pinpoint what leadership is. These characteristics are altered over time depending on societal changes.

Part of being a leader is having excellent ideas and a clear sense of mission or direction. Yet, a mission is useless in day-to-day operations unless it is communicated and accepted by followers (Cronin 1984). Leaders in the 1990s (Brown 1988; Brown and McCool 1987) are made by competition and competence, and those admired the most by others are ethical, effective, and enduring. The essence of leadership in health care today is creativity—knowing what is needed, where health care is headed, mobilizing people and resources, sensing new directions, and welcoming change.

Leadership traits and characteristics have been reviewed extensively since the 1950s (Kellerman 1984). Groner (1986) identified qualities for career success by surveying members of the Hospital Research and Development Institute. Leadership was the top priority for career success followed by decisiveness, integrity, ability to communicate and speak, motivation and attitude, vision, drive, ingenuity, sense of accountability, enthusiasm, knowledge of the field and the institution, personal consistency, appreciation and sensitivity, loyalty, appearance and poise, and community leadership. Bassett and Metzger (1986) emphasize human resources and motivational skills as fundamental hallmarks of successful managers. They list essential leadership traits as the willingness to share power, respect for others, development of subordinates, rewarding above-average contributors, commitment to performance evaluation, and belief in basic values—human dignity, fallibility, and needs.

The common theme for leaders in today's business culture is vision, values, and teamwork. Leaders who have a strong commitment to a central focus achieve their goals and ultimately fulfill their mission. Clinical dietetic managers who want to set one or two basic themes can follow the example of the chief executive officer at SAS airlines who demanded flawless, matchless service (Austin 1988). Food service and nutrition executives should realize the importance of a clear statement of purpose and frequent review of objectives to be sure their vision remains central to daily activities in the department. Top performers exhibit sophisticated management and leadership skills (Schuster 1987) and the ability to sell their message (Finn and Doty 1988).

The *sine qua non* of a high-quality manager is to be thought of as a leader. The state-of-the-art approach for the successful clinical dietetic manager to use to become a leader is to apply the ADVANCE formula. The first step in approaching any situation is to do a thorough analysis or needs *A*ssessment based on prior experience and current information. The clinical manager *D*evelops the solution with a *V*ision of its outcome and with others doing the implementation. Drawing on skills in *A*ccounting, management, and *N*utrition, the manager *C*ommunicates the goals, teaches others, and revises the development plan if necessary. The final step is an *E*valuation of the total process in relation to present goals and directions for the future.

Skills Summary

The quality manager needs numerous qualities and skills discussed in this book. In summary, the high-quality manager

• supervises performance, rather than doing the task; clinical dietetic managers need to set time aside to supervise both professional and support-staff members.

- accepts role ambiguity; productivity parameters often used by practitioners are unrealistic for clinical managers. Work output is not as easily quantified since administrative activities frequently defy measurement.
- makes decisions on a timely basis
- realizes that as managerial experience and skills increase, technical skills may decrease
- delegates important tasks to subordinates to save time, improve morale, and develop managerial skills in others
- allows staff to make autonomous decisions in as many areas as possible
- motivates staff through praise, affirmation, and recognition
- deals with conflict, rather than avoiding it
- evaluates the staff on a consistent basis
- networks with a wide array of individuals both within and outside the institution
- exhibits enthusiasm and a positive attitude
- possesses integrity and high moral standards
- utilizes informal leaders, as well as formal leaders, to manage the department effectively
- evaluates self-performance (Flamholtz 1987)

REFERENCES

Austin, Nancy K. 1988. How to position yourself as a leader. *Working Woman* (November):140–42, 144.

Basset, Lawrence C., and Norman Metzger. 1986. *Achieving excellence.* Gaithersburg, Md.: Aspen Publishers, Inc.

Brown, Montague. 1988. The 1990s: Just around the corner. *Health Care Man. Rev.* 13(2):81–86.

Brown, Montague, and Barbara P. McCool. 1987. High-performing managers: Leadership attributes for the 1990s. *Health Care Man. Rev.* 12(2):69–75.

Calvert, Susan, Hank Y. Parish, and Karen Oliver. 1982. Clinical dietetics: Forces shaping the future. *J. Am. Dietetic. Assoc.* 80(4):350–54.

Cronin, Thomas E. 1984. Thinking and learning about leadership. *Presidential Stud. Q.* Reprint:22–34.

Fargen, D., A.G. Vaden, and R.E. Vaden, 1982. Hospital dietitians in mid-career: I. Career patterns, interests, and aspirations. *J. Am. Dietet. Assoc.* 81:41–47.

Finn, Susan Calvert, and Donald Doty. 1988. How well do you sell? Building a personal winning strategy. *Dietet. Curr.* 15(1):1–4.

Finn, Susan Calvert, and Judith D. Gussler. 1984. Women's issues and dietetics: Implications for professional development. *Dietet. Curr.* 11(1):1–4.

Flamholtz, Eric G. 1987. *The inner game of management.* New York, N.Y.: American Management Association.

Groner, Pat N. 1986. Qualities for career success. In *The effective health care executive,* edited by Terence F. Moore and Earl A. Simendinger. Gaithersburg, Md.: Aspen Publishers, Inc.

Jago 1982. Leadership perspectives in theory and research. *Man. Sci.* 28:315.

Kellerman, Barbara. 1984. *Leadership: Multidisciplinary perspectives.* Englewood Cliffs, N.J.: Prentice Hall, Inc.

LeBouef, Michael. 1984. Rising to the challenge. *Working Woman* (November):35–6.

Muller, Andreas, James Vitali, and Diane Brannon. 1987. Wage differences and the concentration of women in hospital occupations. *Health Care Man. Rev.* 12(1):61–70.

Petroglia, Maria. 1987. Planned change in organizational settings, Course, New York University, Fall 1987.

Rinke, Wolf J., Beatrice D. David, and Walter T. Bjoraker. 1982. The entry-level generalist dietitian: II. Employers' perceptions of the adequacy of preparation for specific administrative competencies. *J. Am. Dietet. Assoc.* 80(2):139–47.

Ryan, Alan S., Mary Beth Foltz, and Susan Calvert Finn. 1988. The role of the clinical dietitian: I. Present professional image and recent image changes. *J. Am. Dietet. Assoc.* 88(6):671–83.

Schiller, M.R. 1984. Current hospital practices in clinical dietetics. *J. Am. Dietet. Assoc.* 84(10):1194–97.

Schuster, Karolyn. 1987. What does the boss want? *Food Man.* (February):23–32.

SUGGESTED READINGS

Adamow, Christine L. 1982. Self-assessment: A quality assurance tool. *J. Am. Dietet. Assoc.* 81(1):62–63.

American Dietetic Association. 1986. *The Competitive edge: Marketing strategies for the registered dietitian.* Chicago: The American Dietetic Association.

Beck, Arthur, and Ellis Hillmar. 1983. The power of positive management. *Personnel J.* 62(2):126–31.

Gardner, John. 1990. Leadership and the future. *The Futurist* (May–June): 9–12.

Munn, Jr., Harry. 1985. Assessing supervisory leadership behavior. *Health Care Supervisor* 4(1):1–9.

Nanus, Burt. 1990. Futures-creative leadership. *The Futurist* (May–June): 13–17.

Owen, Anita. 1984. Challenges for dietitians in a high tech/high touch society. *J. Am. Dietet. Assoc.* 84(3):285–89.

Schuster, Karolyn. 1986. Projecting a positive image. *Food Man.* 68:67–71.

Webster, Richard S., and Susan W. Talbot. 1983. *Management skills for nurses. Moving up: Making the transition to head nurse.* New York: American Journal of Nursing Co.

Part II

Human Dimensions of Managing Dietetic Practice

Chapter 5

Determining Clinical Nutrition Staffing Needs

The organizational structure of the clinical dietetic department is based on the mission of the department and the availability of human resources, space, and technology. This chapter discusses issues in clinical staffing and offers some forms and procedures needed for optimum use of the clinical staff.

The current staffing patterns in hospitals were designed to meet the needs of traditional health care delivery. Clinical dietetic managers in the 1990s and twenty-first century face the challenge of altering their clinical staffing patterns. Outcomes of care need to be considered, and the most economical level of personnel to obtain the desired outcomes must be utilized. To accomplish these objectives, systematic program evaluation will be necessary.

ORGANIZATIONAL PLANS

Six levels of staff are often found in the clinical dietetic department: the clinical dietetic manager, clinical dietetic specialist, clinical dietitian, registered dietetic technician, dietetic assistant, and dietary aide. The department may be situated in the department of food service, as a separate department, or placed organizationally within another department. Figure 5-1 suggests possible configurations for the relationship between the director of food service and the clinical dietetic manager.

The interrelationships between the differing staff levels need consideration. Figure 5-2 diagrams some of the possible staffing pattern models. The strengths and limitations of each configuration need to be identified before determining the best structure for any institution. Principles of organizational management suggest that a limited number of individuals should report directly to the manager. Depending on similarity of tasks and proximity of work settings, this number usually ranges from 6 to 15.

The responsibilities of each position are fundamental to establishing an organizational plan for the department. The plan must follow the pattern of

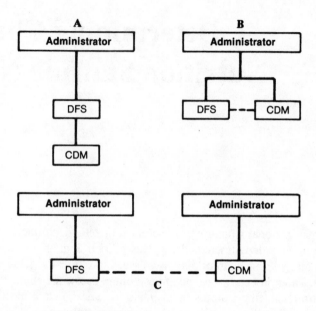

DFS = Director food service
CDM = Clinical dietetic manager

Figure 5-1 Possible Relationships between Food Service Director and Clinical Dietetic Managers

---

normal activities. Does the diet aide provide care to the same units everyday? Is this the case for each member of the staff? If patient reponsibilities vary from day to day, a direct-line relationship of a dietetic technician or dietetic assistant to one dietitian is inappropriate.

SYSTEMS IDENTIFICATION

Consider the departmental systems when establishing staffing patterns. Answering the questions in Exhibit 5-1 will facilitate the analysis of processes, work flow, and how much time is spent on specific functions. The answers may also identify problem areas that could be improved through reorganization of the clinical dietetic unit.

The process of establishing clinical staffing needs requires a thorough job analysis of all positions. Identification of all equipment/material needs, methods, and procedures as well as observation of the functions performed

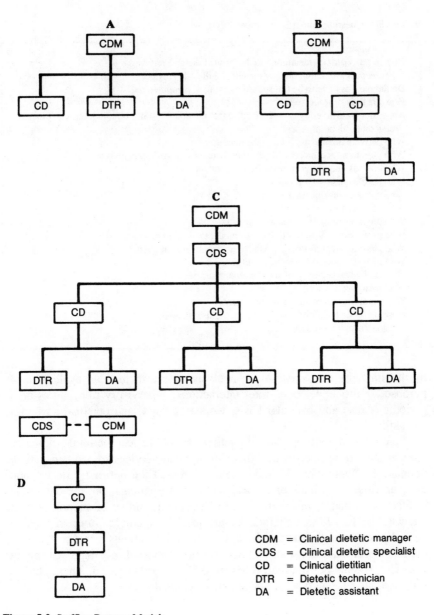

Figure 5-2 Staffing Patterns Models

Exhibit 5-1 Questions about Departmental Systems

How are diet orders transmitted to the clinical dietetic service?
What records are maintained by the clinical dietetic service?
Do the records have to be transposed or are they computerized?
How are menus processed?
Are systems sufficiently standardized so that dietetic assistants or computers can process
    new diet orders into meals?
Who delivers menus and food to the patient?
Who monitors food intake of low-, moderate- or high-risk patients?
Who collects and corrects menus with the client?
Who checks menus for accuracy?
Who provides nutrition screening?
Who documents and where?
Who provides basic nutrition assessments?
Who provides assessments to those at moderate or high nutritional risk?
Who provides the follow-up monitoring to each level of client?
Who provides nutritional supplements?
How is client acceptance of supplements evaluated?
Who monitors tubefeeding?
Who monitors parenteral nutrition patients?
How are procedures different by service or disease entity?
What is the patient turnover rate?

---

by the staff, is necessary. A job analysis should include an evaluation of purpose, significance, co-worker interactions, supervisory role, duties on a periodic (daily) and irregular basis, work standards, and personal attributes and skills.

The clinical department staffing pattern should reflect the total amount of clinical staff time needed to deliver designated services to a given patient population. A number of studies have addressed the optimal ratio of total dietitian time to patients or clinical dietitians to patients, but the data have limited use because information on the level and number of support staff is unavailable. In 1985, the Clinical Nutrition Management Group of Greater New York found the norm to be a ratio of 77 patients per one team of dietitian/technician/assistant. Other studies reported averages of about 100–150 patients per dietitian (Calvert 1982; Sheridan 1979). These studies reflected current practice, not necessarily the ideal.

PROCESS OF PATIENT CARE

Within an institution, care to patients should be uniform. Basic procedures for patient care should be similar, regardless of the service or unit to which each is admitted. More extensive procedures should be designated by patient illness acuity and/or by service. This means that the systems of providing care must be established with current and projected staffing patterns considered. Figure 5-3 is a sample flow chart showing how dietetic services procedures could provide care to each hospitalized patient. In the first step, a dietetic assistant distributes a screening form and menu to each newly admitted patient. The process continues with evaluation of screening data by technician or dietitian, assessment and determination of care level, establishment of monitoring routines, and implementation of a menu processing system. Each separate task or activity can be further elaborated into a policy and procedure. The use of a schematic flow chart for both actual and desired service provides a scenario for future change. The flow chart allows visualization of what is occurring and what should be occurring. This same flow chart can be used as the foundation of a time study or a quality assurance audit.

When developing procedures for patient care, ask yourself these questions. What is the anticipated outcome of each patient encounter, and how is the information about the patient communicated? What forms are needed to facilitate communication or document performance? For example, consider the traditional kardex card. What is its function? Who generates the card? Who discards the card? Is it filed or kept?

Until the diet office is automated and has computer printouts, a kardex system is necessary. If the dietetic assistant is using it to record menu preferences or to check a meal pattern, information on the diet order, likes/dislikes, nourishment needs, and meal patterns may be necessary. If the dietetic assistant is collecting preferences during meal rounds, the kardex needs to be available at mealtimes and may be the appropriate place to record the need for better tray examination for a calorie count or to document that meal rounds were conducted.

The system for documentation by the technician or dietitian also needs to be examined. The documentation form should highlight important information but not duplicate information. The use of noncarbon-required paper might reduce duplication for kardex entries. A notebook sheet or form showing when assessments have occurred and are anticipated and the dates for completion and charting of reassessments may facilitate continuity of care. A sample sheet that dietitians or technicians could use for personal documentation and transfer of care is shown in Exhibit 5-2. The form should be adapted to the particular needs of each facility.

The procedures for chart notes should also be examined. Are templated or standardized chart notes being used? Can they be used? At Memorial Sloan-Kettering Cancer Center, a series of "sticker notes" was designed to eliminate some writing and thereby save time. Exhibit 5-3 shows an incomplete

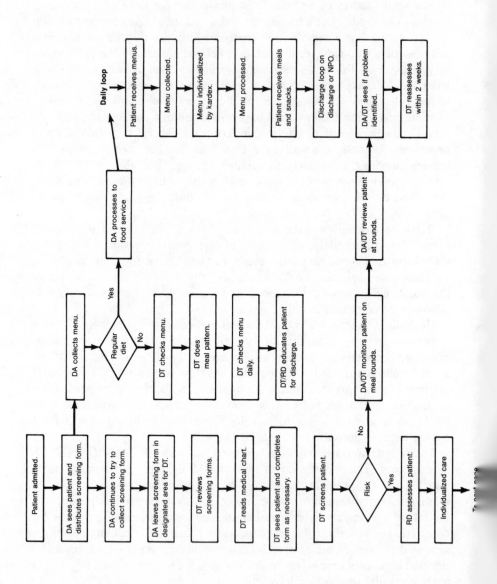

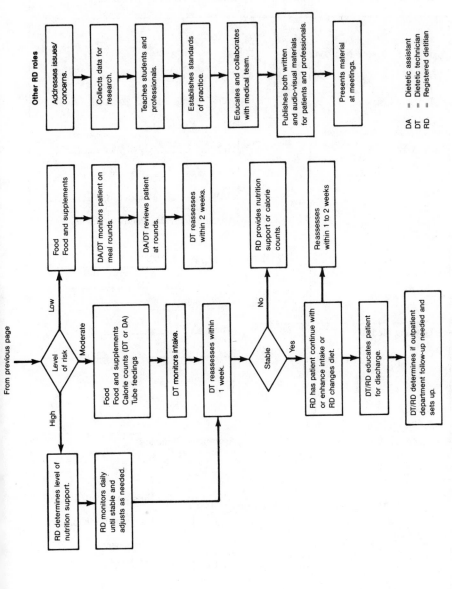

Figure 5-3 Flow Chart of the Process of Patient Nutritional Care

Exhibit 5-2 Documentation Sheet for Use by Dietitians and Dietetic Technicians

Food and Nutrition Service Department
Dietetic Notebook Sheet

Diagnosis: _____

Date Resolved

Problem List:

Adm. Date: _____

Room: _____

Ht.: _____ Usual Wt.: _____

Adm. Wt.: _____ % Change: _____

DBW: _____ Desired Wt.: _____

Appetite: Increase, Decrease, Stable

BP: _____   Temp: _____

Edema/Ascites: _____

Diarrhea: _____   Constipation: _____

Past Diets: _____

Pertinent Med. Hx.

When: _____

Reason: _____

_____

Meds.:

Treatment Plans

_____

Assessment Summary

Lab/clinical data:

Name	Date	Date	Date	Date	Date	Date	Date	Date	Date	Date
A1b										

Done and Charted: _____

Screening Form: _____

Assessment Charted: _____

Reassessment

Antici-
pated   Done   Charted

_____ _____ _____

Frequency of follow-up:
Daily   Weekly   Other

Referred to:
OPD/Specialist

Exhibit 5-2 continued

Date	Diet	Init.

Kcal Counts

Date	Kcal	Prot

Education Given:

Progress Notes: Use problem, goal, action as needed

	Date	Init.

Name: _____

Nourishments

With Meals   *Snacks*

                      3 PM

                      8 PM

Likes	Dislikes/Intol/Allergies

Food Habits

Graph weight change:

8 Kg							
6 Kg							
4 Kg							
2 Kg							
Present Weight							
−2 Kg							
−4 Kg							
−6 Kg							
−8 Kg							

Date _____

Special Facts

Source: Courtesy of Memorial Sloan-Kettering Cancer Center, New York, NY.

Exhibit 5-3 Examples of "Sticker Notes" to Expedite Medical Record Documentation

Dietetic Note

Date _____

S – See Screening Form

O – Diet Rx: _____ (Date: _____)

A – No apparent nutrition risk according to screening criteria. Nutritional discharge problems not anticipated at this time.

P – Follow-up on meal rounds. Reassess within two weeks.

Follow-Up Dietetic Note

Date _____

S – _____

O – Wt. _____ kg as of _____ Last Usual Wt _____ Wt Δ _____

  Diet Rx _____

  Lab _____

  Pt. Ed _____

A – Nutrition Intake: Adequate _____ Inadequate _____ 2°

  to _____

P – Implement _____

  Recommend _____

Clinical Dietetic Note

Date _____

S – _____

O – Diet Rx: _____

  Adm Wt (kg) _____ Usual Wt (kg) _____

  % Wt Change _____ DBW _____ Ht (cm) _____

  Lab: _____

  Current Problems: _____

A – At _____ Nutritional Risk 2° _____

  Needs: _____ Kcal _____ gm protein for wt _____

  Pt. would benefit from: _____

P – 1. Determine if PO intake is adequate via meal rounds.

  Taste-test supplements _____

  Start calorie count _____

  Provide snacks _____ Other _____

  3. Periodically monitor wt./lab data.

  4. Discharge Plan pending treatment care plan.

Exhibit 5-3 continued

Discharge Nutrition Plan

Date _____

_____ Arrange supplement/special feeding
_____ Provide nutrition education material on _____
_____ Provide limited counseling on _____
_____ Provide comprehensive counseling on _____
_____ Refer to out-patient RD for follow-up

_____

_____

Source: Courtesy of Memorial Sloan-Kettering Cancer Center, New York, NY.

---

note for intitial screening, discharge plans, and follow-up dietetic notes. Although not appropriate for all patients, such notes do facilitate documentation on common problems within the organization. The value of the sticker is its placement in the progress notes. The medical records committee of the institution generally requires justification to approve a policy for any addition to the chart, including the use of sticker notes.

Each piece of paper or form needs to have its life-span evaluated from start to finish. Where are overlaps with other forms? Is the overlap essential? Is the information too detailed or insufficient?

SERVICES PROVIDED TO THE PATIENT

When devising staffing needs or re-evaluating staffing patterns, the focus needs to be on outcome. Will the change improve quality, reduce cost, minimize overlap? To determine whether the change will indeed improve quality, ask these important questions:

- What level of care is given to each patient type?
- What is the patient turnover rate?
- What level of personnel should provide the service?
- What type of services are needed for the patient?
- Is the type of service provided necessary?
- Is the type of service provided desired and by whom?
- Is the type of service consistent with the problem?
- What is the result of no service (intervention)?
- Does the patient benefit from the service? How?

COST-CONTAINMENT ISSUES

Cost containment will be one hallmark for patient care over the next few decades. This set of questions focuses on potential cost-containment measures that save money without major sacrifice in the quality of patient care.

- Can lower-level personnel perform the task?
- Can the task be subdivided, with certain portions delegated to lower-level personnel?
- Can middle-management positions be reduced?
- Can the dietitian or technician or dietetic assistant spend more time in direct patient care?
- Can the time per procedure decrease?
- Can the level of the procedure decrease?
- Can the number of procedures decrease?
- Can the use of supplies or enteral products decrease?
- What types of technology can save time or money?

DECISION-MAKING CAPACITY

The final set of questions on staffing patterns is often facility-specific. The level of decision making by the clinical dietitian dictates the level of personnel needed. The more specific the standards of care, the more likely that lower-level personnel can carry out the task. The criteria for writing in the medical record influences what information can be documented by lower-level personnel. A strong commitment to research increases the need for higher-level personnel.

ANALYZING LEVEL OF PERFORMANCE

Deciding which tasks are to be performed by whom is difficult. The role delineation studies conducted in 1989 by the American Dietetic Association provide a base for such decisions (Kane 1990). However, measurement of what exists is different than what should be now and in the future. The clinical dietetic manager needs to use the role studies as a foundation, but should go beyond the identified roles.

McCormick (1979), in his book on job analysis, recommends that job functions be classified as tasks in relation to DATA, PEOPLE, and THINGS. Once the tasks are subdivided into these three primary areas, the complexity of the level of function can be determined. McCormick's model allows categorization of the tasks based on the level of skill needed to perform the task. Statements that focus on analysis, synthesis, and evaluation require higher-level decision making. The higher the level of decision making, the higher the level of personnel needed. DATA activities related to comparing, copying, computing, and compiling information can be assigned to technical-level personnel. Analyzing and innovating are more likely designated as staff dietitian level activities, whereas coordinating or synthesizing is appropriate for the clinical dietetic specialist, manager, or senior dietitian level. PEOPLE tasks, such as taking instruction, serving, and exchanging information, are technical-level duties, whereas dietitians are better prepared for activities involving other people skills. Specialists and managers generally spend considerable time negotiating and mentoring. Activities related to the THINGs scale are done by all levels of dietetic personnel. These include handling and manipulating equipment.

LEVELS OF PATIENT CARE

Can patients be divided into levels of care and then staff needs for each level be determined? In the 1960s and early 1970s, patients were prioritized based on whether they were on regular or special diets. Today, weight status, acuity of illness, and food consumption dictate the level of care.

Acuity levels should be established as policy in each institution. Level one is for all clients and is considered to be the screening phase. Screening is a rapid method of identifying patients with specific problems. It should be as sensitive as possible, using information that is easily available. Screening can be done by a combination of disease category, anticipated treatment, weight change, or weight status. If the screening procedure does not identify nutritional risk, the client is Level I. Level II patients have been identified as at potential or moderate nutrition risk. Based on this evaluation, the patient may be classified as "technician priority." The technician would be responsible for observing day-to-day food acceptance and then comparing intake to a preset standard. For example, one criterion would state, if patient cannot meet two-thirds of caloric needs in 3 days then patient is referred to the clinical dietitian. Level III and IV (high-risk) patients are evaluated by the clinical dietitian or the clinical dietetic specialist who makes a recommendation to the medical team. Alternatively, the clinical dietitian may confer with the clinical dietetic specialist regarding complex cases initially or during the monitoring of care.

The goal of determining levels of care is rapid identification of nutritional care needs. Therefore, screening should be done within 24 to 48 hours of admission, using the lowest level of staff to perform the necessary function.

How are criteria determined for levels of care? Generic standards can be adopted from the literature. However, dietitians may want to set their own criteria for major categories of admissions in their institution. These criteria assist in determining who receives nutritional care, what type of intervention is given, and the amount of time needed for the intervention.

Time studies or productivity studies can be used to document current practice levels. Time studies are generally done in 15-minute increments over 1 to 2 weeks. All activities are converted to a standard unit of time for evaluation. For each of the primary diagnoses at the specific institution, the staff time or levels of service should be documented. The level of service (minimal to comprehensive) should be explicit for each type of procedure. This information allows the clinical dietetic manager to describe the amount of time and type of procedures provided to different diagnoses. The cost per minute of the clinical dietetic specialist or clinical dietitian can determine the cost of the services provided by the clinical staff. Because the cost per minute is higher for the specialist than the dietitian, cost containment results when the dietitian can be used rather than the specialist. Chapter 12 goes into more detail on the costing of services.

Figure 5-4 illustrates the relationship between staffing needs and types of services provided. The top of the cube can be used to categorize the major

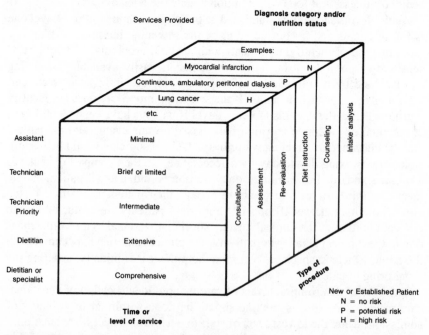

Figure 5-4 Levels of Care That Influence Staffing Needs

Exhibit 5-4 Clinical Staffing Needs Assessment

ENVIRONMENT

Type of institution: _____

Average # of daily admissions: _____/mo = _____/day

Average daily admissions:

Sun _____ Mon _____ Tues _____ Wed _____ Thurs _____ Fri _____ Sat _____

% pts. discharged within 48 or 72 hours: _____%

Average LOS _____ # of beds _____ _____% utilized

By Individual

HOURS AVAILABLE 1 F.T.E. = _____ hrs/wk   *Average Time Taken Yearly*

Position	*Number Currently Available*	*Break Time*	*Sick*	*Holidays*	*Vacation*	*Other*
CDS						
RD						
DTR						
DA						

IN PATIENT CARE/RESPONSIBILITIES (average per person)

TOTAL HRS./WK.	*Staff Meetings*	*C E*	*Rounds*	*Precepting*	*Group Teaching*	*Supervising/ Billing*	*Project Time*
CDS							
RD							
DT							
DA							

HOURS AVAILABLE PER WEEK

Days/Year: 260 days − (Sick) (Holidays) (Vacations) (Other) = _____ days/year

Days x (hrs/wk − break time) = _____ hrs/year   ÷ 52 = _____ hrs/wk.

Number of CDS _____ x hr/wks = _____ hours available for patient care

Number of RD _____ x hr/wks = _____ hours available for patient care

Number of DTR _____ x hr/wks = _____ hours available for patient care

Number of DA _____ x hr/wks = _____ hours available for patient care

Exhibit 5-4 continued

TIME UTILIZATION STUDY RESULTS (List in minutes per task)

Tasks: Direct Clinical	Overall	by Dx	by Service	Level of Personnel			
				CDS	RD	DTR	DA
Nutr. Screening							
Nutr. Assessment							
Follow-up							
Kcal Counts							
Reassessment							
Nutr. History							
Diet Instruction							
Diet Counseling							

Acuity of nutrition: % _____ no risk   _____ potential risk   _____ at risk
Mode of feeding: percent on: oral _____   TF _____   PN _____   NPO _____
Average Minutes Per Person Per Day

	Menu Mod.	Diet Change	Clerical	Meal Rounds	Phone Consults	Other
CDS						
RD						
DT						
DA						

Tasks

	Estimated # Needed Per Day	x Time Needed	= Total Time Per Activity	Hours Per Week	Level of Personnel			
					CDS	RD	DT	DA
Nutr. Screening								
Nutr. Assessment								
Follow-up								
Kcal Counts								
Reassessment								
Nutr. History								
Diet Instruction								
Diet Counseling								

Hours Available Per Week for:

CDS _____   **Hrs. needs/hr. available = # of Staff**
RD _____
DTR _____
DA _____

Exhibit 5-4 continued

Key:	LOS	= length of stay
	FTE	= full time equivalent
	CDS	= clinical dietetic specialist
	RD	= registered dietitian
	DT	= dietetic technician
	DA	= dietetic assistant
	CE	= continuing education

diagnoses and the nutrition status of the typical clients. The side panel identifies the predominant procedures given to each category of patient. Finally, the front of the cube represents the time or level of service needed for each procedure and type of patient. Only after a thorough examination of the patient population and services needed can an accurate staffing pattern be developed.

Exhibit 5-4 can be a helpful tool in thinking through the entire staffing process. Note that levels of care, patient acuity levels, productivity goals, and clinical activities are all summarized on the form. The completion of such a tool is extremely valuable in analyzing staff needs and productivity levels in the department.

REFERENCES

Calvert, Susan, Henry Y. Parish, and Karen Oliver. 1982. Clinical dietetics: Forces shaping its future. *J. Am. Dietet. Assoc.* 80(4):350–54.

Kane, Michael, et al. 1990. Role delineation for dietetic practitioners: Empirical results. *JADA* 90(8):1124–233.

McCormick, E. J. 1979. *Job analysis methods and applications.* New York: American Management Association.

Sheridan, John F. 1979. Results of the Ross Nutritional Assessment Survey. *Dietet. Curr.* 6(6):31–36.

SUGGESTED READINGS

Bureau of Law and Business, Inc. 1982. *How to analyze jobs: A step by step approach.* Stanford, Ct: Bureau of Law and Business, Inc.

Clay, Glenda, Carla Bouchard, and Kay Hemphill. 1988. A comprehensive nutrition case management system. *J. Am. Dietet. Assoc.* 88(2):196–99.

DeHoog, Susan. 1985. Identifying patients at nutritional risk and determining clinical productivity: Essentials for an effective nutrition care program. *J. Am. Diet. Assoc.* 85(12):620–22.

Gael, Sidney. 1983. *Job analysis: A guide to assessing work activities.* San Francisco: Jossey-Bass, Inc., Pubs.

Gobberdiel, Linda. 1986. A new strategy for cost-effective care: Clinical dietetic staffing by diagnosis. *J. Am. Dietet. Assoc.* 86(1):76–79.

McClusky, Kathleen W., Ligia Fishel, and Rebecca Stover-May. 1987. Nutrition priority system: A model for patient care. *J. Am. Dietet. Assoc.* 87(2):200–03.

Noland, Marion S., and Ruth Steinberg. 1965. Activities of the therapeutic dietitian—A survey report. *J. Am. Dietet. Assoc.* 46(6):477–81.

Sheridan, John F. 1979. Results of the Ross Nutritional Assessment Survey. *Diet. Curr.* 6(6):31–36.

Werther, William B. 1989. Involving employees in change, productivity, and the future. *Top. Clin. Nutr.* 2(2):1–14.

Chapter 6

Staff Recruitment, Selection, and Retention

Personnel are the clinical dietetic manager's most precious and most expensive resource. A majority of the budget is designated for salary expenses. To be successful, the clinical manager must apply effectively the principles of personnel management: a selection system, basic planning and organization, a planned orientation, training programs, staff participation, and performance appraisals. This chapter addresses issues in each of these areas.

A quality staff is rarely achieved by accident. Service proficiency is the result of a staff-centered manager who focuses on the needs of the staff while considering the needs of the institution. Figure 6-1 illustrates the foundations for a successful staff.

SELECTION OF STAFF

Few decisions are as long lasting as the clinical dietetic manager's decisions on staff selection. The manager is responsible for the unit's performance, and human resources govern this success. Therefore, the task of staff selection needs to be approached in a systematic way. The major goal of personnel selection is to match the abilities and skills needed for the job to the applicant's qualifications. First, identify the essence of the job and its tasks and review the goals for the position. Then, identify mandatory and advisory credentials, preferences, and needs of the position. Certification credentials can identify minimal competence, peer recognition, and advanced level practice or specialty practice (American Nurses Association 1979).

After the framework for a successful candidate has been developed, the pool of applicants should be examined, and based on a match of their qualifications to the abilities and skills needed for the job, three to five of the best candidates should be interviewed. The strengths and limitations of each

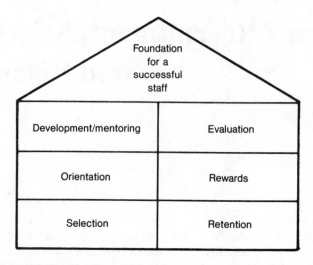

Figure 6-1 Successful Management of Personnel

candidate in relation to institutional needs should be considered. A checklist derived from the job description (Exhibit 6-1) can be used to determine the hiring criteria. This list also facilitates asking uniform questions during each interview. Alternatively, the candidate can do a self-appraisal based on the checklist. Motivational level and communication skills can be added to the checklist. In addition, if a checklist is completed before hiring, this initial data can then be used as a basis for the first evaluation and for subsequent patient assignments, including the type, quantity, and complexity of care.

The better the fit between the candidate and the institution, the higher the probability of job satisfaction. If the individual possesses most of the needed skills before hiring, there will be less need for on-the-job training and close supervision, but the individual may outgrow the position more quickly. On the other hand, a new graduate may be more highly motivated and more easily trained to the manager's style.

Interview

In addition to the checklist, which assists in the identification of the job candidate's skills, an interview establishes how the candidate's qualifications mesh with the clinical dietetic department. Personnel or dietetic services may conduct a screening interview before the full interview.

In the interview, one may want to review the resume and question the candidate on short- and long-term career goals, time gaps on the resume,

Exhibit 6-1 A Checklist for Recruitment and Interviewing

Jobs Requirement	Institutional Need		Interviewee's Extent of Experience		
	Yes	*No*	*Extensive*	*Moderate*	*Minimal*
Mode of Feeding					
Oral					
Enteral supplements					
Tubefeedings					
Parenteral feedings					
Area of Experience					
Medical services					
Surgical services					
Obstetrics					
Pediatrics					
Orthopedics					
Geriatrics					
Intensive care					
Specialty, please list:					
Level of Care					
Quantity of care					
Depth of care					
Type of Communication Skills					
Group teaching: clients					
Group teaching: professionals					
Individual interviewing					
Individual counseling					
Material development					
Written documentation					
Nutrition Care Process					
Data collection					
Assessment					
Plan					
Implementation					
Evaluation					
Leadership Abilities					
Independence					
Resourcefulness					
Other traits					

position development needs, rationale for leaving previous positions, and his or her criteria for career satisfaction. The interview allows assessment of the candidate's previous level and complexity of tasks, extent of job responsibilities, effectiveness in problem solving, and motivational level.

The skills of client interviewing are applicable in employment interviews, using such techniques as open-ended, nondirective questions. As with any interview, listening well and inviting questions are essential. Sample interview questions for a dietetic technician position are found in Exhibit 6-2.

The interviewer must be aware of the legal constraints of applicant interviewing. An inexperienced interviewer should review the Equal Employment Opportunity Commission's (EEOC) Uniform Guidelines on Employee Selection Procedures, as well as state and federal regulations, including the Civil Rights Act, which bars discrimination on the basis of race, color, gender, religion, and nationality; the Age Discrimination Act; and the Rehabilitation Act.

When the interview suggests that the applicant is a strong candidate, explain to the candidate the next step of the hiring procedure, which may include a second interview, tour of the facility with potential peers, requests for samples of previous work, and reference verifications. The potential employee should understand the position, its limitations, and its demands. Convey specific information regarding timelines for final hiring decisions to the applicant. By communicating this information in an open manner, the

---

Exhibit 6-2 Sample Dietetic Technician Interview Questions

1. How was your trip (transportation) here?

2. What do you know about the job/position available?

3A. What experiences have you had to prepare you for the position available?

3B. What educational experiences have helped prepare you for this position?

4. What are your strongest attributes?

5. What is/are your major weaknesses?

6. Why should you be given strong consideration for the position?

7. I would like to pose a few scenarios and hear your response if you don't mind.

8. What questions do you have?

clinical dietetic manager gives the job candidates, whether hired or not, a positive impression. Such a positive impression may facilitate future hiring of the unsuccessful candidate.

A similar process can be used for hiring technicians and assistants. Generally, the interview for these positions is shorter, and the process may be limited to one interview. If the technician or assistant is to report primarily to a specific staff member, that individual should participate in or conduct the interview.

ORIENTATION

The purpose of the orientation process is to expose the new employee to the goals of the institution and department, the physical environment, the staff, and the policies and procedures of the department. Before the orientation period is complete, the skills of the dietitian or technician based on the job description and hiring checklist should be validated. A copy of the job description should be signed by both parties and kept on file. The orientation period should allow both for observation by the employee and of the employee while he or she performs key job responsibilities. Such observation provides helpful information for the evaluation at the end of the probationary period.

The probationary period generally lasts 2 or 3 months. Feedback about performance should be given consistently throughout this period. This evaluation should be developmental or formative for the purpose of skill enhancement. Stepwise increments of both quantity and quality of work should be established to promote successful integration of the new employee. The new employee should be encouraged to perform self-evaluations during this period. A comparison with the clinical dietetic manager's evaluation is an important aid in setting comparable standards.

PERFORMANCE APPRAISAL

Performance appraisal is a process that addresses the past, the present, and the future with the intention of improving outcome. A thorough performance review is an upward spiral. After assessing the past professional growth to the present, planning for future performance is set. The performance appraisal has both an evaluative and a developmental purpose. The evaluative component focuses on past performance. It ascertains the value of the employee to the institution and is the framework used to determine salary, promotion, transfer, or termination. The results of the evaluative portion should be linked to the reward system. A reward can be financial, compensation time, or an award.

The developmental aspect of the evaluation is future-based, focusing on improved performance. The clinical dietetic manager contributes to the achievements of individual staff members through coaching and frequent feedback until the next performance appraisal is due. The goal is to retain staff and set them up for successes. The employee should select a limited number of weaknesses to focus on improving at any given time. These problem areas should be based on the priorities of the unit, as well as the staff member's developmental needs.

Use of the Job Description

To conduct a meaningful evaluation, there must be an accurate job description. The evaluation is a process of comparing the characteristics of the job to the skills of the employee. Therefore, this job description needs to be up-to-date with criterion-based performance standards. These standards need to define what the tasks are, how they should be conducted, when each task is done, and how performance is measured. The same information used for monitoring quality of care should be used in performance evaluation. A sample criterion-based evaluation is in Appendix B.

Often evaluations are based on norm-referenced criteria in which one staff member is compared to another. For example, absenteeism may be related to group norms. In contrast, criterion-referenced evaluations are more outcome based; for example, absenteeism of less than 2 days a year would be considered excellent. Exhibit 6-3 lists some advantages, limitations, and functions of both norm-referenced and criterion-based evaluation. Evaluation of clinical staff should include both techniques. The criterion-based method is most beneficial when performance criteria can be set and achievement measured. Appraisal of the most essential and most time-consuming aspects of any position should be criterion-based. Data used to assess an individual's traits, skills, competency, or performance should be observable and measurable. Less essential items can be based on normative criteria.

When selecting the evaluation tool for performance appraisals, consider the nature of the activity, the degree to which the activity is measurable, the setting under which the performance and evaluation occur, and the availability of evaluation information from other pertinent personnel. Before the evaluation, there needs to be consensus on the purpose(s) of the evaluation. The employee should conduct a self-evaluation before the meeting. Between 30 and 60 minutes should be allowed for the interview/discussion. Generally, clinical staff should receive a probationary evaluation after 2 or 3 months on the job and then an annual or more frequent evaluation.

Exhibit 6-3 Functions, Advantages, and Limitations of Criterion-Referenced and Norm-Referenced Assessment Strategies

	Criterion Referenced	*Norm Referenced*
Functions	Measures achievement through operationally defined performance standards	Compares amount of patient care to other staff (# assessments, etc.)
	Maximizes validity of the job description	Provides consistent evaluation in comparison to others
	Provides consistent evaluations based on criteria	
Advantages	Emphasizes minimal competencies	Compares functions of staff in the hospital.
	Decreases competition	
Limitations	Requires repeat measurements	Increases competition
	Promotes misconception that comparison is unnecessary	Is not consistent over time

The staff member being evaluated needs to take an active role in the evaluation process. This can include self-appraisal of performance in relation to departmental goals, the job description, and the objectives set by the employee in the previous year. Self-assessment can be used in comparison to standards of practice and standards of professional responsibility.

Many institutions have their own evaluation form for all employees, which must be adapted for a clinical staff, generally from the job responsibility list. Exhibit 6-4 lists some of the major categories useful for evaluation. These characteristics are then scored on a scale from outstanding to unacceptable. It may be a 5-point scale of outstanding or exceptional, good or commendable, adequate or competent, marginal, and unacceptable. Establishment of generic descriptors can help standardize the interpretation of these terms. Competency levels for each point on the scale need to be developed. For example, what number of patient interactions is needed per week for "outstanding" performance? Or what percentage of the patients on the service need to be seen for an "acceptable" rating? A sheet for comments is critical.

Information Analysis

Once the purpose and system of performance appraisal are determined, data collection procedures and the frequency of obtaining data should be established. Because the evaluation must be as objective and equitable as possible, data from productivity reports and actual observation of performance throughout the evaluation period are essential. Staff participation in the evaluation process and the development of the job descriptors and criteria for success facilitates acceptance of the evaluation.

The clinical dietetic manager should not rely on a singular criterion or source for the evaluation. Multiple sources of data need   to be collected and analyzed. What feedback can subordinates provide? Peers? Students? Physicians? Other allied health personnel? Clients? Is this information documented anywhere? If not, can it be compiled in a folder throughout the year and summarized for the evaluation?

Evaluation Errors

Nauright (1987) identified six common errors in nursing evaluation:

1. going easy on poor performers; being lenient
2. holding standards too high, especially for the best performers
3. giving everyone the same evaluation, rather than discriminating among individuals
4. rating one individual high in all areas because he or she is particularly good in key areas
5. rating individuals based on current performance, rather than throughout the evaluation period
6. guessing about performance, rather than using objective data

The cost and time required for employee reviews must be reasonable. One system that can facilitate evaluation is keeping a diary of significant events and findings throughout the year. The entire evaluation system should not be so complex that it cannot be conducted on a scheduled basis, usually in a 30- to 60-minute time frame depending on the length of employment and needs of individual staff.

Quality Evaluations

Providing consistent and objective evaluations is an important part of being a clinical dietetic manager. To improve one's ability to evaluate staff, especially during initial evaluations, a review of the process should be conducted by the clinical dietetic manager's supervisor or by the human resources department.

The outcome of any evaluation should be a process of skill development. Recommendations on how to strengthen weaknesses, pointers on how to use

Exhibit 6-4 Categories for Clinical Staff Evaluation

Topics	Subtopics
Knowledge	Expertise Diversity Guidance needed
Quantity of work	Volume of tasks Timeliness of work
Quality of work	Handling of routine cases Handling of complex cases Recommendations for diet change Use of different modes of feeding
Communication	Oral Written Computer ability Educator
Ability to relate to	Clients/patients/families Peers Subordinates Manager Health care team
Productive work hours	Absenteeism Lateness Dependability
Professionalism	Adaptability/flexibility Cooperativeness Motivation Sensitivity Leadership Judgment Integrity Loyalty Assertiveness Organization Creativity Initiative Delegation Mentoring Strategic planning Ability to stay within budget
Development	Ability to learn Potential for advancement Future goals
Scholarship	Data collection Collaborative research Principal investigator Publications Presentations

strengths more effectively, and objectives for the following year should be offered. Performance goals should include such areas as improvement in direct patient care, counseling or teaching, research, record keeping, and contributions to the organization's goals. These performance goals should be a combination of ongoing, problem-solving, and innovative objectives. Overall, staff development programs should be based on the collective needs of the staff. Individual skill development can then be planned in relation to the departmental plan.

Performance Discrepancies

Magee (1964) discussed a method to address performance discrepancies systematically. First, judge performance against clear standards. Second, decide if the discrepancy is important enough to discuss during the performance review. If not, ignore it. If it is important, explore why expectations are not being met. Are the expectations unclear? Is feedback lacking? Is the practitioner lacking practice or knowledge? Third, provide constructive criticism. Discuss the positives first and then the discrepancy. Be specific and clear about the expectations. Fourth, try to inspire the person to improve by involving the employee in a plan of development. Fifth, if a problem is still anticipated, the next question on the decision tree concerns whether there is a skill deficiency. If yes, then train or retrain. If the individual does not acquire the skill, then reassign the task or the individual's job responsibilities. Figure 6-2 is a decision-tree model describing the above process.

The situation is more complex when the individual has the skill, but is not performing up to capacity. Such a situation has a motivational component. Poor performance can be caused by a combination of obstacles blocking the behavior, lack of consequences for not performing the behavior, some form of punishment for doing the task, or lack of reward for performing the task (Blackley 1989).

The clinical dietetic manager's expectations of the staff assist in establishing staff performance level. Subordinates tend to do what they believe is expected of them, which is consistent with the concept of self-fulfilling prophecies. Staffs need to be challenged to perform, and the expectations must be achievable. Unrealistic expectations do not lead to superior performance because when the goal is too high, the employee can give up trying. When a staff member repeatedly fails to meet performance expectations, retention of the staff member becomes a problem.

Discipline

Performance discrepancies occur in every work environment. To minimize these discrepancies, training programs and consistent feedback are

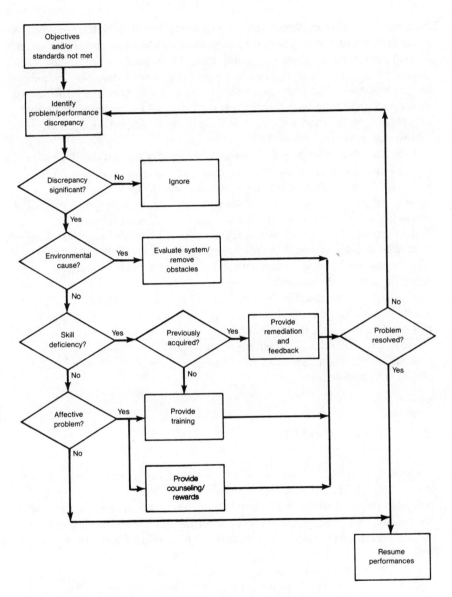

Figure 6-2 Model for Analyzing Practitioner Performance Problems

necessary. When a problem arises, a counseling session with the employee is needed. If the problem is not correctable, verbal warnings need to be given. If the problem persists, written warnings and a suspension are given. If the employee decides not to follow the suggestions, termination may be necessary at this point. For example, a dietetic assistant is consistently instructed to conduct meal rounds on one floor at each meal. Yet, the assistant continually skips large blocks of patients daily. This problem, when not corrected, causes a deterioration in patient care.

Firing a subordinate is a difficult task, especially one on the professional level. When doing so, remember the manager's primary obligation is to the institution. Termination does not mean the individual is not creative, successful, or a good practitioner. Rather, the individual may just not suit the needs of the institution. When the weaknesses of the individual are identified, if a performance improvement plan cannot be established, termination should be quick and handled professionally. Procedures should be checked with the human resources (personnel) department to guard against litigation regarding wrongful discharge.

Maintaining the confidence and respect of the discharged employee is essential both for the employee and for the clinical dietetic manager. A factual statement that the individual has stepped down should be provided immediately. In addition, other employees should be reminded of their importance to the institution, and they should observe that the dismissed employee is treated well.

STAFF DEVELOPMENT

The staff development plan should be based on the needs of the total staff. It represents an investment in human potential. Obviously, the longer the estimated retention of the staff members, the more time there will be available for staff development. Major expenditures of staff development money from the institution may require commitment of individual employees to the institution.

The development plan can be established for a short duration or an extended period of time. A 1-year plan is reasonable, but the clinical dietetic manager may want to tie the departmental 5-year plan to staff development by setting up a 5-year plan for the staff. If for example, the department plans to incorporate a clinical dietetic specialist into the department in 3 years, the plan can delineate how to upgrade a clinical dietitian into that position through formal staff development planning. In this way, both the professional staff member and the institution have successful outcomes.

JOB SATISFACTION

The clinical manager has an important role in promoting job satisfaction. An effective team is generally a satisfied team in which all players are content with their specific positions.

Few studies are available on job satisfaction for the clinical dietetic team. Stone et al. (1981) examined dietitians in the early years of their career and found that job satisfaction was linked to their ability to use professional judgment, have initiative, and have the feeling of accomplishment. Calbeck et al. (1979) found that increased autonomy enhanced job satisfaction for food service directors. In a study by Crissey et al. (1988), job satisfaction was higher when the dietitian was assigned few ancillary job duties, such as telephone answering, meal correction, screening procedures, and meal rounds. As would be expected, clinical dietitians prefer to concentrate their time on comprehensive assessment, counseling, and instruction. Job satisfaction is also related to the employee's perception of the importance of his or her position.

RETENTION

The cost of turnover is high. Yet, clinical dietetic practitioners are leaving their jobs at a rapid rate. In 1988, dietitians in acute care in New Jersey were surveyed on their job status. Twenty-five percent planned to leave their job within the next year (Crissey et al. 1988). The clinical dietetic manager needs to examine this trend and its causes and determine how his or her institution compares to the study findings. With the decreasing pool of available practitioners and the high cost of replacement in terms of advertising, insufficient staff for a number of weeks, and needed training, staff retention is critical.

Is termination or leaving the result of unrealistic expectations? Lack of rewards for success? Poor work conditions? Crissey et al. (1988) found the major reasons for employee turnover to be a desire for more money, more responsibility, or an easier commute. Two of three of these problems are within the clinical manger's ability to manipulate; successful use of these variables may increase retention.

A sense of appreciation is often a top-ranked goal among workers. A formal employee recognition program can go a long way toward demonstrating appreciation of individuals in the department and key collaborators outside the unit. Informal compliments, thank you notes, and an occasional simple gift also contribute to the feeling of need and appreciation. Job satisfaction contributes to employee retention. Retaining quality employees and using the skills of each individual make for a quality dietetic team.

REFERENCES

American Nurses Association. 1979. Credentialing in nursing: A new approach. *Am. J. Nurs.* 79(4):674–83.

Blackley, Joanne. 1989. How to fine tune your management skills. Presentation at the University of Medicine and Dentistry of New Jersey, Newark, June 15, 1989.

Calbeck, Doris C., Allene G. Vaden, and Richard E. Vaden. 1979. Work-related values and satisfactions. *J. Am. Dietet. Assoc.* 75(4):434–40.

Crissey, Janice, et al. 1988. Unpublished dietetic intern research project. University of Medicine and Dentistry of New Jersey, Newark.

Magee, J.F. 1964. Decision trees for decision making. *Harvard Bus. Rev.* 2(4):126–38.

Nauright, Lynda. 1987. Toward a comprehensive personnel system: performance appraisal. Part IV. *Nurs. Man.* 18(8):67–77.

Stone, P.K., A. Vaden, and R. Vaden. 1981. Dietitians in the early establishment stage of their careers. *J. Am. Dietet. Assoc.* 79(1):30–33.

SUGGESTED READINGS

Blomberg, Robert, Elizabeth Levy, and Ailene Anderson. 1988. Assessing the value of employee training. *Health Care Man. Rev.* 13(1):63–70.

Bushardt, Stephen C., and Aubrey R. Fowler. 1988. Performance evaluation alternatives. *J. Nurs. Admin.* 18(10):40–44.

Davidowitz, Ester. 1987. The Art of constructive criticism. *Working Woman* (May): 102–03.

Drucker, Peter. 1985. Getting things done: How to make people decisions. *Harvard Bus. Rev.* (July-August): 22–26.

Falvey, Jack. 1986. Fire early, fire often. *Working Woman* (January): 25–26.

Fulmer, William E. 1981. Step by step through a union campaign. *Harvard Bus. Rev.* 59(4):94–102.

Hamel, Gerald L. 1984. Employee discipline Seminar sponsored by Resource Applications, Inc.

Livingston, J. Sterling. 1988. Pygmalion in management. *Harvard Bus. Rev.* 121–130.

Lawler, Therese. 1988. The objectives of performance appraisal—or where can we go from here? *Nurs. Man.* 19(3):82–88.

Sullivan. C. 1985. *Management of medical foodservice.* Westport, CT. AVI Publishing Co., Inc.

The College and University Personnel Association. 1981. *Interview guide for supervisors.* Washington, D.C.: College and University Personnel Association.

Wiatrowski, Michael, and Dennis Palkon. 1987. Performance appraisal systems in health care administration. *Health Care Man. Rev.* 12(1):71–80.

Chapter 7

Professional Development

One of the significant challenges of management is to facilitate the growth and development of subordinates. This responsibility flows from four factors that have an impact on the practice of dietetics.

1. Academic preparation becomes outdated within a few (3–5) years after graduation. Dietitians and dietetic technicians must keep pace with new information or their knowledge soon becomes obsolete.
2. Entry-level education does not prepare graduates for advancement in the field. It is assumed that professionals will embark on a program of continuing development to master the knowledge, skills, and attitudes needed for specialization and promotion in nutrition care.
3. Dietetic practice is continually changing in response to trends in health care delivery. To remain strong in a competitive environment, practitioners must learn to provide high-quality services to diverse populations.
4. New skills are needed for management, research, and education. These skills are essential for promotion to leadership positions in dietetics.

Clinical dietetic managers are called upon to foster professional development both for themselves and their personnel. This chapter deals with concepts, activities, and strategies to facilitate performance in this area.

Professional development is like an umbrella encompassing personal development; career planning; and continuing, inservice, and graduate education. All aspects are important. It is a mistake to focus on only one or another fragment of professional development and ignore the other dimensions. A glossary of terms associated with professional development is shown in Exhibit 7-1.

Graduate education is one important dimension of professional development. It prepares professionals to think critically, substantiate practice with a

Exhibit 7-1 Glossary of Terms Used in Professional Development

---

Career planning: the process of determining long-range goals and sequential steps for achieving or improving one's career aspirations

Competence: the ability to carry out a specific task or tasks according to predetermined standards of performance

Continuing education: formalized learning experiences designed to (1) expand knowledge, (2) develop skills further, or (3) strengthen or modify practitioner attitudes or values

Inservice education: programs and learning experiences offered by an employer to assure competence to do the assigned job at a given organization or institution

Personal development: planned growth in character and/or personal life. Personal development complements professional development. It addresses such qualities as creative thinking, vocabulary, self-confidence, positive self-concept, personal relationships, emotional maturity, enthusiasm for life, positive thinking, stress management, constructive behavior, values, and self-motivation.

Professional development: a planned approach to identifying educational needs and opportunities to facilitate career improvement, personal growth, self-fulfillment, and possibly upward mobility and increased responsibility

---

strong theoretical base, and assume positions that call for specialization or independent practice.

Ordinarily, continuing education programs are less rigorous than graduate studies. These programs are often shorter and usually require little independent study on the part of learners. Topics are specific and often are related to everyday professional practice. Evaluation of continuing education is usually done through self-reporting, rather than through structured external assessment, such as written or practical examinations. Continuing education and graduate education complement each other.

The purposes of spending time and effort in self-improvement are the same whether the activity is categorized as continuing education, professional development, or personal growth:

- maintain an up-to-date knowledge base
- sharpen skills for improved performance
- learn new information to increase understanding of concepts or scientific theory
- develop new skills for career advancement
- deepen positive attitudes and clarify values
- strengthen personal commitment and motivation
- stimulate creative thought and conceptual thinking
- expand one's sphere of influence through networking and social contacts

• energize one's spirit, thereby recapturing a sense of purpose
• maintain registration, licensure, or certification

PATTERNS OF DEVELOPMENT

Margaret Sovie (1982) developed a model for professional development in nursing that can be aptly applied to the field of dietetics (Exhibit 7-2). This model provides a framework for designing educational goals and learning experiences that foster growth beyond entry-level practice. Each developmental phase is described below as it applies to clinical dietetics.

Not all dietitians progress through the developmental phases at the same rate. Figure 7-1 shows that some take a fast track, whereas others take longer to attain the necessary competence to advance in the profession.

Exhibit 7-2 Overview of Professional Development: Phases and Characteristics

---

PHASE I: PROFESSIONAL IDENTIFICATION/1 TO 3 YEARS

The entry-level dietitian characteristically enters the workforce with minimal clinical competency. Development focuses on orientation and inservice education. Skills are needed to

• understand hospital/department policy/procedures
• learn patient care practices and hospital organization
• internalize professional expectations
• deliver nutrition services effectively to a designated patient population
• identify specific areas of development and define career goals

PHASE II: PROFESSIONAL MATURATION/3 TO 5 YEARS

The dietitian at this level has selected a specialty area for practice and achieved professional recognition. Continuing education focuses on advanced practice and development for career advancement. Dietitians in this phase have

• career orientation: goals and direction
• holistic view of patient care delivery
• institutional perspective on most issues
• desire to take on increased responsibility and assume greater accountability
• awareness of alignment between job and personal growth/career satisfaction

Professional development at this phase includes self-direction and independent study. Focus is more goal oriented. Emphasis is on skill building, continued growth, enrichment, and stimulation.

Exhibit 7-2 continued

PHASE III: PROFESSIONAL MASTERY/(PROFESSIONAL EXPANSION WITH STABILITY)

Professionals at this phase are

• self-directed in most areas of learning
• professionally involved in committees or projects outside their prescribed job
• professionally involved in organizations outside the institution that enhance and utilize current skills and help maintain currency of information
• change agents within the department and institution
• committed to dietetics as a career and to the organization
• seeking to accept additional responsibilities

At this phase professional development is individualized according to specialty areas and career interests.

Source: Adapted from *Journal of Nursing Administration,* Vol. 12, No. 12, pp. 5–10, with permission of J.B. Lippincott, © 1982 and *Journal of Continuing Education in Nursing,* Vol. 19, No. 2, pp. 68–72, with permission Slack, Inc., © 1988.

Dietetic technicians have growth needs similar to those of dietitians. At entry levels, technicians engage in routine activities under close supervision. With further development, technicians assume greater responsibility for patient care, education, management and research.

Professional Identification

This first phase of professional development, lasting 1 to 3 years, is a time of orientation and inservice education. During this period new dietitians both internalize the science and master the art of dietetic practice. They finally realize the ramifications of their career choice.

Through a planned program of orientation new dietitians become familiar with hospital and departmental policies and procedures and see the institution as a whole. They study the standards of practice and develop behavioral patterns consistent with expectations. They begin to function as members of the health care team and develop confidence in their roles as team members.

During this phase of professional identification new dietitians become proficient in their job functions and responsibilities. This period of development is marked by refinement of skills that characterize meritorious performance.

Another aspect of professional identification is active participation in local and state dietetic associations. Attendance at meetings, committee assign-

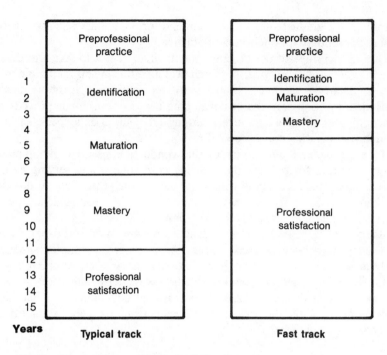

Figure 7-1 Timelines for Phases of Professional Development

ments, career guidance, and public relations activities enhance feelings of group solidarity. Such involvement often leads to volunteer work on other projects, such as nutrition hotlines, health fairs, food exhibits, food pantries, public education, and school nutrition programs.

Career planning occurs during this phase of professional development. As new dietitians become proficient in their professional roles, they should look ahead and define their desired career path. Although most students have been introduced to the idea of writing long-range career goals, most are unable to articulate their aspirations until they have personally experienced dietetic practice. Role models and mentors are extremely important during this phase of development. Guidance and support are essential in helping new professionals map out career goals and make steady progress toward fulfillment of their aims.

Professional Maturation

The second phase of professional development is characterized by specialization and preparation for career advancement. This is the time for enrolling in a graduate degree program and for obtaining specialty certification as appropriate for one's area of practice.

During this stage of development the dietitian begins to take a leadership role in professional practice. In the clinical area this means taking the initiative to identify and solve complex nutritional problems. It means creating expanded nutrition services or developing new systems for improved care, functioning at an advanced level, earning recognition as a specialist in the field, and expanding one's scope of responsibility.

Taking a leadership role often implies conducting research, giving presentations, writing for publication, chairing committees, and serving as a resource person for others both within and outside the profession. At this stage dietitians should expect to provide education for dietetic students, nurses, physicians, pharmacists, and other health professionals.

It take several years to attain credentials, engage in diverse experiences of increasing magnitude, exercise judgment in numerous complex situations, and fine tune qualities inherent in professional maturation. After 3 to 5 years at this level, the dietitian should evaluate his or her personal readiness for advancement to the next phase of professional development. If additional knowledge or skills are needed for advancement, a strategy should be developed to obtain them.

Professional Mastery

The third phase of professional development, professional mastery, is characterized by goal achievement. Dietitians who reach this stage of development are established in their careers. They are recognized for their expertise and are prepared to make significant contributions to the profession. They have "made it."

Any aspect of dietetics is a legitimate choice for professional mastery: management/administration, education, clinical specialization, teaching, writing, consultation, entrepreneurship, research, or private practice. There are numerous options and opportunities within the profession for ambitious, energetic, and innovative dietitians. The profession needs to keep its young talent. Clinical managers can facilitate that process by guiding clinical dietitians in career paths that maximize the use of individual capabilities and promote fulfillment of personal aspirations.

Once individuals attain professional mastery they do not simply stand still. Rather, they keep expanding the scope of responsibilities and experiences. They provide leadership in dietetic practice, education, governance, accreditation, research, administration, or other realms of influence. These leaders are involved in policy formulation. They sit on key committees and hold office in state or national associations. They are often invited to give presentations or write manuscripts as an opportunity to share their expertise.

ROLE OF THE CLINICAL DIETETIC MANAGER

The clinical dietetic manager plays a major role in the professional development of dietitians and support staff within the unit. Although each individual maps a personal career path, the manager can facilitate the process of goal development and goal achievement by

- setting the tone for development through role modeling and by insisting that subordinates engage in a program of personal growth and career development
- providing for the assessment and evaluation of continuing education needs and activities in the department, involving dietitians and technicians in the process
- facilitating personal growth of both dietitians and technicians by asking for copies of career goals and monitoring their progress toward goal achievement
- channeling information and providing growth opportunities consistent with individual needs of dietitians and dietetic technicians
- providing inservice education and/or continuing education opportunities to satisfy some development needs of employees
- making committee appointments or recommendations for project leadership based on professional development needs

ASSESSMENT OF STAFF DEVELOPMENT NEEDS

Assessment of staff development needs falls into two primary categories: (1) individual professional development needs and (2) departmental inservice and continuing education needs. Since techniques and resources vary greatly for each category, these assessments are discussed separately.

Individual Needs Assessment

Identifying individual strengths and liabilities is primarily a self-assessment activity. Mentors, supervisors, and friends can assist with this process, but in the end, each person must recognize his or her own areas of needed growth to achieve personal and career goals.

Several popular books are available to guide self-assessment in one or another dimension of personal or professional life. These self-help books can be particularly helpful in identifying areas for personal growth and development (see Suggested Readings).

The Pennsylvania State University Office of Continuing Professional Education in cooperation with the Pennsylvania Dietetic Association has initiated a comprehensive program of practitioner needs assessment (Chernoff et al. 1983). A state survey indicated that clinical dietetic practitioners desired more training in all phases of the nutrition care process (Kris-Etherton et al. 1983). Focus group interviews were deemed an effective method of determining professional developmental needs while use of a conference display area to obtain needs assessment data was less effective (Klevans and Parrett 1990). Based on the results of these projects, state-of-the-art self-assessment prototypes for various areas of practice are under development (Babjak 1990; Dougherty and Tower 1989).

Another method of individual assessment is based on the Sovie model for professional development presented earlier in this chapter. An overview, modified from Barr and Desnoyer (1988), is shown in Exhibit 7-3. Clinical dietetic managers can work with staff members to identify their phase of development and determine specific developmental needs.

Exhibit 7-3 A Guide to Professional Development Needs and Activities for Dietetic Personnel

Dietetic Technician (Basic)	
Patient Nutrition Care	*Research/Scholarship*
Menu system	Quality assurance data collection
Patient food service	
Screening	*Service*
Assessment	Member of local, state, national
Diet instructions	organizations
Nourishments/supplements	Attendance at local professional meetings
Documentation	
Mealtime problem solutions	

Dietetic Technician (Advanced)	
Patient Nutrition Care	*Management*
Nutrition assessments	Supervisory skills
Patient education	Orient, direct, appraise
Computerized nutrient data	Communication
Documentation	Motivation
Patient care as assigned	Sanitation and safety
Specialty unit coverage	*Research/Scholarship*
	Data collection and entry
	QA collection and analysis

Exhibit 7-3 continued

Education	*Service*
Education and training of food service workers and students regarding menu and patient care systems	Plan local or state conferences Attend national meetings Hold office Serve on committees

Dietitian Phase I/1 to 3 Years

Patient Nutrition Care

Policies, procedures, and standards for patient nutrition care

Competence in delivery of dietetic services to diverse population

Processes for assessing, planning, intervening, evaluating, documenting, and problem solving

Familiarity with sphere of activity: unit management, health care team functions, medical practices, hospital systems and resources, coordination of patient care

Referral systems for continuity of care

Knowledge, skills, values, attitudes, and beliefs needed for meritorious performance

Management

Skills to manage area
Use/revise policies/procedures
Maintain standards
Supervise subordinates
Comply with state and federal regulations
Enforce sanitation and safety standards
Maintain equipment and furnishings
Manage space and work flow
Maintain positive human relations
Prepare effective reports/written communication

Research/Scholarship

Apply research findings to clinical practice
Participate in institutional studies

Education

Patient education:
Effective counseling for diverse patient population
Group counseling
Group teaching
Professional education:
How to plan and direct learning experiences
Role modeling
Evaluating own clinical performance

Service

Attend local/state professional meetings
Serve on local/state committees
Volunteer for activities

Dietitian Phase II/3 to 5 Years

Patient Nutrition Care

Develop competence in specialty area and advanced practice: complex cases, team consultation, diet recommendations and prescriptions, problem solving
Develop new protocols
Establish standards of practice
Encounter and solve ethical dilemmas
Continuing education in specialty area
Increased accountability

Management

Conceptualize and coordinate nutrition services
Personalize leadership philosophy and style
Market nutrition services
Sit on institutional policy-making committees
Manage quality assurance
Provide leadership for hospital nutrition services policy formulation

Exhibit 7-3 continued

Justification of nutrition services
Effective use of technology

Education

Patient education:
  Develop educational materials
  Audit/evaluate systems
Professional education:
  Hold clinical faculty appointment
  Develop teaching materials
  Serve on educational committees
  Teach dietetic classes in specialty area
  Provide inservice education to nurses, residents, and other health professionals

Prepare reports, write business plans

Research/Scholarship

Assist in planning research studies
Submit abstracts for poster sessions/short research presentations
Assist in planning research studies

Service

Consult with outside groups
Attend national meetings/conferences
Chair committees
Hold office in local/state organizations
Serve on national committees
Mentor others

Dietitian Phase III

Patient Nutrition Care

Competence for career placement:
  Advanced practice
  Clinical education
  Clinical management
  Research
Expanding scope of responsibility
Leadership in clinical practice, patient care, standards of practice

Education

Patient education (in specialty area):
  Design new programs
Professional education:
  Teach staff development seminars/classes in specialty area
  Hold clinical faculty appointment
  Initiate educational programs

Management

Plan innovations in departmental organization and management
Direct policy review and formulation
Supervise professional staff
Make major contributions to institutional committees
Participate in institutional problem solving
Contribute to departmental planning and evaluation
Do manpower/productivity studies
Do strategic planning in specialty area

Research Scholarship

Design and carry out research studies
Present papers at national conferences/meetings
Publish research and other papers
Initiate project grants and proposals

Service

Hold state/national offices
Consult with outside groups
Provide state/national leadership in specialty area
Mentor others
Maintain effective network

Source: Adapted from *Journal of Continuing Education in Nursing*, Vol. 19, No. 2, pp. 68–72, with permission of Slack, Inc., © 1988.

Departmental Needs Assessment

The clinical dietetic manager provides inservice and continuing education opportunities for personnel in the department. Such programs should be designed to meet specific developmental needs of the dietetic staff.

To determine appropriate topics for these programs first clarify the purpose of continuing education programs within the workplace (Smith and Elbert 1986, 67-106). There are generally two main purposes. The first is to ensure that dietitians and dietetic technicians meet institutional standards of practice, including

* procedures for safety and sanitation
* components of the nutritional care process, such as screening, assessment, dietary intervention, patient counseling, documentation, and patient evaluation
* application of research findings
* innovations in practice
* new treatment modalities

The second purpose of continuing education at the workplace is to satisfy individual professional growth needs (Bell 1986).

To satisfy either purpose, needs assessment data can be obtained from a variety of sources, including

* interviews with nurses, dietetic administrators, and food service managers
* review of patient care records/audits regarding malnutrition, documentation, assessment procedures, etc.
* review of patient satisfaction data
* review of quality assurance studies and reports
* results of Joint Commission or other outside evaluations
* needs assessment survey of staff members
* topic analysis of current literature
* identification of mandatory continuing education programs for institutional licensure or accreditation (Bell 1986; Sanger 1987)

Clinical dietetic managers can use the results of either individual or departmental assessments to determine institutional continuing education needs. Programs and activities can be established internally, or they can be coordinated with those of the broader professional community.

Continuing education needs of staff differ. Therefore, clinical nutrition managers who take their staff development responsibility seriously attempt to provide educational opportunities for personnel at different stages of professional development.

Inservice and continuing education programs for dietetic technicians should focus primarily on the patient nutritional care process, supervision, and patient education. Continuing education for dietitians covers a broad range of topics and must provide for greater depth as one achieves career advancement.

Program planners often emphasize nutritional topics in designing programs for clinical dietitians. Although these are certainly important, neither dietitians nor their clinical managers should ignore the need for skill development in administration, education, and research.

The sample checklist presented in Exhibit 7-4 can be used as a framework to

- identify individual continuing education needs
- design a sequence of inservice programs
- conceptualize development needs of individual dietitians
- justify attendance at conferences or workshops
- allocate resources to support the purchase of certain continuing education materials or to pay program registration fees for qualified dietitians

Clinical dietetic managers should not ignore their own continuing educational needs while providing development opportunities for staff members. Although strategies for meeting development needs are the same for all groups, appropriate content and topics will differ among managers and the clinicians, researchers, educators, and the diverse personnel for whom they are responsible.

CONTINUING EDUCATION ALTERNATIVES

After the needs assessment, individual dietitians and the clinical manager must decide on strategies to be used for personal and departmental continuing education. Exhibit 7-5 offers a partial list of opportunities and techniques for individual staff development, and Exhibit 7-6 gives some departmental continuing education alternatives.

Journal clubs, journal reviews, and nutrition rounds are popular in-house methods of continuing education. They combine the advantages of minimal costs and individual involvement to foster the application of current research

Exhibit 7-4 Sample Checklist to Assess Inservice and Continuing Education Needs

Possible Topics	Critical to Current Practice Needs		Needed by Staff	
	Yes	*No*	*Yes*	*No*
CLINICAL PRACTICE				
Screening for nutritional problems	____	____	____	____
Research in clinical practice	____	____	____	____
Patient care documentation	____	____	____	____
Interdisciplinary team care	____	____	____	____
Coping with illness and death	____	____	____	____
Procedures for discharge planning	____	____	____	____
Use of technology in clinical dietetics	____	____	____	____
Cost-benefit methodologies	____	____	____	____
MANAGEMENT				
Organizing	____	____	____	____
Directing	____	____	____	____
Planning	____	____	____	____
Staffing	____	____	____	____
Coordinating	____	____	____	____
Controlling	____	____	____	____
EDUCATION				
Precepting students	____	____	____	____
Patient nutrition education	____	____	____	____
Effective diet counseling	____	____	____	____
Educating nurses and medical students	____	____	____	____
RESEARCH				
Developing research proposals	____	____	____	____
Writing an abstract	____	____	____	____
Getting started in clinical research	____	____	____	____
Initiating collaborative research	____	____	____	____
Designing research studies	____	____	____	____
Using statistics	____	____	____	____
GENERAL				
Setting of goals and priorities	____	____	____	____
Stress management	____	____	____	____
Public speaking	____	____	____	____
Ethical issues in dietetics	____	____	____	____
How to use the personal computer	____	____	____	____
Time management	____	____	____	____

Exhibit 7-5 Professional Development Opportunities for Individuals

Attendance at conferences/workshops
Attendance at lectures or meetings of the local professional associations
Attendance at state and national meetings of professional associations
Enrollment in courses or a graduate degree program
Participation in hospital teaching rounds
Enrollment in self-study programs
Completion of continuing education exercises published in professional journals
Use of self-assessment examinations, such as the one published by the American Society for Parenteral and Enteral Nutrition
Listening to audio- or videocassettes
Reading new books, professional journals, and relevant lay publications
Service on professional committees
Participation in offering workshops or seminars
Completion of a traineeship or practicum
Participation in collaborative research projects
Writing manuscripts for publication
Career counseling; working with a mentor

and trends to everyday practice. Guidelines for organizing these programs are given in Exhibit 7-7.

Many hospitals financially support attendance at continuing education events. To facilitate accountability in this regard, a form may be used for requesting attendance at outside continuing education events including anticipated costs and reimbursements.

JUSTIFYING THE COST OF CONTINUING EDUCATION

The ultimate purposes of continuing education are to improve cost effectiveness and the quality of patient care. Improved employee morale and job satisfaction and career advancement are also legitimate reasons to support continuing education, even if the learning opportunities do not affect patient care directly. To what extent should the clinical manager support the cost of continuing education activities that fall in either of these two categories?

First, the institution should fully support those activities that are essential for individuals to meet the demands of their jobs. Ordinarily, these activities are considered as inservice education. Such programs are generally offered at the institution, and attendance is required. Examples might include emergency routines, introduction to new policies, use of new or revised forms or procedures, safety measures, and the like.

Exhibit 7-6 Educational Activities within a Department

Journal clubs

Circulation/sharing of journals and new books within a department

In-house continuing education programs taught by various institutional personnel

Continuing education programs planned and offered by the institution for a broad audience

Encouragement of reading by copying and circulating the table of contents of pertinent journals and new books

Attendance at grand rounds or other in-house programs offered by other departments

Assignment of projects or research that requires extensive study and examination of scientific literature

Maintenance of a professional loaning library of audio tapes, videocassettes, study kits, or popular nutrition books

Funding to support individuals to attend pertinent programs in specialized areas of clinical practice, management, research, or education

Arrangement of an exchange program for staff members to visit other hospitals or organizations to discuss procedures and methods with professional colleagues

Policies that promote attendance at continuing education events during scheduled work time

Use of educational records for staff evaluation

Designation of an education coordinator in the department to serve as a consultant and to plan and promote continuing education of staff members

Provision of adequate resources for continuing education (equipment, space, personnel, registration fees, library, etc.)

Involvement of staff in the evaluation of professional development programs and activities

Provision of a mentoring system to guide and support development of staff members

Second, institutions generally provide at least the partial cost of continuing education programs directly related to an employee's job performance, even if such programs are offered outside the institution. Paid time off work, partial registration fees, and part of the travel costs are generally covered if it can be demonstrated that program objectives are congruent with one's area of practice.

Third, since dietitians are expected to maintain a current knowledge base, it is reasonable to expect the institution to provide at least partial support for programs and activities generally related to foods, nutrition, dietetics, health care, and service delivery. This category of support may include the purchase of books, journal subscriptions, and tapes, as well as organization of journal clubs, encouraging attendance at grand rounds, and payment of registration fees for university classes.

Fourth, since dietetic practitioners have a personal responsibility for maintaining their professional credentials, they should also contribute to the costs of membership in professional societies and of attendance at local and state

Exhibit 7-7 Guidelines for Establishing Journal Clubs, Journal Reviews, and Nutrition Rounds

---

JOURNAL CLUB

Objective: Systematic and comprehensive review of a specific area

Role of Clinical Dietetic Manager

- Determine the frequency of presentations and the length of presentation.
- Set up chairpersons for the year.
- If applying for ADA Continuing Education credit, find out approval procedures and deadlines for your state. Obtain forms and submit the proposed program by the established deadlines, which are often 1 to 2 months before the presentation.

Role of Journal Club Chairperson

- Select the topic. Obtain approval through clinical dietetic manager.
- Research the topic.
- Prepare a bibliography.
- Organize the presentation, i.e., what are the objectives?
- Assign articles to participants.
- Finalize outline of the presentation, handouts, and audiovisual materials.
- Give presentation; moderate discussion of topic.
- Submit attendance roster to ADA for credit.

JOURNAL REVIEW

Objective: Broad-based awareness of clinical literature

Role of Clinical Dietetic Manager

- Determine number of clinical staff available. Do you want to include dietetic technicians?
- Determine the number of journals to be used. Keeping abreast of three per person is feasible.
- Make a list of the most pertinent journals to follow. Go to the library to see if journals are available.
- Have dietitians/technicians select journals to review.
- Schedule dates for journal review articles to be submitted.
- Determine the best method for circulating articles.
- Designate categories, such as pediatric, maternal, or renal, and prepare bibliography of submitted articles periodically.

Exhibit 7-7 continued

- Give each staff member a bibliography for future reference.
- Maintain a file of articles or other system of making articles available to dietitians/technicians.

Role of Dietitians/Technicians

- In the month scheduled to submit articles, go to the library, scan assigned journals and make one or two photocopies of pertinent articles, depending on procedure implemented.
- Mark articles "Journal Review, month/year."
- Give copy of articles to clinical dietetic manager or designee.
- Scan bibliography for MUST READ articles. Obtain articles and read on a timely basis.

NUTRITION ROUNDS

Objective: Utilize and enhance clinical skills

Role of Clinical Dietetic Manager

- Determine frequency of meetings.
- Set aside time for nutrition rounds.
- Assign dietitians to select and present cases.

Role of Clinical Dietitians

- Select case and accumulate data on patient.
  1. pertinent medical facts
  2. past history
  3. hospital course
  4. socioeconomic data
  5. medications, tests
  6. nutrition profile
  7. history of nutrition management
  8. present assessment and plan
- Make a 10–20 minute case presentation.
- Answer questions and moderate discussion of patient management.
- Formulate new patient assessment and care plan if warranted.
- Document new interpretations/plans in the medical record.

Source: Adapted with permission from *Dietitians in Critical Care Newsletter,* Vol. 7, No. 8, pp. 1–3, © 1986.

meetings. Employers often pay these costs for employees who are official representatives, officers, exhibitors, speakers, or recruiters. In this case institutions support the contribution made, rather than the opportunity to pursue educational objectives.

Fifth, institutions may give limited release time with pay for dietitians to engage in career advancement programs, but the direct costs of such programs are generally borne by individuals. Although institutions may benefit from such programs, it is usually the individual who has most to gain from involvement in professional development activities unrelated to work performance. However, if clinical ladders or other career tracks have been developed, institutions may gladly support dietitians to attend programs that will help prepare them for advancement to specified positions.

Are the personal and institutional direct and indirect costs of dietetic continuing education justifiable in relation to the benefits derived? Within the nursing profession it has been suggested that such costs are an expensive burden and that the benefits are somewhat tenuous (Rizzuto 1982). A recent study of dietitians revealed a difference between expected and actual economic benefits of continuing education (Partlow et al. 1989). In order of importance, actual economic benefits were learning up-to-date information, preparing to handle increased job responsibilities, gaining new qualifications, increasing job earnings or qualifications, qualifying for a new job, and qualifying for reentry into the field. Becoming informed about some subject, improving interest or skill in learning, gaining from self-improvement, developing positive feelings of worth, and developing self-reliance or independence were considered especially important noneconomic benefits.

Evaluation can be either formative or summative: these types are also referred to as process and outcome. Generally, formative or process evaluations are conducted at the time of training to evaluate learner response to a particular program. Summative evaluations go a step further as they attempt to determine whether (1) participants met the learning objectives of the instructor, (2) participants transferred their new knowledge or skills to job situations, or (3) training had a positive impact on job performance (increased efficiency, saved time, or improved quality of care).

No outcome evaluations of continuing education were found in the dietetic literature. However, nursing research documents that training programs can result in improved patient education (Martin et al. 1986) and managerial performance (Blomberg et al. 1988). Summative evaluation of continuing education in dietetics is therefore a fertile area for research.

REFERENCES

Babjak, Patricia. 1990. Self-assessment: Build on your strengths and improve your weaknesses. *CDR Messenger,* Office on Dietetic Credentialing. (Summer):1–4.

Barr, Norma J., and Janet M. Desnoyer. 1988. Career development for the professional nurse: A working model. *J. Cont. Educ. Nurs.* 19(2):68–72.

Bell, Eunice A. 1986. Needs assessment in continuing education: Designing a system that works. *J. Cont. Educ. Nurs.* 17(4):112–14.

Blomberg, Robert, Elizabeth Levy, and Ailene Anderson. 1988. Assessing the value of employee training. *Health Care Man. Rev.* 13(1):63–70.

Chernoff, Ronnie, et al. 1983. Continuing education needs assessment and program development: An alternative approach. *J. Am. Dietet. Assoc.* 83(6):649–53.

Dougherty, Darlene A., and Joyce B. Tower. 1989. New projects to help practitioner competence. *J. Am. Dietet. Assoc.* 89(7):977–78.

Klevans, Deborah R., and Joan L. Parrett. 1990. Continuing professional education needs of clinical dietitians in Pennsylvania. *J. Am. Dietet. Assoc.* 90(2):282–86.

Kris-Etherton, P.M., Carl A. Lindsay, and Ronni Chernoff. 1983. A profile of clinical dietetics practice in Pennsylvania. *J. Am. Dietet. Assoc.* 83(6):654–60.

Martin, Deborah A., et al. 1986. The impact of professional education on nursing behavior in the practice setting. *J. Cont. Educ. Nurs.* 17(2):40–42.

Partlow, Charles G., Marian C. Spears, and Charles R. Oaklief. 1989. Noneconomic and economic benefits of continuing education for dietitians. *J. Am. Dietet. Assoc.* 89(9):1321–24.

Rizzuto, Carmela. 1982. Mandatory continuing education: Cost versus benefit. *J. Cont. Educ. Nurs.* 13(3):37–43.

Sanger, Monica T. 1987. Overcoming the dilemma of continuing education. *J. Nurs. Staff Dev.* 4(3):169–74.

Smith, Howard, and Norbert F. Elbert. 1986. *The health care supervisor's guide to staff development.* Gaithersburg, Md.: Aspen Publishers, Inc.

Sovie, Margaret D. 1982. Fostering professional nursing careers in hospitals: The role of staff development: Part 1. *J. Nurs. Admin.* 12(12):5–18.

SUGGESTED READINGS

Agristi-Johnson, Clair, Kathleen Dwyer, and Maria Steinbaugh. 1988. Nutrition support practice: A study of factors inherent in the delivery of nutrition support services. *JPEN* 12(2):130–34.

American Dietetic Association, Committee on Goals of Education for Dietetics, Dietetic Internship Council. 1969. Goals of the lifetime education of the dietitian. *J. Am. Dietet. Assoc.* 54(2):91–93.

American Dietetic Association. 1986. *Communicating as professionals.* Chicago: American Dietetic Association.

American Dietetic Association, Council on Practice Continuing Education Committee. 1988. Continuing Education: Keeping pace with the changing scene. *J. Am. Dietet. Assoc.* 88(10):1224–25.

Barber, Elaine D. 1987. Developing and maintaining a climate of support for staff development. *J. Nurs. Staff Dev.* 4(3):150–53.

Barnard, Janet. 1986. Managerial obsolescence: How to keep it from happening to you. *Supervisory Man.* 31(4):14–25.

Bennis W., and Bert Nanus. 1985. *Leaders: The strategies for taking charge.* New York: Harper and Row.

Blanchard, K., and S. Johnson. 1982. *The one-minute manager.* New York: Berkley Books.

Blanchard, K. and Norman Vincent Peal. 1988. *The power of ethical management.* New York: William Morrow and Co., Inc.

Blanchard, K. William Oncken, and Hal Burrows. 1989. *The one-minute manager meets the monkey.* New York: William Morrow and Co., Inc.

Bliss, E.C. 1984. *Doing it now.* New York: Bantam Books.

Brown, W.S. 1985. *13 fatal errors managers make and how you can avoid them.* New York: Berkley Books.

Buchholz, S., and T. Roth. 1987. *Creating the high-performance team.* New York: John Wiley and Sons, Inc.

Chorba, T., and A. York. *Winning moves: Career strategies for the eighties.* New York: Anchor Books.

del Bueno, Dorothy J. 1982. A clinical ladder? Maybe. *J. Nurs. Admin.* 12(9):19-22.

Flemming, Laura K., and Ann M. Apking. 1986. The supervisor's role in a training needs analysis. *Supervisory Man.* 31(5):40–43.

Flournory, Icilda C. 1984. Planning for continuing education: Goal setting and self-assessment. *J. Am. Dietet. Assoc.* 84(8):926-28.

Garfield, C. 1986. *Peak performers: The new heroes of American business.* New York: William Morrow and Co., Inc.

Heider, J. 1985. *The Tao of leadership.* New York: Bantam Books.

Hopkins, T. 1984. *Official guide to success.* New York: Warner Books.

Johnson, S. *One minute for myself.* New York: Avon Books.

Johnson, S. and L. Wilson. 1984. *The one-minute sales person.* New York: William Morrow and Co., Inc.

Josefowitz, N. 1985. *You're the boss.* New York: Warner Books.

Marsh, Karen. 1985. Increase your professional networth. *Nurs. Success Toady* 2(11):19-21.

O'Sullivan Maillet, Julie. 1986. Three techniques for clinical staff development. *Dietit. Crit. Care Newsl.* 7(8):1,3.

Rinke, W. 1989. *The winning foodservice manager: Strategies for doing more with less.* Gaithersburg, Md.: Aspen Publishers, Inc.

Rosenbaum, B.L. 1987. *How to motivate today's workers.* New York: McGraw-Hill Book Co.

Scheele, A. 1979. *Skills for success.* New York: Ballantine Books.

Snyder, John R., M. Rosita Schiller, and Jack L. Smith. 1985. A comparison of career-entry administrative competencies with skills required in practice: Implications for continuing education. *J. Am. Dietet. Assoc.* 85(8):934–38.

Thompson, A.M. and M.D. Wood. 1980. *Management strategies for women.* New York: Simon and Schuster.

Waitely, D. 1978. *The psychology of winning.* (Audio-cassette series.) Chicago: Nightingale-Conant Corporation.

Chapter 8

Team Building

Because clinical dietetic managers need to spend more time managing than producing, their job is to build an effective team that produces the desired outcomes. Cohesive teams are facilitated by collaboration and networking with the staff and other members of the health care team, a focus on outcomes and problem solving, the use of techniques to enhance job satisfaction, and a uniform, consistent management style.

COLLABORATION AND NETWORKING

Teamwork means collaboration. This internal networking or collaboration starts within the clinical dietetics department and extends to other departments, committees, the local community, the state, similar national groups, and other organizations. This type of teamwork can be expressed through brainstorming, completing questionnaires sent out by other groups, sharing recent articles, or referring someone to a position (Ross Laboratories 1989). For networking to flourish, the question, "What can I do for you?" must take priority over the question, "What can you do for me?"

Collaboration is a delicate balance of sharing aspirations and plans, building cooperative work relationships, and improving on each other's thoughts and ideas. Successes, and occasional failures, within the group, need to be shared openly. Collaboration has a synergistic effect when approached systematically. Its logical expression in daily practice is found in problem solving, definition of action plans, incorporation of change, and definition of responsibilities and rewards.

PROBLEM SOLVING

The effective manager is a problem solver who involves the team in problem identification and solution. Figure 6-2 provides an overview of techniques for problem solving issues related to practitioner performance. The art of problem solving begins with a clear statement of the problem. More often then not, departmental problems can be attributed to deficiencies in training, attitudes, or the work environment. If the problem is training, educational program needs should be assessed and new training opportunities initiated. If the problem is attitudinal, human relations skills are needed to investigate facts, counsel workers, and discipline those who may need it. If the problem is environmental, systems must be evaluated and manipulated. Managers should track their problems to identify the type most frequently encountered and then work proactively in their weakest area.

Numerous team-building skills are necessary for effective problem solving. Through the use of facilitative skills used in observation, analysis, decision making, and action, collaboration can be strengthened and even the most difficult problems can be solved.

ACTION PLANS

The clinical dietetic manager writes a departmental plan based on institutional goals, departmental goals, and staff goals. However, this activity is not done in isolation. A team needs to participate in identifying both the goals and the outcomes. Especially for professional staff, a voice in creating the action plan is even more important than having an overall knowledge of the plan. After all, it is the clinical staff who will bring the plan to fulfillment.

All dietetic team members should contribute in some way to departmental goal setting. Exhibits 8-1 and 8-2 show how individual activities are planned and used as a basis for the annual report. In this model the annual report provides both a summary of individual goal accomplishments for the year and an account of quality standards in the department. These examples focus on dietetic technicians, but the same strategies can be used for all staff members.

Team building needs additional emphasis when personnel are unionized. Antagonism between manager and unionized staff is common, especially during times of labor negotiations. To deal with these stresses, positive relationships must be built with an emphasis on problem solving. A strong central focus, such as specific departmental problems, can unify the staff and facilitate team building during periods of external conflict. Problem identification and action planning, with follow-up evaluations, help create a cohesive work group bound together by common departmental goals and expectations.

Exhibit 8-1 Examples of Annual Objectives (Dietetic Technician)

Objectives for 199___

Name: _____   Date: _____

Objectives	Activity	Responsible Person	Target Date
1. To increase assessments and charting by 15%	Assess new admissions within 72 hours of referral	Self	Ongoing
2. To compile a technician's training manual	Gather all information necessary to train a technician in clinical dietetics	Self and other DTs	April
3. To finish writing an article on the role of the technician in clinical practice	Summarize the job responsibilities of a technician and how a RD/technician team can complement each other.	Self	June
4. To expand my education	Enroll in a course	Self	Fall

Exhibit 8-2 Example of Annual Report Based on Annual Objectives

ANNUAL REPORT

To:
      Chief Clinical Dietitian
From:
Subject: Annual Report, 19___
Date: September 30, 19___

I. OBJECTIVE PLANNED:
  A. To write and have published an article on the RD/technician experience.
  B. To take required course for ADA Plan IV/V certification.
  C. To train DTs from _____ in their supervised practice experience.
    1. **Activities Completed, When & By Whom:**
      a. Article published in DPG newsletter, "The Role of the DT," Sept.
      b. Completed a course in biochemistry in May   .
      c. Training manual for DT compiled
    2. **Objective Planned:**
      a. To continue taking courses to expand my education
      b. To increase assessments and charting
    3. **Other Accomplishments, When & By Whom:**
      1) Taught nutrition series: "High Pro/Cal" presentation
      2) Manned cafeteria booth —"Garnishes," June   .

INCORPORATING CHANGE AND INNOVATION

A good manager is a good change agent, one who facilitates innovative and creative activity within the team. To be an effective change agent, the clinical dietetic manager must be committed to any anticipated change; develop the support and resources needed; provide training before, during, and after the change; and monitor performance after incorporating the change.

Teamwork happens when individuals collaborate to address common concerns. For effective change to occur, all or at least most team members need to concur with the change. Marris (1975) suggests that each individual must work through change themselves:

> However reasonable the proposed changes, the process of implementing them must still allow the impulse of rejection to play itself out. When those who have power to manipulate changes act as if they have only to explain, and when their explanations are not at once accepted, shrug off opposition as ignorance or prejudice, they express a profound comtempt for the meaning of lives other than their own. For the reformers have already assimilated these changes to their purposes, and worked out a reformulation which makes sense to them, perhaps through months or years of analysis and debate.

Loucks-Horsley and Hergert (1985) explain six stages of reaction to a change or innovation (Exhibit 8-3). The clinical dietetic manager should identify the stage of concern demonstrated by individual staff members and

---

Exhibit 8-3 Typical Expressions of Concerns about an Innovation

Stages of Concern	Expressions of Concern
6 Refocusing	I have some ideas about something that would work even better.
5 Collaboration	I am concerned about relating what I am doing with what other nutritionists are doing.
4 Consequence	How will my use affect patient status?
3 Management	I seem to be spending all my time in getting material ready.
2 Personal	How will using it affect me?
1 Informational	I would like to know more about it.
0 Awareness	I am not concerned about it (the innovation).

Source: Adapted from *Teachers College Record,* Vol. 80, No. 1, pp. 36–53, with permission of Columbia University, © 1978.

determine how best to interact with each one to facilitate personal acceptance of any change.

DELINEATION OF RESPONSIBILITIES AND REWARDS

Collaboration requires that the primary responsibility for a project and the tasks of all members be defined clearly. Just as the success of a baseball team depends on nine different players with different skills, a successful clinical dietetic staff team needs to use the unique skills of each staff member. These skills must be identified and congruent responsibilities delineated.

Resentment can occur when one member of the staff feels another member is encroaching on his or her area of responsibility. It is especially likely to occur among staff members whose responsibilities are similar or when one position has more prestige than another. In the first situation, the clinical manager should help clarify divisions in the gray area, defining boundaries and limits. When role conflicts occur among staff dietitians, clearly spelled-out criteria for referrals to the clinical dietetic specialist or technician need to be set and re-evaluated often. All individuals need to feel they are carrying a comparable workload and using to the maximum their level of expertise and qualifications. In the second situation, the staff need to know the criteria for appointment to the more prestigious position and the possibility of attaining that position. Advancement needs to be based on ability and not perceived to be a result of favoritism.

An effective manager earns the trust of the staff. The team must think that the manager has a uniform, consistent approach to both criticism and reward. When counseling is needed to improve performance, the behavior, not the individual, is criticized constructively. These disciplinary discussions should focus on problem solving, not personality. As the criticized area(s) improve, give positive feedback. Establish and use objective criteria when granting any rewards. This is true whether the recognition is a bonus, career advancement, or simply a pat on the back.

DELEGATION

Delegation is part of the process of establishing responsibilities—knowing who has what responsibilities and who has the ultimate responsibility. Successful delegation stretches your staff members' skills, increasing managerial time for other tasks and thereby increasing productivity. The use of yearly objectives as a structured method of delegation can facilitate the fair allocation of activities and professional skill development. A file system of due dates and progress by individual and project can help the manager stay on top of staff projects. Listening to any problems with the task assignment and offering advice is important. However, remember that responsibility and autonomy are delegated along with the job assignment.

Delegation is often hampered by a manager's fear of losing control and the knowledge that he or she can do the activity with greater dexterity and accuracy. Too often, managers limit delegation to gathering information and suggestions while he or she makes the final decision. Other managers allow some participation from the staff in the delegated activity. The more efficient manager allows the staff member to make autonous decisions, requesting consultation on difficult obstacles but generally relying on reports about the outcome of delegated projects. An example would be delegating to a dietitian the project of improving the screening system of the hospital. The first type of manager would encourage data collection and possible suggestions, but limited decision making. The second would delegate data gathering, some staff participation, and limited decision making. The more efficient manager would make only the final decision to implement or would allow a pilot implementation of the project with progress reported by the dietitian.

LEADERSHIP STYLES

In 1973 Tannenbaum and Schmidt (Sullivan 1985) developed a continuum of leadership to identify major leadership styles. The styles range from a manager-centered leadership style where the manager makes a decision and announces it to a subordinate-centered style where the manager permits subordinates to exercise freedom within limits. Although each style and the points between them are useful, leaders who are staff-centered and allow autonomy seem to have a higher chance of achieving professional staff satisfaction.

Sharing the power and influence of the responsibilities of the clinical manager with the clinical staff fosters collaboration. Power can be shared by having the clinical staff plan the agenda and chair staff meetings on a rotating basis. Having the chairperson as secretary at the previous meeting can facilitate continuity of the meetings. Assigning various staff to different committees within the department, institution, and professional community enhances the influence of the department and expands awareness of the internal and external environment affecting the department.

Effective clinical management means knowing who are the informal leaders and the formal leaders and utilizing both. Leaders tend to accomplish decision making by consensus, are frequently contacted by others for advice, and have the ability to influence others. A manager should strive to become a

Exhibit 8-4 Why a Manager Should Become a Leader

Let's Get Rid of Management

People
don't want
to be
managed.
They want
to be led.
Whoever heard
of a world
manager?
World leader,
yes.
Educational leader.
Political leader.
Religious leader.
Scout leader.
Community leader.
Labor leader.
Business leader.
They lead.
They don't manage.
The carrot
always wins
over the stick.
Ask your horse.
You can *lead* your
horse to water,
but you can't
manage him
to drink.
If you want to
manage somebody,
manage yourself.
Do that well
and you'll
be ready to
stop managing.
And start
leading.

Source: © United Technologies Corporation 1986.

leader. A leader instills confidence in the employees, showing consideration for the entire picture: environment, task, and individuals. A leader provokes enthusiasm from the team, examines the long-range projections, and overcomes obstacles. An effective leader creates future leaders. (See Exhibit 8-4.)

MENTORING

Mentors can make a significant contribution to the career development of their proteges (Ross Laboratories 1989). Bunjes and Canter (1988) note that the outcome of mentoring in dietetics is a practitioner with increased skills, knowledge, abilities, power, visibility, and credibility. These, of course, are the goals of staff development and enhance the clinical team effectively.

Mentoring relationships ordinarily last 5 years and progress through somewhat structured phases of initiation, cultivation, separation, and redefinition. It is likely, then, that different mentors play key roles in facilitating growth through the different phases of development from career entry through professional recognition, career advancement and finally professional satisfaction.

Clinical dietetic managers can serve as mentors to others. Just as importantly, they need mentors to assist and guide them in their own leadership roles. Areas of need may be lack of decision-making experience, insecurity, insufficient management expertise, or inadequate preparation in one or another aspect of clinical management. Vance (1982) noted that primary benefits of the mentor relationship are

- preparation for a leadership role
- career advancement and success
- greater personal satisfaction
- increased self-confidence
- enhanced self-esteem

The effective clinical dietetic manager nurtures professional growth through mentoring. This process allows job expansion and satisfaction for both the manager and the dietetic staff.

REFERENCES

Bunjes, M., and D. Canter. 1988. Mentoring: Implications for career development. *JADA* 88(6): 705–07.

Loucks-Horsley, S., and L. Hergert. 1985. *An action guide to school improvement*. Andover, Mass.: The NETWORK, Inc.

Marris, P. 1975. *Loss and change*. New York: Anchor Press.

Petroglia, Maria. 1987. Planned change in organizational settings. Course at New York University, New York.

Ross Laboratories. 1989. *Linking strategies for dietitians: Networking, liaison building, and mentoring*. Columbus, Ohio: Ross Laboratories.

Sullivan, C. 1985. *Management of medical foodservice*. Westport, Conn.: AVI Publishing Co., Inc.

Vance, Connie N. 1982. The mentor connection. *J. Nurs. Admin.* 12(4): 7–13.

SUGGESTED READINGS

Blake, Robert R., and Jane S. Mouton. 1983. Developing a positive union-management relationship. *Personnel Admin.* (June):23–32, 140.

Calbeck, Doris Cudney, Allene G. Vaden, and Richard E. Vaden. 1979. Work related values and satisfactions. *J. Am. Dietet. Assoc.* 75(4):434–40.

Hoover, Loretta. 1983. Enhancing managerial effectiveness in dietetics. *J. Am. Dietet. Assoc.* 82(1): 58–61.

Januz, Lauren. 1989. How to get on top of your job. *Executive Female* (March–April): 18–19.

Langholz, Edna. 1984. Organizing and conducting meetings in the workplace. In *Handbook for healthcare food service management*, edited by James Rose. Gaithersburg, Md.: Aspen Publishers, Inc.

Ross Professional Development Series. 1989. *Linking strategies for dietitians: Networking, Liaison Building, and Mentoring*. Columbus, Ohio: Ross Laboratories.

Stone, P. K., A. Vaden, and R. Vaden. 1981. Dietitians in the early establishment stage of their careers. *J. Am. Dietet. Assoc.* 79(1): 30–33.

Swindall, Linda. 1985. Delegate, delegate! *Working Woman* (July): 18–19.

Chapter 9

Ethical and Legal Issues

Dietitians often encounter situations with legal and/or ethical ramifications. Ethical decision making may concern denial of nutritional support to trauma victims, AIDS patients, the terminally ill, or those in a permanent vegetative state; the use of aggressive nutritional therapy after other treatments have been discontinued; and refusal of a patient to accept nutrition and hydration. Ethical dilemmas occur within the full range of dietetic responsibilities, including nutritional charting; disagreements with other health care professionals regarding treatment interpretations and protocols; alleged mistreatment of employees; lack of discretion in sensitive management situations; or observed dishonesty among coworkers. This chapter deals with legal and ethical issues of special concern to clinical dietetic managers in clinical, managerial, and educational situations.

CONCEPTS IN ETHICS

Ethics is derived from the study of philosophy, primarily human morals, character, and behavior. Ethical behavior is fundamentally a code of conduct that conforms to moral standards within a society.

Kenneth Blanchard and Norman Vincent Peale (1988), authors of *The Power of Ethical Management*, suggest asking three questions to test the ethics of an action or decision: (1) Is it legal?, (2)Is it balanced (fair and equitable)?, and (3) How will it make me feel about myself? Would I want to broadcast the results? Quite simply, ethics is doing what we think is right.

Health care is subject to the special tenets of medical ethics since life-and-death issues are often at stake. Patients place themselves and their lives in the hands of hospitals and health care professionals. In turn they expect to receive high-quality personalized treatment; have their best interests protected; and be perserved from pain, complications of illness, physical or mental harm, and even death. Respecting this trust, hospital personnel need to conduct themselves according to established ethical norms.

Codes of Ethics

Professional groups have codes of ethics to guide the professional conduct of their members. These codes conform to ethical norms of the society, but also address specific concerns of each professional group.

A Code of Ethics for the Profession of Dietetics (1988) applies to all dietetic practitioners and puts forth guidelines for professional practice and conduct. Ethical principles delineated in the code address "commitments and obligations of the dietetic practitioner to self, client, society, and the profession."

The code provides general guidelines for moral decisions and assures peer evaluation of violators. In most instances, however, prescriptions in the code are so general they are of little use in specific situations. Thus, it is essential to engage in a decision-making process when faced with ethical dilemmas in dietetic practice.

Morality

Morality is basic to any discussion of ethics. The concept refers to what is deemed befitting, good, and appropriate behavior for human beings as persons (McInerny 1987). Morality deals with the "shoulds" and "oughts" of human behavior. Personal values and ethical dilemmas are often rooted in moral development and norms for human behavior. For example, some physicians assert that the value of respect for life demands assisting at the death of patients who wish to die, rather than allowing prolonged suffering in hopeless cases. On the other hand, many religions, and society in general, prohibit euthanasia on any grounds. A health care professional, forced to take sides in such a situation, would face the dilemma of supporting individual moral assertions or widely held societal norms.

Dietitians' values may be in conflict with those of the public or even other health care professionals. For example, a dietitian may recommend the use of tubefeedings for a homebound debilitated patient unable to consume sufficient calories to maintain weight, but the caregiver may object to the inconvenience involved in this mode of feeding. A physician might recommend continued aggressive nutritional therapy for a terminal patient, whereas the dietitian may place a priority on the patient's comfort and desire to allow the disease to take its natural course. In these and similar cases the dietitian is expected to defend the importance of food and nutrition in relation to health.

No other health care provider is likely to have the same commitment to this fundamental value (Thomasma 1979).

Values in conflict are at the center of ethical analysis. "Right" and "good" ethical decisions promote the interests and fundamental rights of individuals while maintaining the proper order of values inherent in the situation (Thomasma 1979).

Ethical Principles

Many ethical decisions are based on the fundamental principles of autonomy, beneficence, fidelity, and justice (Matejski 1982). These principles are briefly discussed here.

Individuals have the right of self-determination. That is, they are free to decide what is best for themselves and make autonomous decisions based on personal beliefs and values.

When a dietitian "knows what is best" in a situation but finds the other person unwilling to conform, adhering to the principle of autonomy may present problems. For example, it is unethical during a labor strike for a dietitian to force employees to cross picket lines even though personnel may be needed to provide nutrition services. In clinical practice a dietitian cannot ethically coerce a terminally ill patient to accept insertion of a nasogastric tube even though enteral feedings would improve nutritional status.

Informed consent is based on the principle of autonomy. Even though patients are unable to diagnose and treat themselves they remain in control of their own health care. Patients authorize physicians and other health care professionals to

- determine what is necessary to maintain optimum health
- administer appropriate services when self-care is impossible
- prepare patients to care for themselves whenever they can

This authorization can only occur when patients are fully aware of their condition, as well as the options, ramifications, and probable effects of treatment.

Another important aspect of autonomy is decision making for incompetent patients. In some cases patients make their wishes known through legal documents, such as living wills or durable power of attorney. In other situations surrogate decision makers or the courts step in to serve as proxies to protect the best interests and personal desires of the patient.

Beneficence obligates professionals to avoid inflicting harm, to prevent others from doing harm, to obliterate harm or evil when present, and to do good to others. Patients and employees expect to be protected from harm or even the risk of harm while in the health care institution. Such elements as infection control procedures, security guards, lighted parking lots, and risk management programs demonstrate administrative commitment to this principle.

How are people treated when their interests are in competition with those of the institution or other individuals? Justice mandates impartial and fair treatment, but it also allows difference of proportionality based on such indexes as needs, merit, effort, or contribution. Justice is of major concern in the allocation of limited health care resources (Bell et al. 1985; Luce 1990). Not only must one determine which patients have the greatest need or merit but the interests of individual patients must also be balanced against the needs of the health care institution or society as a whole.

Fidelity includes the obligations to honor one's contracts and promises and to be truthful. Implicit in this principle are reliability, faithfulness to one's word, and fulfillment of expectations and obligations.

Fundamentals of Law

In the delivery of health care the responsibilities of providers are delineated in two types of law: contract law and tort law (Rosoff 1982, 167). These laws spell out both patient rights and the duties of health care professionals.

Contract law provides for delivery of competent services according to established standards. The bases for contract law among dietetic practitioners are the ADA Code of Ethics and institutional standards of practice.

Tort law prohibits any wrongful act, injury, or damage for which a civil action can be sought. Clinical dietetic managers and their subordinates must guard continually against conduct and decisions that, even unintentionally, may be illegal.

Every dietitian should carry malpractice liability insurance. It is particularly important in states where dietitians are licensed and have a legally defined scope of practice. Even if dietitians are covered under a hospital's group policy, it is wise to have an individual professional liability insurance policy.

A DECISION-MAKING MODEL

The principles, guidelines, and other considerations offered throughout this chapter can facilitate ethical decision making. In addition, use of a structured model can ensure decisions that are congruent with individual rights, as well as personal values and ethical norms. The following model was synthesized from various publications (Anderson and Glesnes-Anderson 1987; Bunting and Webb 1988) and can be used to guide the decision-making process.

- Identify the problem. Clarify exactly what is at issue and the nature of the resulting decision. Use assessment data or other pertinent information to define the problem clearly.
- Delineate personal values, legal standards, and ethical positions pertinent to the case. Identify any ethical or legal dilemmas inherent in the situation.
- Develop alternatives for resolving the dilemmas. Be creative; try to think of innovative ways to approach the problem. Examine and categorize the alternatives. Rule out alternatives that are undesirable.
- Predict possible consequences of acceptable alternatives. Look at the outcomes, benefits, and burdens that each alternative will accrue to each person involved in the case.
- Prioritize acceptable alternatives. Determine which option offers the greatest benefit with the least burden to those involved.
- Develop a plan of action. In clinical cases the plan will likely include treatment goals, communication with the medical team, counseling of patients or caregivers, criteria for evaluation, and implementation plans. The plan should also be documented appropriately in the medical record. In other cases the plan should include a statement of desired outcomes, meetings with administrators and persons involved in the case, guidelines for action, methods for monitoring implementation, evaluation strategies, and reporting mechanisms.
- Implement the plan. Carry out the established plan, monitor evaluative criteria, and document outcomes as appropriate.
- Evaluate outcomes. Use previously determined criteria to asses the effectiveness of the treatment or action. Reassess the problem and goals to determine the need for alterations or the creation of new problems.

CLINICAL APPLICATIONS

Widely published court actions regarding withdrawal of nutritional support have stimulated public interest in current ethical dilemmas (Ostling 1987). Cases of negligence for failure to provide timely and adequate artificial nutrition have been reported in the literature (Major 1986; Spencer and

Palmisano 1985). For dietitians to be sued for failure to provide reasonable nutritional care under a given set of circumstances, the charge must demonstrate four elements: (1) the duty to provide specified services (as spelled out in such documents as licensure laws, diet manuals, accreditation standards, policies and procedures, dietetic standards of practice, or federal regulations), (2) failure to carry out one's duty, (3) proof that damage of some type is caused, and (4) the damages are a direct result of negligence (Glantz 1987).

Denial of Nutritional Support

Major deliberations should precede the decision not to initiate nutritional support or to withdraw feedings when no longer appropriate. Dresser and Boisaubin (1985) suggest five considerations when making the decision to withhold or withdraw nutritional support.

1. Withhold nutrition if there is medical certainty that the person's condition is not likely to improve even if aggressive measures are taken.
2. Continue palliative care even after life-sustaining measures are withdrawn.
3. Continue feedings when there is any indication that withdrawal of nutrition and hydration would contribute to increased pain or discomfort of the patient.
4. Let the patient's wishes concerning treatment guide decisions regarding nutritional support.
5. Be sensitive to lingering questions regarding the discontinuation of nutritional support, such as the sedative effects of dehydration, hunger pains, and feelings of adandonment that may accompany nonfeeding.

Dietitians should be careful to establish clearly stated nutritional goals and to evaluate the effectiveness of treatment plans regularly. If goals have not been realized and the benefits of feeding no longer outweigh the burdens commensurate with it, withdrawal of nutritional support should be considered. Clinical dietetic managers would do well to monitor nutritional care planning and goal setting to ensure both conscientious practice and avoidance of litigation.

Concerns over when and where to document often arise in clinical practice. Exhibit 9-1 contains some essentials for charting in the medical record. Anderson and Green (1990) also suggest that progress notes should be clear, accurate, and concise with sufficient detail to allow recollection of all services provided.

Exhibit 9-1 Guidelines for Medical Record Documentation

1. Use BLACK ink.
2. Put direct patient quotes in the "S" of the "SOAP" method.
3. Place only FACTS in the medical record. Impressions must be clearly stated as such.
4. Complete ALL spaces on the forms. BLANKS indicate a failure to complete the form, which can suggest negligence (the date was ignored).
5. Use only standard abbreviations.
6. Date ALL entries. The TIME of the note should be stated when appropriate.
7. Print your name and title below your signature, if your handwriting is poor.
8. Do NOT obliterate anything in the medical record. To void a word/statement, cross it out with a single line, write "void," and initial it. If appropriate, explain the rationale for voiding the information in a subsequent note.
9. Document indications for diagnostic and treatment procedures that may pose a potential risk to the patient, e.g., the need for a feeding tube or TPN.
10. When noting a future return visit in your "Plan," use a calendar date, NOT "next Thursday."
11. Complete and place dictated or transcribed reports/forms in the chart in a timely fashion.
12. Do NOT go back and insert a progress note entry drafted later. If necessary, write an addendum and date it.
13. Date ALL missed appointments, lack of patient compliance, and the fact that the patient was counseled on the consequences of poor compliance.
14. Do NOT make uncomplimentary comments about patients or significant others in the chart.
15. Do NOT place anything in the medical record that has no bearing on the patient's care.
16. Do NOT use the medical record to criticize prior care or incompleteness of care of/ by other providers.
17. Be COMPLETE, ACCURATE, and LEGIBLE in documenting all information.

Source: Reprinted with permission from *Dietitians in Critical Care Newsletter,* Vol. 6, No. 5, p. 33, © 1984.

Advance Directives

By 1990, 41 states and the District of Columbia had enacted natural death acts authorizing the use of living wills (Orentlicher 1990). These legal documents allow competent adults to give legally binding instructions that, in case they are diagnosed as terminally ill and are unable to give directions concerning their care, no "extraordinary treatments" shall be provided that will merely prolong the act of dying (Mishkin 1986).

Twenty-five living will statutes make some mention of artificial feeding. Some indicate that artificial feeding can be withdrawn under certain circumstances. Others consider artificial feeding as "comfort care" and stipulate that it may not be rejected under the law (Society for the Right to Die, 1988).

Despite clear directives from patients, some hospitals and physicians refuse to honor living wills for fear of litigation from opposing family members (McLeod 1990). Also, some state laws allow withdrawal of feeding tubes and other life-support measures only when death is imminent.

Courts are often requested to rule in specific cases when a family member or guardian requests the withdrawal of feeding tubes. In the United States there are approximately 10,000 patients in a persistent vegetative state who are being kept alive by enteral feeding (Wallis 1986). For some of these individuals, advance directives may prevent sustaining of life "that in no way approximates what anyone's view of life ever was before the invention of the respirator and the feeding tube" (Greenhouse 1989). The 1990 Supreme Court decision on the Cruzan case will have a major impact on decisions in this regard (Friedrich 1990).

Durable power of attorney affords competent adults an opportunity to designate one or more agents to make decisions on their behalf in the event of subsequent incapacity. If the person creating the power of attorney specifies that nourishment and hydration may be withheld, such a directive is sufficient legal authority to deny such interventions (Mishkin 1986).

Both clinical dietetic managers and staff dietitians must keep informed about natural death acts and any other state legislation addressing the issue of nutritional support. Attitudes and practices in this arena have changed during the past decade (Sprung 1990). Current legal documents can facilitate ethical decision making when the need arises.

Is Nutritional Support "Extraordinary" Care?

In the past many ethical decisions were based on the concept of obligatory "ordinary" care and optional "extraordinary" measures. In modern health care these distinctions are clouded. What seems ordinary for one may be both ethically and morally unnecessary according to the judgment of another (Strong 1981).

It is now commonly accepted that the conventional term of "extraordinary" must be defined in its relationship to any given patient. "Proportionality" is a more appropriate term in decisions based on the nature of treatments. Accordingly, food and water may be withheld from patients when the following occurs:

- The treatment is futile and the patient will die regardless of what is done.
- There is no benefit to the patient or any obligation to caregivers, family members, or the general society.

• There is a disproportionate burden in terms of cost, pain, risk, or inconvenience for the patient (Lynn and Childress 1983).

Dietitians have a responsibility to participate in deliberations about the
benefits and burdens of nutrition support. The ADA Position Paper on Nutrition Support for the Terminally Ill (1987) offers guidelines for the dietitian's
role in this regard.

Economic Considerations

Despite economic constraints, health care must be provided within current
ethical guidelines. Tough choices are required: priorities must be established
and patient rights protected, especially when costs are high or when care is
rationed (Pownall 1989). May (1986) cited several types of ethical issues
facing dietitians that have fiscal implications: nutritional support for the
terminally ill, use of costly specialized nutritional support for the uninsured,
early discharge of patients who need specialized nutritional support, and
reductions in quality care due to staff shortages and budget cuts.

Today's health care environment exacerbates ethical dilemmas of institutions dealing with financial problems. Net benfits of health care must be
maximized for the total community. At the same time, there must be equal
opportunity for all persons to receive the same level and complexity of care.
In the balance of health care priorities, the wishes of an individual patient
may have less weight than the demands of social justice, especially at a time
when there are increasing numbers of both chronically ill elderly and patients
in a permanent vegetative state (Boisaubin 1984; Veatch 1984, 1986).

Hospital Ethics Committees

Many hospitals have initiated institutional ethics committees to

• educate physicians, health care workers, and the public
• provide consultation regarding policies and particular cases
• counsel patients, physicians, administrators, and health care personnel
• make decisions in specific cases involving complex ethical or moral
  issues
• develop policies to guide ethical decision making within the institution
  (Avard et al. 1985; Walters 1985)

Clinical dietetic managers can seek guidance from ethics committees when
making difficult ethical choices. Also, dietitians should be encouraged to

serve as members or as consultants to ethics committees. Both the nutrition services unit and the ethics committee can receive mutual benefits from regular and substantive interactions, particularly in regard to the nutritional care of patients.

MANAGEMENT APPLICATIONS: ROLE OF THE CLINICAL DIETETIC MANAGER

Management activities often raise ethical issues that are very different from those encountered in patient care. As a manager, you can foster an ethical climate by doing the following (Goddard 1988):

- Identify ethical attitudes desired among the staff. Such attitudes might include honesty, sound judgment, conscientious attention to policies and details, and concern for and respect of others.
- Select employees with the desired values; nurture desired attitudes and values in all subordinates.
- Incorporate ethics in the job evaluation process; demonstrate a renewed attention to its applications in nutrition services.
- Establish a work environment that reinforces ethical attitudes and behaviors: mention ethical norms frequently in discussions, meetings, decisions, and training programs.
- Exhibit ethical leadership and an upright value system; never compromise your personal integrity.

Although the responsibility for ethical decision making often rests with individual dietitians, there are several actions the clinical dietetic manager can take to promote and enhance such decisions in the nutrition services unit.

First, maintain departmental copies of institutional policies regarding such issues as personnel matters, use of life-sustaining measures, clinical research, and educational programs. Be sure each dietitian has a copy of policies and guidelines related to his or her area of practice. Clinical dietitians should be familiar with institutional policies for the nutritional care of terminally ill and comatose patients.

Second, evaluate personal and staff dietitian competence to deal with ethical dilemmas. Review basic knowledge, skills, values, and attitudes expected of dietitians and assess areas where development is needed.

Third, offer regular inservice programs for dietetic personnel on ethical or legal issues. Such programs might include discussions and interpretations of institutional policies, analysis of position papers and guidelines, laws regarding personnel or patient rights, analysis of case studies, and legal precautions to be used when dealing with ethically sensitive issues. Case studies similar to the ones shown in Exhibits 9-2 and 9-3 may be used as a basis for discussing ethical issues.

Fourth, when individual dietitians are faced with making difficult ethical decisions, involve others in helping define the problem, clarify issues, and develop alternative solutions. The exercise can be instructive for members of the staff and exremely helpful to the dietitian accountable for the decision.

Fifth, provide resources for dietitians. A few good articles or books on the subject added to the clinical nutrition library may go a long way toward

---

Exhibit 9-2 Case Presentation for Discussion of Ethical Issues in Nutritional Services

A.B. is a 66-year-old single male. He is a retired dishwasher and lives alone in an apartment.

Past Medical History

Mild mental retardation	Hernia repair × 6
Obese	Infection at hernia site
Smokes cigarettes (1 ppd)	Hemorrhoidectomy
Current medications:	Bilateral broken elbows
"water pills"	Bleeding ulcer

Day 1   Admitting diagnosis: Nutrition and edema control
Ht.: 6'   Wt.: 302#   Diet order: 600 Kcal
Medications used during hospitalization: Lasix, Aldomet, Procardia, Keflex, multi-vitamin with iron
Physician notes
   Difficulty losing weight
   Low ventral hernia
   To evaluate and "force" diet
Nursing notes
   Some inability to understand/follow instructions
   Some confusion/agitation
   Responds slowly to questions

Day 2   Wt.: 298#
Dietitian note
   Menus modified for 600 Kcal
   Offering "free foods" as snacks

Day 4   Wt.: 293#
Physician note
   Fecal impaction relieved
   Patient depressed and disgusted

Day 5   Wt.: 296#
Physician note
   Continue encouraging weight loss

Exhibit 9-2 continued

Day 6   Wt.: 289#
Physician note
Very frustrated and angry over dietary restrictions
Cellulitis showing little or no improvement
Will have dietary service help patient with diet
Nursing note
Frequently requests snacks
Dietitian note #1
(On 600 Kcal) . . . will not get adequate nutrients needed for bodily functions.
Patient extremely upset
Dietitian note #2
Explained exchanges . . . meal plan with low-calorie snacks.
Patient extremely agitated and hostile . . . understanding of meal plan is questionable
. . . written information given . . . simple, adjusted to patient.

Day 7   Wt.: 287#
Physician note
Weight down to 287#
Will look into . . . binder to take tension off area. . . .

Day 8   Wt.: 286#

Day 9   Wt.: 288#

Day 10   Wt.: 284#
Physician note
Discharged. Cellulistis improving . . . D/C on antibiotics and present diet. Hope to
repair hernia if weight loss continues.

Source: Case prepared by Doug Maier, R.D., L.D., Mount Carmel Medical Center, Columbus,
Ohio.

giving dietitians confidence and easing the weight of ethical decision making.

Sixth, take the initiative to have dietitians appointed as members or as consultants to ethics committees or other ethical/legal groups whose work may affect nutrition services.

Seventh, provide encouragement, empathy, and support for individual dietitians engaged in complex ethical decision making. Usually such decisions are finalized over the course of several days. Depending on the clarity of the issues and the ethical conflicts involved, some dietitians may experience sleepless nights, irritability, and mental distraction during the decision-making process. Encouragement and understanding may help sustain the decision maker's courage and fortitude.

Eighth, be sure decisions involving ethical and legal issues are documented accurately and appropriately in the departmental and/or in the patient's medical record. The clinical dietetic manager should provide guidance regarding the wording and timeliness of the documentation.

Exhibit 9-3 Case Study: Professional Responsibility

Mary is a diet technician at Good Samaritan Hospital. Her responsibilities include supervising the tray line, checking menus, and reviewing medical charts to determine diet orders. Her first task every morning is to review medical charts to determine changes in diet orders for the lunch menu. While reviewing a particular patient's chart, Mary noticed the diagnosis "Acquired Immune Deficiency Syndrome." Looking further she found that the patient was in isolation, and precautions should be taken regarding the transmittal of bodily fluids. Mary happened to notice the name on the chart and realized that the patient (Joe) was a prominent member of the community. Immediately, Mary went to the dietitian's office and reported her findings to Sue, the chief clinical dietitian. In casual conversation, Sue told local members of the dietetic association of her findings. Eventually, Joe lost his job. Mary and Sue continue to practice at Good Samaritan Hospital.

1. What is the underlying problem in this case study?

2. How can the spread of this information be stopped?

3. Comments:

Source: Courtesy of Rebecca Gould, University of Utah, College of Health, Salt Lake City, Utah.

Ethical Power

In *The Power of Ethical Management* (Blanchard and Peale 1988, 44–80) five principles are given to guide personal behavior. These simple rules can help turn potential ethical problems into management opportunities.

1. Have a clear purpose. Know who you are and who you want to be. Let your purpose, *not your calendar*, run your life.
2. Take pride in yourself. Strong self-esteem will enhance dealings with others.
3. Have patience; think positively. Believe that everything will always work out for the best.
4. Be persistent. When your patience runs out, let your commitment take over to keep you focused on your purpose.
5. Keep things in perspective. Nurture your spiritual inner self to keep control over your task-oriented external self. If you take time to reflect, many problems can be worked out to the satisfaction of all concerned.

These five principles can also be applied in organizations to foster positive relations with employees and to enhance problem solving in the work situation. When dealing with either potential or current employees, clinical dietetic managers have ample opportunity to exhibit ethical behaviors. A few examples can be cited as a basis for reflection:

- During employment or counseling interviews, avoid bias, unlawful inquiries, breach of confidentiality, bribery, or unjust treatment.
- Be sure personnel policies are interpreted with the same stringency or latitude for all. Be fair, consistent, objective, and honest in dealings with both professional and support personnel.
- Be supportive and loyal to employees; provide guidance, but be careful not to infringe on individual rights.
- Distribute rewards and merits to those who deserve recognition. Be attentive to evaluation reviews so that workers receive salary increases on schedule.
- Know and follow labor laws, antidiscrimination practices, and union contracts.

Relationships with Institutional Operations

Many nutrition service units are embarking on new ventures to increase revenue or achieve personal satisfaction through a business enterprise. Both the "business of dietetics" and the operation of a food service system entail numerous ethical issues. In addition to maintaining sound business practices and objectivity, the clinical dietetic manager needs to observe caution in the following areas:

- *Dealings with vendors.* Base purchases on price, quality, and delivery according to the needs and interests of the institution. Avoid bribery and prejudice. Obtain the maximum value for each dollar expended (Spears and Vaden 1985, 171). Refuse offers of gifts, paid vacations, or personal incentives. When you know someone is "on the take," discuss your concerns with the individual; in extremely serious cases consider filing a complaint with the appropriate authorities.
- *Patient food service.* Watch for accuracy in posting and delivery of menu items, portion sizes, product quality, patient selections, and dietary prescriptions (Neville and Chernoff 1988).
- *Revenue-producing operations.* Be sure charges are justified and that service complies with established standards of quality and advertised characteristics. Be truthful in advertising and marketing, business cards, and directory listings. When counseling patients or employees, maintain

confidentiality and guard against infringing on individual rights and human dignity (Bartley 1987, 170–74).

- *Use of facilities.* Take care not to vandalize property or to use resources illegally for personal advantage. Guard against such actions as use of the copy machine, postage, and office supplies for personal use. Institutional systems should not be used to build one's private practice or identify patients for referral to one's personal business enterprise.
- *Administration.* Be truthful and accurate in reporting activities and needs. Keep the good of the whole organization, as well as the department, in mind when making decisions that will have far-reaching effects.

RESEARCH AND EDUCATION APPLICATIONS

A multitude of ethical issues confront the dietetic manager who conducts research, oversees clinical investigations, or directs educational programs. Hospitals that participate in educational programs should assure establishment and adherence to codes of honor to prevent such actions as cheating, plagiarism, destruction of intellectual resources, or theft of library materials. Disciplinary action and appeals procedures are generally included in these policies. In addition, students should be taught to develop the skills, knowledge, values, and attitudes necessary for ethical conduct in dietetic practice (Schiller 1989).

REFERENCES

Anderson, Gary R., and Valerie A. Glesnes-Anderson. 1987. Ethical thinking and decision making for health care supervisors. *Health Care Supervisor* 5(4):1–12.

Anderson, Sara L., and Richard A. Green. 1990. Dietitians, depositions, and the law: Issues in practice. *Dietet. Curr.* 17(1):1–4.

Avard, D., G. Griener, and J. Langstaff. 1985. Hospital ethics committees: Survey reveals characteristics. *Dimensions* 62(2):24–26.

Bartley, Katharine Curry. 1987. *Dietetic practitioner skills.* New York: Macmillan Publishing Co., Inc.

Bell, Stacey J., et al. 1985. Allocation of feeding pumps: An ethical question. *J. Am. Dietet. Assoc.* 85(6):697–99.

Blanchard, Kenneth, and Norman Vincent Peale. 1988. *The power of ethical management.* New York: William Morrow and Co.

Boisaubin, Eugene V. 1984. Ethical issues in the nutritional support of the terminal patient. *J. Am. Dietet. Assoc.* 84(5):529–31.

Bunting, Sheila, and Adele Webb. 1988. An ethical model for decision-making. *Nurse Practitioner* 13(12):30–34.

Code of ethics for the profession of dietetics. 1988. *J. Am. Dietet. Assoc.* 88(12):1592–96.

Dresser, Rebecca, and Eugene Boisaubin. 1985. Ethics, law, and nutrition support. *Arch. Inter. Med.* 145(1):122–24.

Friedrich, Otto. 1990. A limited right to die: The Court affirms the principle, but not for Nancy Cruzan. *Time* 136 (July 9): 59.

Glantz, Leonard H. 1987. Withholding and withdrawing treatment: The role of the criminal law. *Law, Med. Health Care* 15(4):231–41.

Goddard, Robert. 1988. Are you an ethical manager? *Personnel J.* 67(3):38–47.

Greenhouse, Linda. 1989. Does right to privacy include right to die? Court to decide. *The New York Times.* (July 25)

Luce, John M. 1990. Ethical principles in critical care. *JAMA* 263(5):696–700.

Lynn, Joanne, and James F. Childress. 1983. Must patients always be given food and water? *Hastings Center Rep.* 13(5):17–21.

Major, Victoria H. 1986. Legal aspects of nutrition support of the terminally ill. *Top. Clin. Nut.* 1(4):45–50.

Matejski, Myrtle. 1982. Ethical issues in the health care system. *J. Allied Health* 11(2): 131–39.

May, William W. 1986. Economics and ethics. *J. Am. Dietet. Assoc.* 86(10):1355–358.

McInerny, William. 1987. Understanding moral issues in health care: Seven essential ideas. *J. Prof. Nurs.* 3(5):268–77.

McLeod, Don. 1990. Matter of life and death: Supreme Court soon will rule on who can decide. *AARP Bull.* 31(5):1, 8–9.

Mishkin, Barbara. 1986. Withholding and withdrawing nutritional support. *Nutr. Clin. Pract.* 1(1):50–52.

Neville, Janice, and Ronni Chernoff. 1988. Professional ethics—everyone's issue. *J. Am. Dietet. Assoc.* 88(10):1285–87.

Orentlicher, David. 1990. Advance medical directives. *JAMA* 263(17):2365–67.

Ostling, Richard N. 1987. It is wrong to cut off feeding? *Time* (February 23):71.

Position of the American Dietetic Association: Issues in feeding the terminally ill adult. 1987. *J. Am. Dietet. Assoc.* 87(1):78–84.

Pownall, Mark. 1989. When care has to be rationed. *Nurs. Times* 85(5):16–17.

Rosoff, Arnold. 1982. Legal and ethical issues. In *Clinical care of the terminal cancer patient* edited by Barrie Cassileth and Peter Cassileth. Philadelphia: Lea and Febiger.

Schiller, M. Rosita. 1989. Ethical behavior: Areas of competence. *Dietitians Nutr. Supp. Newsl.* 11(2):9–11, 15.

Society for the Right to Die. 1988. *Questions and answers about the right to die.* New York: Society for the Right to Die, Inc.

Spears, Marian C., and Allene Vaden. 1985. *Foodservice organizations: A managerial and systems approach.* New York: John Wiley and Sons, Inc.

Spencer, Robin, and Donald Palmisano. 1985. Specialized nutritional support of patients—a hospital's legal duty? *Qual. Rev. Bull.* 11(5):160–63.

Sprung, Charles L. 1990. Changing attitudes and practices in forgoing life-sustaining treatments. *JAMA* 263(16):2211–15.

Strong, Carson. 1981. Can fluids and electrolytes be "extraordinary" treatment? *J. Med. Ethics* 7(2):83–85.

Thomasma, David. 1979. Human values and ethics: Professional responsibility. *J. Am. Dietet. Assoc.* 75(5):533–36.

Veatch, Robert. 1984. Autonomy's temporary triumph. *Hastings Center Rep.* 14(5):38–40.

———— 1986. DRGs and the ethical reallocation of resources. *Hastings Center Rep.* 16(3): 32–40.

Wallis, Claudia. 1986. To feed or not to feed. *Time* (March 31):60–61.

Walters, LeRoy. 1985. Biomedical ethics. *JAMA* 254(16):2345–48.

SUGGESTED READINGS

Artificial nutrition and hydration. 1987. *News from the Society for the Right to Die* (January): 1–7.

Christensen, Paula. 1988. An ethical framework for nursing service administration. *Adv. Nurs. Sci.* 10(3):46–55.

Horan, Dennis. 1986. Failure to feed: An ethical and legal discussion. *Issues Law Med.* 2(2):149–55.

Isaacs, Barbara. 1984. 17 essential points of medical record documentation. *Dietitians Crit. Care Newsl.* 6(5):33.

O'Rourke, Kevin. 1986. The AMA statement on tube feeding: An ethical analysis. *America* 154(15):321–24.

Paris, John J. 1986. When burdens of feeding outweigh benefits. *Hastings Center Rep.* 16(1):30–32.

Rosner, Fred. 1988. Withdrawing fluids and nutrition: An alternate way. *Bull. NY Acad. Med.* 64(5):363–75.

Schiller, M. Rosita. 1988. Ethical issues in nutrition care. *J. Am. Dietet. Assoc.* 88(1):13–15.

Standards of Professional Responsibility. 1983. *J. Am. Dietet. Assoc.* 83(6):702–03.

Strand, Gerald. 1987. *Proverbs* provides guidelines for management in the next century. *Health Progr.* 68(8):63–66.

Thomasma, David, Kenneth Micetich, and Patricia Steinecker. 1986. Continuance of nutritional care in the terminally ill patient. *Crit. Care Clin.* 2(1):61–70.

Welch, H. Gilbert, and Eric B. Larson. 1988. Dealing with limited resources. *N. Engl. J. Med.* 319(3):171–73.

Wenston, Sylvia R. 1987. Applying philosophy to ethical dilemmas. In *Health Care Ethics*, edited by Gary Anderson and Valerie Glesnes-Anderson. Gaithersburg, Md.: Aspen Publishers, Inc.

Part III

Structural Environment for Managerial Decision Making

Chapter 10

Quality Assurance

Quality assurance "is a dynamic, systematic process that assures the delivery of high-quality care to clients being served" (Lintzenich 1987, 123). A mechanism of setting standards of care, evaluating achievements, and providing accountability, quality assurance (QA) is a routine part of nutrition service and health care operations. Early quality assurance programs were often annual studies or audits that focused on food production activities. In the 1980s, the Joint Commission recommended that the focus on quality assurance shift to ongoing monitoring and clinically oriented issues. With ongoing monitoring, the distinction between quality control activities and quality assurance may blur; however, quality monitoring adds the dimension of identifying patterns and trends in service delivery. Quality improvement, the enhancement of the status quo, is the ultimate outcome.

The quality assurance plan should reflect what the nutrition service department is striving to achieve. Key issues should be monitored continuously; less important issues less frequently.

To assist in problem identification, clinical dietetic managers need to determine what data are necessary to demonstrate the quality of nutrition services. The goals of the department help identify the desired outcomes of the service. Definition of the major clinical functions of the dietetic service is essential for the development of indicators of both volume and quality of work performed. The development of a concise report that measures the quality of dietetic service takes time and effort, but is essential to justification of staff and continuing services.

Hospital QA professionals can help clinical dietetic managers in this data collection effort. They can help determine what information to collect, how often to collect it, and the methods to use to obtain the data. QA professionals can also help with analysis and determining the department's future directions.

149

Numerous clinical processes can be monitored, including the amount of service provided as assessment or counseling; number of follow-ups, including telephone calls after diet counseling; level of care; number of diet changes recommended by the clinical dietitian and written by the physician; or identification of food allergies. Links between clinical dietetics and food production can also be monitored through an analysis of the congruity between menu selection and nutrient needs. Many of these areas have been examined for years; quality assurance plans document the evaluation of the nutrition care process.

QUALITY INDICATORS

Each department needs to establish its own indicators of quality. First, make a list of four to eight items that capture the most meaningful data based on the volume of work performed. Then list four to eight items that could indicate quality of performance. Ask yourself these questions: Could this information serve as a justification for the clinical dietetic staff? Are the data available or how can the data be collected? How much data needs to be collected and how often? Exhibit 10-1 shows sample volume of work, quality indicators, and appropriateness indicators. A system can be established to tabulate and compile this information (Exhibit 10-2) on a monthly or other predetermined schedule. A realistic standard performance level should then be established. If the volume or quality indicator drops below its standard performance level (i.e., less than 75 percent of the criteria), an action or further investigation should be taken. Monthly reports suggest trends and help ensure that the department is maintaining its expected performance. Unusual results may trigger the recognition of potential problems that need to be resolved.

AUDITS AS RESEARCH

Audits, a method of inquiry, should address specific problems, as well as identify characteristics in groups of patients. Some of the audit findings deserve to be published and shared with others. For example, Feitelson et al. (1987) reviewed the quality of care given to tubefed patients. In a retrospective study of all patients tubefed in 1984 they found that two-thirds of the tubefeeding days were accounted for by 14 percent of the patients receiving enteral nutrition support. The results of the audit produced questions for future audits, such as the need for home care of enteral feeders. In another study, McMillin and Jasmund (1985) demonstrated how nursing and dietetic

Exhibit 10-1 Volume, Quality, and Appropriateness Indicators

VOLUME INDICATORS

Total number of patients seen
Total number of patients seen by key
  diagnoses
Number of nutrition screenings
Number of basic assessments
Number of comprehensive assessments
Number of follow-up contacts
Number of reassessments
Number of brief diet instructions
Number of diet counseling sessions
Number of tubefeedings/parenteral
  feedings
Number of diet changes recommended
Number of group classes
Number of individuals attending group
  classes
Average length of stay

QUALITY INDICATORS

Percentage of time that nutrition
  evaluation is completed
Timeliness of nutrition evaluation
Number of diet changes implemented by
  team based on clinical dietitian
  recommendation
Number of feeding complications, such as
  clogged tubes

Number of malnourished patients at
  admission and discharge
Number of delays in feeding patients
Number of patients NPO more than 3
  days
Number of patient complaints
Number of staff complaints
Patient questionnaire results
Percentage of food consumption
Number of patients readmitted within 30
  days for malnutrition

APPROPRIATENESS INDICATORS

Number/percent of assessments based on
  thorough data collection
Number/percent of assessments
  appropriate for diagnosis
Number/percent of implemented plans
Number/percent of evaluated plans
Number/percent of requested diet
  instructions given
Number/percent of timeliness of initial
  care
Number/percent of timeliness of follow-
  up care
Number/percent of diet orders that are
  implemented inappropriately
Number/percent of enteral feedings that
  are advanced appropriately

departments can work together to investigate and solve a problem of insufficient documentation of weights and heights. Another audit by Dowling and Cotner (1988) led to the design of a monitoring system to evaluate and improve the accuracy of foods served on patient trays.

Monitoring nutrition services can identify trends in both the processes and outcomes of care. It also allows collection of data to evaluate whether intervention by a dietitian makes a difference. Exhibit 10-3 illustrates a retrospective quality audit used to identify baseline information on the incidence of dietitian-recommended diet change and whether the change was actualized.

Exhibit 10-2 Summary of Clinical Nutrition Care Audit, Memorial Sloan-Kettering Cancer Center

---

Reviewer: _____

Date: _____

Staff member: _____

Number of charts reviewed: _____

Number of charts with initial evaluation and documentation: _____

Percent with initial documentation: _____

Number of charts with discharge plan: _____

Percent with discharge plan: _____

Number of charts with follow-up documentation: _____

Number of charts requiring follow-up documentation: _____

Percent with follow-up documentation: _____

Quality of documentation: ( ) Excellent   ( ) Satisfactory
                                   ( ) Good   ( ) Unsatisfactory

Positive points in documentation: _____

Unsatisfactory points and improvement suggestions:

Source: Courtesy of Department of Dietetics, Memorial Sloan-Kettering Cancer Center, New York, NY.

THE QUALITY ASSURANCE PROCESS

To meet the requirements for the Joint Commission and other regulatory groups, the QA program should be established by a departmental group as an integral part of the institution-wide quality assurance program. QA program implementation requires the completion of these ten steps.

1. Identify or define the problem.
2. Establish a method to evaluate the problem.
3. Set a timeline for data collection.
4. Collect the data.

Exhibit 10-3 Data to Study Effectiveness of RD Recommendations

Topic: Effect of RD recommendations on MD diet and the nutritional status of patients
Problem: To determine whether RD recommendations have a significant impact on MD's diet orders

MD Initial Diet Order and Date	RD Recommendation for Diet Change and Date	MD Response and Date	Parameters Causing RD recommendations	Actual Change

Source: Courtesy of Clinical Nutrition Managers of Greater New York, Bronx, NY, 1986.

5. Analyze the results.
6. Discuss the findings and make conclusions.
7. Suggest alternatives to rectify the problem.
8. Try a solution that seems feasible.
9. Develop a system to monitor the success of the proposed solution.
10. Implement a system to reevaluate the plan at least annually.

The Problem

A problem is anything that deviates from what is expected and cannot be explained easily. In the problem selection step solvable situations are chosen that will improve patient care or outcomes when the problem is resolved. The problem can be identified from multiple sources: the nutrition committee, patient care committees, medical rounds, infection control audits, medical record reviews, direct observation, staff or client complaints, regulatory surveys, discussions within the department, or findings in a check of adherence to specific policies and procedures.

To determine if the problem is actually present, the problem's dimensions need to be described. What is the extent of the problem? What are the implications of the problem if it is not solved? Will patient complaints increase? Will the complication rate or length of stay increase? Will staff members be at risk for legal actions? Once problems are identified, priorities need to be set based on the answer to this question: Which problems can be solved and which solutions will have the biggest or most crucial effect on patient care?

Evaluation of the Problem

The method of problem evaluation is chosen based on the cause of the problem. The evaluation mechanism can be retrospective or prospective and ranges on a continuum from very elaborate to extremely simple. If the problem has little impact on patient care, the problem needs minimal review time. The larger the number of patients affected or potentially affected, the more elaborate the review. Other considerations are the duration of the problem, the relationship to other problems, and how complex the investigation needs to be.

Data Collection

Before gathering data the value of the data to the problem needs to be identified. Will the data collected truly address the problem? Generally, the fastest and least costly method of data collection that addresses the problem appropriately is used. A commonly used method is review of a small percentage of the total sample. Data are collected from three sources: documents, such as medical records and reports; direct observation; and interviews.

Studies may be used to examine past performance (retrospective studies) or present activities (prospective studies). Retrospective studies review patient comment surveys, productivity reports, and medical records. Prospective evaluative mechanisms include random reviews of accuracy of diet orders, spot checks of menus for accuracy, quantity and quality of nutrition assessments and evaluation plans, time/temperature studies, or specific data collected over a period of time.

Monitoring tools should be devised to facilitate data collection. They should be specific to the problem under review and be simple to use. The monitoring tool or technique should be tested on a pilot basis before it is finalized.

Exhibit 10-4 shows an example of a quality assurance form used to evaluate whether nutritional care is documented appropriately. Evaluations of charting quality can be conducted on individual staff members throughout the year, randomly throughout the institution, or by specific conditions or other parameters, such as infections.

The timeline for evaluation of the problem needs to be set based on the acuteness of the situation, the time available, and when the solutions are needed. A reasonable time frame for conducting a QA audit is 1 to 4 weeks. Data collection should have a pre-established endpoint, either within a given period of time or a specific number of cases.

Data collection can be done by the clinical dietetic manager, clinical dietitians, technicians, or assistants. Data that can be objectively collected with a limited number of gray areas of judgment are best collected by the dietetic technician or dietetic assistant. Such data deal with frequency of procedures, timeliness of events, or similar audits that quantify care. Quality monitoring data that must be evaluated during collection require the skill of the clinical dietitian or clinical dietetic manager. Judgments on the appropriateness of assessment and comprehensiveness of care plans and interventions require peer or supervisory review.

Analysis of Data

Process criteria or guidelines for the care of general conditions and specific disorders developed by the specialty areas provide a foundation for the establishment of audit criteria. Each criterion needs an acceptable standard to measure actual performance. Figure 10-1 illustrates criteria assessment based on the level of nutritional risk.

Exhibit 10-4 Clinical Nutrition Care Audit

Date: _____

Floor: _____

Key:
N =
Y =
X =

	Chart #: Date of Adm:	Chart #: Date of Adm:	Chart #: Date of Adm:	Chart #: Date of Adm:	Chart #: Date of Adm:	Chart #: Date of Adm:	Chart #: Date of Adm:	Chart #: Date of Adm:	Chart #: Date of Adm:	Chart #: Date of Adm:
Diagnosis										
Nutrition screening completed										
Assessment completed within 72 hours										
Use of SOAP format										
Pertinent S & O data										
Diet dated										
Assessment of nutrition status stated										
Parameters listed are evaluated										
Percent weight change noted										
If moderate/severe risk, Kcal and protein needs stated										
Amount of oral supplement charted										

Assessment based on S & O										
Plan based on assessment										
Education plan if necessary/outcome criteria										
Discharge plan										
Dated and signed										
Diet change recommended										
Follow-up notes as stated or										
High risk within 1 week										
No risk within 2 weeks										
Subsequent follow-up notes										
Implementation Explained										
Evaluation of outcome included										
Reviewer's Name: _____										

Source: Courtesy of Memorial Sloan-Kettering Cancer Center, New York, NY.

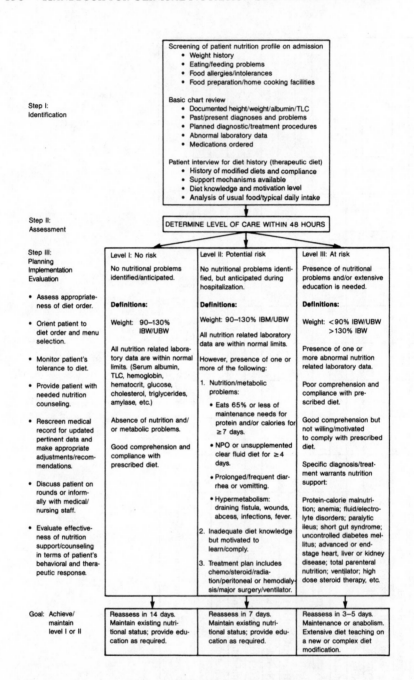

Figure 10-1. Quality Assurance: Patient Management by Risk level. *Source:* Courtesy of New York University Medical Center, New York, NY.

Data compilation should be done by technical personnel. Data entry into a computer facilitates the ability to sort it in many ways and to gain multiple perspectives for reviewing the data. Once the data are compiled they need to be analyzed by the quality assurance committee to determine if the results are valid, the information is complete, and there is enough information to form recommendations. Do the findings suggest that there is a problem and identify its potential causes? Can the problem or parts of the problem be solved? Can responsible parties be identified?

Possible solutions and the implications of each alternative need to be determined. Both the feasibility of the solutions and their implications on other areas need to be discussed. The actions to correct the problem and the extent of the problem need to be documented on the quality assurance reports generated by the department. The results of each investigation should include the problem identified and the cause(s) of the problem: knowledge, performance, or systems. Is lack of knowledge the root of the problem? Is poor performance due to insufficient time or attitude? Are policies and procedures inadequate or not enforced?

Corrective Actions

Finally, the potential solution or corrective action needs to be implemented. A timeline for the implementation is essential. All actions taken as a result of the investigation need to be documented. Measurable objectives, the expected change, and the responsible parties for implementation should be identified. A timeline also needs to be established to monitor the original problem and its corrective action and to evaluate whether the situation has improved. The extent of desirable change needs to be identified clearly as well. For example, if the dietitians' chart notes were written on a timely basis only 25 percent of the time, an increase to 100 percent in a short period of 3 months is unlikely. Rather the goal may be an increase to 40 percent. The audit procedure should only be repeated if necessary.

Quality monitoring systems should enhance evaluation of patient care processes and the outcome of patient care. Efforts should be made to implement fully the solutions or corrective actions or change will not result. If the problem was lack of knowledge, an inservice or continuing education program should be provided for the staff. If performance is the problem, reasons for the performance deficit need exploration. If the problem is systemic, a systems analysis or a revision in procedures should occur.

Quality Assurance Reports

Clinical dietetic managers need to submit QA reports to their immediate supervisors or administrators. This information is sent to a quality assurance committee or department that oversees the overall operation of the institution.

The quality assurance process is begun with a reasonable number of quality and volume indicators to monitor and a reasonable number of problems to tackle. A successful system of monitoring and evaluating quality care should be planned, with staff agreeing on the indicators of care.

REFERENCES

Dowling, Rebecca A., and C. Cotner. 1988. Monitor of tray error rates for quality control. *J. Am. Dietet. Assoc.* 88(4):450–53.

Feitelson, Marion, Larry H. Berstein, and Walter Pleban. 1987. Tube feeding utilization: A quality of care review. *J. Am. Dietet. Assoc.* 87:73–74.

Lintzenich, Joanne. 1987. Attaining quality assurance. *Food Man.* (May): 123–24.

McMillin, Bonnie A., and Joanne M. Jasmund. 1985. A quality assurance study of height and weight measurements. *Qual. Rev. Bull.* 11(2):53–57.

SUGGESTED READINGS

Ford, Deborah A., and Michelle M. Fairchild. 1990. Managing inpatient clinical nutrition services. A comprehensive program assures accountability and success. *J. Amer. Dietet. Assoc.* 90(5):695–704.

Greenley, Hugh. 1986. Continuous monitoring and data-based quality assessment for ancillary and support department managers. Presentation at University of Medicine and Dentistry of New Jersey, 18 February.

Kaskel, Phyllis, and Tessie Pia-Geronimo. 1987. Quality assurance: An overview. *Dietitians Nutr. Supp. Newsl.* (September): 3, 4, 10, 11.

McNab, Helen, et al. 1987. Dietetic quality assurance practices in Chicago-area hospitals. *J. Am. Dietet. Assoc.* 87(5):635–37.

Ream, Elisabeth. 1987. Surveys: Opportunities for excellence. *Clin. Man.* 3(11):41–44.

Renner-McCaffrey, Jo, and Anna Hendricks Leyshon. 1989. *Quality assurance in hospital nutrition services.* Gaithersburg, Md.: Aspen Publishers, Inc.

Chapter 11

Productivity and Cost Containment

The need for dietetic services will be examined carefully throughout the next decade. To survive, dietetic practitioners will have to engage in activities that result in observable outcomes. These authorized activities must be done at the lowest cost without sacrificing quality. Both showing effectiveness and controlling costs require data collection and reporting by the department. This chapter discusses how to collect data on clinical dietetic productivity and reviews current knowledge regarding the cost benefit of clinical dietetics.

COMPONENTS OF PRODUCTIVITY

Productivity is a measure of the efficiency with which services are provided or produced. Productivity management can be applied to both personal and professional growth (McEwan and Messersmith 1987). Two preliminary steps are necessary to establish baseline productivity data for a clinical dietetic service. The first is to identify patients at nutritional risk at a given point in time. Pre-established criteria are set, often including height for weight, usual weight, serum albumin, hemoglobin, and disease state. Those at nutritional risk are identified by conducting a retrospective chart review, analyzing ongoing screening data, or doing a 1-day chart review of inpatient medical records. Step two measures the dietetic staff necessary to provide care based on the appropriate risk level of each patient and the procedures to be performed. The priority for dietitians is to give more intensive care to those in greatest need (DeHoog 1986).

CUTS is an acronym representing the factors to consider in containing costs and monitoring productivity in a clinical dietetic service. *C* denotes the collection of meaningful data. *U* is utilizing the data effectively to measure what is needed; generally this means measuring staff performance. *T* stands for the time and task allocation that allows a comparison of productivity over time. *S* represents the standards for assessing the quantity and quality of nutritional care provided, a description of what should be. Underlying this framework are two essential research principles: solid documentation or record keeping and sound interpretation of the data.

Productivity often is measured as a ratio of output (patient care) per unit of input (dietitian's time) or a comparison of outcomes produced based on resources invested (time-task allocation compared to salaries of dietetic staff). Effectiveness, in relation to productivity, implies the capability of producing the desired outcomes—doing the correct things at the correct times. In addition to labor, inputs in nutritional care are equipment, materials, and management. Outcomes are the end results of activities performed by professional staff, not the activities themselves. Nutritional outcomes are alterations in the health status of the patient. To collect productivity data it is important for managers to know

- the number of patients requiring various levels of care and at what cost
- operational costs for identifying nutrition intervention, patient education materials, and counseling in relation to total costs for food, labor, and supplies
- potential for reimbursement and revenue-producing activities
- whether nutrition intervention results in reduced lengths of stay (Ross Laboratories 1984).

MATCHING PROFESSIONAL LEVEL AND JOB FUNCTION

A major step toward increasing productivity is ensuring that staff members are engaged in activities congruent with their educational background and salary levels. For example, basic assessments and screening procedures are well-defined tasks that are within the scope of responsibility of the dietetic technician or dietetic assistant. Screening is a simple process with yes/no decisions that lower-level personnel can perform. Yet, often the clinical dietitian does screening and basic assessments. In a 1988 study of New Jersey hospitals, Crissey found that the clinical dietitians spent a large percentage of their time doing basic assessments: nearly a third of the dietitians spent 10 to 14.9 hours per week in this activity (Crissey 1988). Having dietitians perform basic assessments, as well as other technical tasks shown in Table 11-1, is poor utilization of time, money, and talent. The adage is "today's professional is tomorrow's technician," and in dietetics, this certainly is the case.

Each institution must decide which tasks are appropriate for each staff level. As a department examines levels of staff functions, it is necessary to

Table 11-1 Activities of New Jersey Dietitians, 1988

Appropriate Level	Duties	%	Hours per Week
DT level	Phone answering	83	0–4.9
		4	5–9.9
DT level	Screening	45	0–4.9
		23	5–5.9
		26	10–14.9
RD level	Comprehensive assessment	27	0–4.9
		37	5–5.9
		18	10–14.9
RD level	Counseling	37	0–4.9
		34	5–9.9
		28	10–14.9
RD level	Instruction	46	No instruction
		51	0–4.9
DT level	Meal rounds	72	0–4.9
RD level	Teaching	71	No teaching
		19	5–9.9
		9	0–4.9
DT level	Basic assessment	23	0–4.9
		24	5–9.9
		32	10–14.9

% does not equal 100% because some respondents did not select any hours.
DT = Dietetic technician, RD = Registered dietician.

Source: Courtesy of Janice Crissey, Department of Dietetics, New York University Medical Center.

review all tasks and indicate who currently does and who should do each task. Exhibit 11-1 provides a basic format for conducting such a study. Another foundation for assigning responsibilities is the role delineation study of the American Dietetic Association published in 1990.

TIME UTILIZATION REVIEW

Actual time spent in an activity needs to be evaluated periodically through observation or self-recording. Observation is time-consuming and generally not recommended because the process may be intrusive to the staff.

To use the self-reporting method, begin by having the staff record all their activities for 1 to 2 weeks. Several days are recommended for this time

Exhibit 11-1 Review of Type of Personnel and Job Function: Current Functions and Projected Goals

Task	Actual				Ideal			
	RD	DT	DA	FSW	RD	DT	DA	FSW
1. Educate patients on the following diets: List type of diet _____ _____ _____ _____								
2. Provide nutrition consults								
3. Assess patients on special diets or with special conditions List: _____ _____								
4. Perform screening assessments on the following categories of patients _____ _____ _____ _____								
5. Gather subjective and objective data for assessments. Which information? _____ _____ _____ _____								
6. Identify patients at high nutritional risk.								
7. Assess patients at high nutritional risk.								
8. Plan routine hospital diets.								
9. Plan nonroutine hospital diets. Which ones? _____ _____ _____ _____								
10. Aid patient with menu selection Diet: regular sodium controlled combination diet modified consistency Kcal controlled low fiber other:								
11. Check appropriateness of menu selection.								

Exhibit 11-1   continued

12. Plan between-meal nourishment.								
13. Order between-meal nourishment.								
14. Tally or order special menu items.								
15. Do daily meal rounds.								
16. Collect Kcalorie count information.								
17. Calculate Kcalorie counts.								
18. Chart on high nutritional risk patients potential nutritional risk patients minimal nutritional risk patients								
19. Chart calorie counts.								
20. Chart recommendation for diet changes.								
21. Monitor high nutritional risk patients potential nutritional risk patients minimal nutritional risk patients								
22. Conduct reassessment on high risk cases potential risk cases minimal risk cases								
23. Provide basic group education.								
24. Educate students in clinical dietetic practice.								
25. Educate students on diet calculation. basic complex combined								
26. Develop research protocols.								
27. Collect research data.								
28. Develop written educational tool and audiovisual education tools								
29. Attend medical team rounds or discharge rounds.								
30. Set criteria for assessment, risk, monitoring.								
31. Participate in the following committees: Quality Assurance menu development formulary patient care other:								
32. Other activities on job descriptions								

RD = Registered Dietitian
DT = Dietetic Technician
DA = Dietetic Assistant
FSW = Food Service Worker

review as record keeping may only be realistic after the first few days when staff have become comfortable with the process. A form similar to the one shown in Exhibit 11-2 may be used for data collection. Thorough completion of this type of form may take 30–40 minutes daily. Completed forms provide the clinical dietetic manager with a wealth of information on the number of procedures, as well as how much time is spent on screening, basic assessments, comprehensive assessments, follow-up care, meal rounds, group teaching, meetings, kilocalorie counts, meal patterns, and staff conferences. Results of the study can then be used to estimate the time standards and costs for the various types of care given. Attendance and punctuality records must also be considered in the estimations.

Once the time per task is determined, a cost value can be assigned to the activity, as discussed in Chapter 12. Direct and indirect time, as well as nonproductive time—answering the phone, walking to the unit—should be calculated when assigning a cost value. Services can also be costed by disease category of the patient to determine what units would require more in-depth staff assignments.

The Clinical Nutrition Management Group of Greater New York examined time utilization of dietitians in 1985 and found less than 50 percent of time was spent in direct and indirect clinical activities (Touger-Decker 1985) (Fig. 11-1). Clerical time, which included documentation, consumed over one-third of the clinical dietitian's time. Surprisingly, time allocations were similar to those reported in a study 20 years earlier (Noland and Steinberg 1965) with about one-third of the time spent in doing written communications, although the shift in types of clerical functions is dramatic.

Exhibit 11-2 Dietitian Time Utilization Review

For a period of 2 weeks, the RDs/DTs complete the following time utilization review daily.

INDICATE AMOUNT OF TIME AND/OR NUMBER OF EACH

Thorough counselings: # _____ time: _____
Mini-counseling or review # _____ time: _____
Initial assessments # _____ time: _____
Thorough assessments # _____ time: _____
No. of diet orders requested to be changed: _____
Types of diets: _____

Designing meal patterns: _____ time: _____
Checking technicians/assistant menus: _____ time: _____

Exhibit 11-2 continued

Conferring with support staff on patients: _____ time: _____
Educating professional staff: _____ time: _____
Setting up and conducting group teaching: _____ time: _____
Time to chart group teaching: _____ time: _____
Educating or evaluating interns: _____ time: _____
Time developing teaching tools: _____ time: _____
Time spent on continuing ed: meetings, readings, etc. _____
Time spent on dept. meetings: _____ # _____
Time spent on follow-up of nutritional care: _____
Time spent dealing with food problems: _____
Time spent acting as Diet Assistant: _____
Time spent picking up menus (special) _____
                              (regular) _____
Calorie counts # _____ time: _____
Patients seen outpatient: # _____ time: _____
Transfer summaries sent: # _____ time: _____
OTHER: _____ time: _____

COMPLETE SCHEDULE FOR DAY

8		1	
8:15		1:15	
8:30		1:30	
8:45		1:45	
9		2	
9:15		2:15	
9:30		2:30	
9:45		2:45	
10		3	
10:15		3:15	
10:30		3:30	
10:45		3:45	
11		4	
11:15		4:15	
11:30		4:30	
11:45		4:45	
12		5	
12:15		5:15	
12:30		5:30	
12:45		5:45	

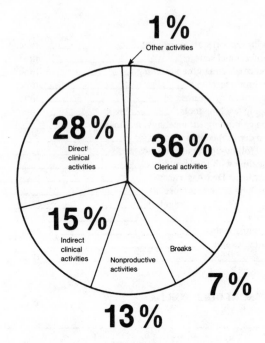

Figure 11-1 Use of Clinical RD Time in 1985, New York City

In a related study Huyck and McNamara (1987) found that six clinical dietitians and two dietetic technicians spent 22 percent of their time in direct patient contact. Dietetic personnel in this study devoted 33 percent of their time to medical records, including documentation of nutritional care plans and follow-up.

A clinical manager should evaluate time usage within the institution and decide what is appropriate in that setting. Determining the appropriate amount of time the dietitian should spend in direct or indirect patient care is essential for developing staffing goals and patterns.

DEPARTMENTAL PRODUCTIVITY

Departmental productivity may be calculated by the clinical dietetic manager weekly, monthly, or quarterly. Examples of various statistical report sheets are shown in Exhibits 11-3 to 11-6.

Reports can be used simply to record activity. However, an effective clinical manager will also use report results to set goals and evaluate performance of individuals or the entire group. If the information is computerized, it can be sorted in various ways to pinpoint problems or improve-

Exhibit 11-3 Inpatient Clinical Statistics

Year ___ Service ___ Patient Name	Chart #	Diagnosis	Level of Nutrition Risk			Date of Admission	Screening and Initial Assessment	Comprehensive Nutrition Assessment	Education on In-House Diet	Comprehensive Counseling	Follow-up and Re-assessment	Follow-up	Limited Nutrient Analysis	Follow-up	Brief Diet Instructions for Discharge	Discharge Plan
			N	P	H											

*N = no risk; P = potential risk; H = high risk.
Source: Courtesy of Memorial Sloan-Kettering Cancer Center, New York, NY.

Exhibit 11-4 Daily Activity Form

Dietitian/Technician: _____

Daily Assignment
Primary Floors _____   Primary Plus Secondary Coverage for: _____
(indicate ✔)

Daily: _____
Weekend: _____
Date: _____

Initial Assessments			Follow up Intervention			Diet Counselings		D/C Summaries	
Client	Unit	Status*	Client	Unit	Comment	Client	Unit	Client	Unit

* *Indicate Level of Risk*

No. of Diets Confirmed _____   No. of Tubefeeding Problems _____   Meal Rounds (Unit) _____

Units → Menu Modification _____   No. of Clients Visited _____

(List Units)

TIME

Inservices:

Intern Training _____   Attended _____   Quality Assessment—Menus

Medical Rounds _____   Provided _____   Unit Reviewed _____

Staff Meetings _____   Outside Seminar _____   Menus Satisfactory _____

Kardex Updating _____   Other: _____   Menus Unsatisfactory _____

Projects: _____   (State on back, errors)

  Specify _____

Source: Courtesy of University of Medicine and Dentistry of New Jersey, Department of Food and Nutrition Services, Newark, NJ.

Exhibit 11-5 Activity Summary Report

Report for month of: _____   Submitted by: _____   # of Work Days _____   Date: _____

Date	1	2	3	4	5	6	7	8	9	10	11	12	13	14	15	16
Nutritional assessments*																
Diet counselling																
Follow-up intervention																
D/C summaries																
Tubefeeding problems																
Diet confirmations																
Meal rounds/# of patients visited																

Date	17	18	19	20	21	22	23	24	25	26	27	28	29	30	31	Grand total
Nutritional assessments																
Diet counseling																
Follow-up intervention																
D/C summaries																
Tubefeeding problems																
Diet confirmations																
Meal rounds/# of patients visited																

*Indicate total per day and then total for month.

Source: Courtesy of University of Medicine and Dentistry of NJ, Department of Food Nutrition Services, Newark.

Exhibit 11-6 Outpatient Daily Statistics

Patient's Name	Chart Number and Physician's Name	Diagnosis	Diet	Date	Charge	Full Consult	Group Counseling	Prescribing Formula	Dispensing Supplement Formula	Follow-up Evaluation	Brief Office Visit	Telephone Conference

Source: Courtesy of Memorial Sloan-Kettering Cancer Center, New York, NY.

ments in performance. Lack of standardized terminology for the services provided by dietitians and technicians has made group comparisons difficult. Standard nomenclature for nutrition services, recommended by the American Dietetic Association in 1984, may be found in Appendix C.

Continuous productivity reporting should give valuable information but should not be so extensive that it is a burden to collect and analyze. Any collected data should provide useful information needed for decision making or accountability. Which types of diagnoses require which types of care? Are levels of severity and quantity of services congruent? How much of the dietitian's time is spent on basic assessments or assessment in general? Do dietitians use equivalent amounts of time for similar tasks?

Quantity alone is only part of the productivity story, enabling evaluation of the process of nutritional care. To assess outcome criteria, quality of care must also be evaluated. Quantity and quality of care must be balanced, and the overriding principle should be the achievement of positive patient outcomes. Staff evaluation and performance appraisals discussed in Chapter 6 assist the clinical manager in making decisions about quality of care.

Costing out services is meant to increase efficiency of nutritional care delivery. Productivity studies may reveal that certain nutrition activities can be accomplished more efficiently. Are all the data collected useful in making decisions about nutritional care? If not, what can be eliminated? Can the service be performed as well by a dietetic assistant as by a dietetic technician? Can services be combined with other activities; for example, at meal rounds or providing nutrition supplements with medications?

Are the right factors being measured? Improving patient care is the objective of nutritional care. Measurable outcomes of counseling should be patients' knowledge, attitudes, and behavioral change. Changes in clinical indicators also reveal outcomes of care by the dietitian. Physical well-being and financial savings can also be achieved. Ask the following questions and quantify the results:

- How often do dietitians' actions result in diet changes?
- What are the results of the diet changes?
- How frequent are recommendations for feedings made by the dietitian?
- How often are the proposed changes implemented?
- Does intervention by the dietitian alter patient outcomes?

COST CONTAINMENT

Cost containment establishes specific expenditure goals or "caps" and assists planners in making budgetary decisions. Budgets and operating expenditures are adjusted to meet these goals by the end of specified fiscal periods. Caps usually are placed on a department by administration or through government funding formulas to control spending (Conklin 1984). The prospective payment system (PPS), signed into law in 1983, instituted a capitation system into health care based on 468 diagnostic-related groups (DRGs). The prospective payment system requires justification of the costs of providing services and, for clinical dietetic managers, of staffing requirements as well.

ProPAC, the Prospective Payment Assessment Commission, has examined cost containment over the past 10 years and found that hospital prices are continuing to rise under the PPS. Costs per patient case have been increasing at a rate of 10 percent each year (ASPEN, 1988). The major change in hospital fiscal allocations has been a greater emphasis and investment in outpatient services.

Changes observed by clinical managers since the inception of the DRG system have included higher patient turnover, increased acuity levels of patients, greater use of enteral products and less use of parenteral nutrition, downsizing of staff, and departmental reorganization (Stokes 1986). Clinical managers have found it necessary to provide more detailed productivity reporting to administrators to justify new and continuing positions. Some institutions now allow the clinical nutrition services staff to provide nutrition assessments, consults, and education only by order of the physician.

When asked to give recommendations for containing costs, the clinical dietetic manager needs to identify services that could be eliminated or reassigned to other departments. The usual cost-containment options are to cut either salary or operating expenses. If the decision is to reduce costs through decreasing work hours, this may be accomplished through attrition, not filling a position, or delaying the hiring of replacement personnel. During periods of staff reductions, the remaining workers should not be overburdened. Either services must be reduced or the time used to accomplish certain procedures must be decreased.

JUSTIFYING STAFFING NEEDS

Time expenditure reports and estimated time per activity provide essential data to the justification of services. Staffing needs change over time, and the reason for the changes must be documented well. The clinical manager must succinctly present the rationale for change and the outcome of implementing or not implementing the change. Variables that could change staffing needs include

- change in bed capacity
- change in type of meal service

- change in regulations
- inability to carry out current regulations
- decreased length of stay and increased total number of patients admitted monthly
- increased acuity of nutritional status with additional time providing in-depth care
- increased community service
- increased time allocated to research

Once a staffing need is defined, estimate the number of hours required per week and determine the desired level of staff activity. Information on the procedures used at similar institutions may be helpful in arriving at an appropriate rationale. Costs should be identified and alternatives delineated based on the clinical manager's recommendations. The justification may be for immediate change or a gradual change. The reason for the change needs to be discussed with the staff and immediate supervisors. Consensus on the need and value to the service can facilitate the change in staffing patterns.

COSTS AND BENEFITS OF CLINICAL DIETETIC SERVICES

Legislators, administrators, and government agencies use the costs and benefits of nutrition services to justify continued funding. Hospital administrators are particularly interested in how to measure the effectiveness of the dietitian and how dietitians contribute to costs incurred per patient or per case (Edmundson 1986). Administrators should understand the time required to provide nutrition services at the appropriate level: basic care by dietetic assistants, intermediate care by dietetic technicians, and comprehensive care by dietitians and specialists. Recording times and tasks within one's own facility and comparing results to published studies help determine time standards for care levels or DRG categories. Time standards provide a framework for assigning costs to specific services or care levels, allocating staff by priority standards (e.g., care levels, DRG categories, diet order, or acuity level), and instituting a data base for fee-for-service.

Cost-benefit analysis (CBA) compares the cost of intervention to its benefits, with both costs and benefits represented in dollar figures. The cost-benefit ratio may indicate a positive, negative, or neutral effect. A neutral effect means that the costs are the same as the benefits. Generally, decision makers only consider implementing a program or a service when the benefits of the program exceed the costs. However, caution should be exerted in the interpretation of cost-benefit analysis. Tradition, ethics, politics and long-term benefits or public pressure may intervene in the decision-making process, particularly when instituting large-scale community programs or preventive services. A difficulty in using cost-benefit analysis with nutrition and health programs is the lack of data for translating benefits—extended-life span, quality of life, old versus young, male versus female—into dollar amounts. Therefore, cost-effectiveness analysis (CEA) is easier to use when evaluating health and nutrition programs. The costs are designated in monetary terms, but the benefits are stated as outcomes; for example, patient' days or improved quality of life.

Costs and benefits fall into three categories: direct, indirect, and intangible. Direct costs are those directly related to the program, service, or intervention. They are usually derived from the budget of the department and consist of personnel, equipment, educational materials, other supplies, space, and overhead. Indirect costs are those that may be incurred in addition to direct costs; for example, cost of travel for participants to receive treatment and loss of participant income due to treatment time. Intangible costs should be considered, but are not measurable in dollars, e.g., participant loss of dignity, pain and suffering and a decrease in quality of life parameters (Conklin 1984).

Direct benefits are outcomes associated with a service or intervention that can be related directly to savings or avoidance of expenditures. These savings can be the costs averted if the program had not been undertaken— hospital costs, physicians' services, costs of medications, and the extended life of an individual who remains productive to society. Indirect benefits are difficult to quantify because several assumptions must be made—that the service or intervention reduces pain and suffering or morbidity and mortality. Intangible benefits again are not measured in dollars, but should be figured into the overall outcomes of the service. Intangible benefits include the alleviation of pain and suffering, improved quality of life, and improved independence and control for patients.

A growing dietetics literature is examining the cost-benefit analysis of nutrition services. Exhibit 11-7 lists useful publications—most published since the late 1970s—that can help you develop procedures for determining costs and benefits and collecting productivity data. The 1979 monograph, *Benefits of Nutritional Care,* raised awareness of cost-benefit issues and stated some cautions about tackling the calculations with insufficient documentation and missing data. The 1980s saw continued pressures to cut costs and to measure the productive time of clinical dietetic staff. Revenue-generating functions were encouraged, and articles began to appear on fee-for-services in inpatient and outpatient settings. These recent publications emphasize costing methods and the need to market what is done and to conduct economic analyses (cost-benefit analysis). Exhibit 11-8 provides a

Exhibit 11-7 Selected References for Productivity and Costing Procedures in Clinical Dietetic Management

Reference	Purpose	Tools/Examples
Costs and Benefits of Nutritional Care. Phase 1. American Dietetic Association 1979.	First comprehensive literature review in ambulatory nutrition care	Model on cost benefit in dietetics applied to various age groups and selected diseases
Management of the Clinical Dietetics Staff in Financial Management of the Hospital Food Service Department, American Hospital Association 1983.	Measuring performance of the clinical staff and productivity	Task-time allocation procedures for budget preparation
Financing Hospital-Based Nutrition Services, Ross Laboratories 1984	Experience in establishing fees for inpatient and outpatient services	Four examples of time studies; charge indexes/logs and DRG study for services and time
Cost-Benefit/Cost-Effecitve-Analysis: A Practical Step-by-Step Guide for Nutrition Professionals, Bertram Associates 1984.	Method to implement cost-benefit analysis and cost-effectiveness analysis; definitions and annotated bibliography	Cost-effectiveness worksheets. Ten-Step Process for identifying costs and benefits. Example: effect of dietary intervention on hypertension in outpatient clinic
Costing Nutrition Services: A Workbook, Splett and Caldwell and Dept. of Health and Human Services 1985.	Simplified process to identify the cost of nutrition services in seven steps	Focus on prenatal nutrition services. Time and costing worksheets for calculating direct, indirect, and personnel costs
Productivity Management for Nutrition Care, American Dietetic Association, ADA Members with Management Responsibilities in Health Care Delivery Systems 1986.	Description of a productivity management system for internal usage and to establish a mechanism for future comparisons	Productivity ratios; data collection forms and service area productivity; nine forms for recording productivity of staff and by service area with computer spread sheet example
Benefits of Nutrition Services: A Costing and Marketing Approach, Ross Laboratories 1987.	Review of financial trends: use of a cost-effectiveness process for dietitians with focus on	Matrix of nutrition services benefits for inpatient and home care case studies; comparing cost

Exhibit 11-7 continued

	data collection, analysis and marketing results, for decision makers and users of nutrition services	benefit for prospective payment system and fee-for-service payment
The Costs and Benefits of Nutrition Services: A Literature Review, A supplement to the Journal of the American Dietetic Association, Disbrow 1989.	Updated literature review of cost benefit/cost-effective studies and reports related to nutrition services	Summary of reports that identify economic, cost, and benefit analyses and extensive bibliography

Exhibit 11-8 Documenting Cost-Effective Nutrition Services: Getting Started

STEP I. DEFINE THE PROGRAM OR INTERVENTION TO BE INVESTIGATED.
    A. Questions to be asked
        1. What has administration been emphasizing lately? Where is your service vulnerable?
        2. What have you and your work colleagues been doing that is
           a. successful in terms of patient care outcomes
           b. successful in terms of reducing the use of resources (labor, material costs, etc.) while still achieving the same outcomes
           c. questionable with regard to the amount of effort involved in achieving little or no results—and you want to change it
        3. What type of changes have been made in your department that have also been made at other facilities?
           a. Is there a possibility of a group study within your practice group?
           b. Where can resources and ideas be pooled for mutual benefit?
    B. Once a project has been identified, decide to whom the results of the study will be marketed.
        1. Who is your target audience for the study? From whose point of view do you want the program to be cost effective?
        2. Settle on a specific accounting perspective
           a. patient
           b. hospital or funding agency
           c. society
STEP II. READ AND GATHER INFORMATION.
    A. Review methodology for cost-benefit analysis/cost-effectiveness analysis (CBA/CEA)
    B. Research in subject area of interest to help with
        1. establishing measurable outcomes and proxy measures that correlate highly with desired outcomes

Exhibit 11-8 continued

        2. thinking through your research design to uncover all associated benefits (outcomes) and costs, especially those that are indirect and intangible

        3. other methodological issues

STEP III.   DEFINE METHODOLOGY FOR THE STUDY.

    A. Determine baseline data.

        1. What pertinent information is already being gathered by accounting and medical records? Are these departments willing and able to collect additional information for you?

        2. What are the outcomes and costs associated with what you are presently doing?

        3. Are retrospective data available to compare what you are doing now with a previous time period (before this procedure or treatment)? Caution: data must be comparable and collected in the same way! If so, GO TO STEP VI.

    B. Establish outcome measures for a prospective study.

STEP IV.   DETERMINE PROGRAM EFFECTIVENESS

    A. If not efficacious—STOP. Rethink the use of resources for achieving desired outcomes OR decide on alternative uses for the same resources.

    B. If effective,

        1. Calculate the magnitude of the outcomes in relation to an average outcome per patient.

        2. Make sure the results are meaningful in terms of your accounting perspective.

STEP V.   DETERMINE THE COST OF ACHIEVING THE OUTCOMES.

    A. Calculate the pertinent costs from your accounting perspective.

        1. Direct costs—budget plus overhead costs not directly mentioned in the budget. All use of resources must be considered even though you do not pay for them, e.g., volunteer labor. This will make your calculation conservative in terms of cost effectiveness.

        2. Indirect costs—any pertinent opportunity costs or real costs not reflected on the budget

        3. Intangible costs? You cannot include these in the calculations, but they can be mentioned in the discussion, particularly if your new procedure reduces these.

STEP VI.   CALCULATE THE COST-EFFECTIVENESS RATIO.

    A. Compute total cost of program ÷ Total outcome = $ per unit outcome

    B. Compare the programs under investigation—the one that is most cost effective is the one that delivers the most outcome for equivalent cost or the same outcome for the least cost.

STEP VII.   CALCULATE THE SAVINGS TO THE ORGANIZATION GENERATED BY THE PROGRAM

    A. If the outcome of a treatment or program directly affects the potential financial reimbursement of the organization (as with reduced length of stay), you will want to pinpoint this effect by conducting a benefit-cost analysis from the viewpoint of the HOSPITAL. This would be similar to a business conducting a profitability analysis.

    B. For this procedure

        1. Benefits or outcomes are the reduction in patient days and other ancillary costs per patient resulting from your EFFECTIVE program.

Exhibit 11-8 continued

    2. These benefits/pt. are valued by using the per diem hospital rate, actual material costs, etc. Caution: Always keep your accounting perspective in mind—what is a benefit to one may be a cost to another!

    3. Costs/pt. are calculated in the same way.

    4. Calculation of the savings generated

        a. Subtract the costs from the benefit dollars to yield a net benefit figure per patient.

        b. Determine the number of patients who will be treated with the DRG related to this procedure.

        c. Multiply net benefits by number of patients to give an annual savings generated.

STEP VIII. COMMUNICATE RESULTS TO THE TARGET AUDIENCE.

    A. Prepare succinct written presentation with executive summary, costs and outcomes, comparison of ratios/alternative, and suggested plan for action.

    B. Request response/reaction on the results and approval for implementation.

Source: Martha T. Conklin, Presentation to The Clinical Nutrition Managers of Greater New York, April, 1987.

blueprint for initiating cost-effectiveness and cost-benefit studies in the clinical management arena.

COST EFFECTIVENESS OF NUTRITIONAL SUPPORT

Efforts to prove the cost effectiveness of nutritional support are beginning to have an impact on patient care. It is not sufficient to tell administrators that nutritional support is cost effective. Administrators should be informed of how much the average length of stay (ALOS) was diminished by aggressive nutritional support (Buzby 1988).

Malnutrition, if left untreated, can increase health expenditures. It exists in 30–50 percent of hospitalized patients. Although malnutrition is not classified as a DRG, it is a comorbidity that increases reimbursement for costs incurred (Huyck and Fairchild 1987). Comorbidities or complications are defined as conditions that, when present, extend the length of stay by at least 1 day in 75 percent of all patients. The comorbidities associated with malnutrition in the DRG scheme are kwashiorkor, nutritional marasmus, protein-calorie malnutrition, and vitamin K deficiencies (see Appendix D).

REFERENCES

American Dietetic Association, 1990. *Role delineation for registered dietitians and entry-level dietetic technicians.* Chicago: American Dietetic Association.

American Society of Parenteral and Enteral Nutrition. 1988. Ten years of health cost containment. *PENLine* (February):7.

Buzby, Karen. 1988. Cost effectiveness of nutrition support. *Dietitians Nutr. Supp. Newsl.* 10(6):11, 15.

Conklin, Martha T. 1984. Cost effectiveness of nutrition intervention. In *Nutrition Assessment,* eds. Margaret D. Simko, Catherine Cowell, and Judith A. Gilbride. Gaithersburg, Md.: Aspen Publishers, Inc.

Crissey, J., L. Manera, D. Morris, and V. Revinski. 1988. Dietetic intern research project. University of Medicine and Dentistry of New Jersey, Newark.

DeHoog, S. 1986. Identifying patients at nutritional risk and determining clinical productivity: Essentials for an effective nutrition care program. *J. Am. Dietet. Assoc.* 85(12):620–22.

Edmundson, R. William. 1986. Clinical services departments in hospitals become revenue generating departments. *J. Am. Dietet. Assoc.* 86(11):1521–22.

Huyck, Norma, and Michele Fairchild. 1987. Provision of clinical nutrition services by diagnosis-related groups (DRGs) and major diagnostic categories (MDCs). *J. Am. Dietet. Assoc.* 87(1):69–70.

Huyck, Norma, and Patricia McNamara. 1987. Monitoring accountability of a clinical nutrition service. *J. Am. Dietet. Assoc.* 87(5):620–23.

McEwan, Celine W., and Ann Messersmith. 1987. Productivity management: Applying it personally and professionally. *J. Am. Dietet. Assoc.* 87(5):581–83.

Noland, Marion S., and Ruth Steinberg. 1965. Activities of the therapeutic dietetian—a survey report. *J. Am. Dietet. Assoc.* 46(6):477–81.

Ross Laboratories. 1984. *The cost-effectiveness of nutrition support: Selected references with annotations.* Columbus, Ohio: Ross Laboratories.

Stokes, Judy. 1986. Beyond formula tube feeding equipment. *Clin. Man.* 3(6):1–4.

Touger-Decker, Riva. 1985. *Clinical dietetic staffing needs assessment survey 1985 abstracts: Directions for action.* Chicago: American Dietetic Association.

SUGGESTED READINGS

Disbrow, Doris. 1989. The costs and benefits of nutrition services: A literature review. *J. Am. Dietet. Assoc.* 89 (Suppl. 4):3–66.

Finn, Susan C. 1988. The value of cost-benefit analysis in marketing nutrition services. *Clin. Man.* 4(2):5–8.

Kaud, Faisal A. 1983. Management of clinical dietetics staff. In *Financial management of the hospital food service department.* Chicago: American Hospital Association.

Mirtallo, Jay, et al. 1987. Cost-effective nutrition support. *Nutr. Clin. Pract.* 2(4):142–51.

Regenstein, Marsha. 1989. Reimbursement for nutrition support. *Nutr. Clin. Pract.* 4(6):194–202.

Report of the Fifth Ross Roundtable on Medical Issues. 1984. *Financing hospital-based nutrition services.* Columbus, Ohio: Ross Laboratories.

Rose, James. 1986. Fee for service: Concepts and finances. *Hosp. Food Nutr. Focus* 2(11):1,4–7.

Schaffarzick, Ralph. 1985. Technology assessment and health benefits determination. *Qual. Rev. Bull.* (July): 222–25.

Shankin, Carol, et al. 1988. Documentation of time expenditures of clinical dietitians: Results of a statewide time study in Texas. *J. Am. Dietet. Assoc.* 89(4):485–87.

Simko, Margaret, and Martha Conklin. 1989. Focusing on the effectiveness side of the cost-effectiveness equation. *J. Am. Dietet. Assoc.* 89(4):485–87.

Smith, Alice E. 1984. Reimbursement for clinical nutrition services. *J. Am. Dietet. Assoc.* 84(3):328–30.

Smith, Philip, and Alice Smith. 1988. *Screening for hospital malnutrition.* Deerfield, Ill.: Clintec Nutrition Company.

Splett, Patricia, and Mariel Caldwell. 1985. *Costing nutrition services: A workbook.* Chicago: Dept. of Health and Human Services, Region V.

Chapter 12

Managing Fiscal Affairs

Historically clinical dietetic managers have focused on services needed by the patient with little concern for the budget. Today, clinical managers are aware that budgets dictate what services can be provided and that accurate budget projections are essential to the process of establishing goals and objectives. Financial management is an integral part of clinical dietetic management whether the clinical dietetic budget is a portion of the food service department budget or a distinct budget. Separate budget lines for clinical dietetics are the basis for monitoring and adjusting costs and portraying a true picture of available services.

Revenue generation and fee-for-services can offset some costs and help with decisions on resource allocation. Cost-effectiveness and cost-benefit analyses are outgrowths of a sound financial management system. Evaluation of the outcome of services and the methods of delivering patient care can improve the cost and quality of patient care.

A CASE FOR SURVIVAL

A budget for clinical dietetic services is an organized plan for a specific period that forecasts activity and income, determines expenses, and concludes with the overall financial position. The financial plan is an essential tool for setting goals and measuring accomplishments. Although a variety of budget styles exist, all budgets serve as the basis for coordinating the activities of a department or segment of a department. Clinical managers should use whatever accounting procedures have been approved in their institutions. Whatever the accounting procedures used at the institution, a good budget facilitates the goals of the department, is tied directly to short- and long-range plans, provides a systematic review of the operation, and includes all costs.

In a world of dwindling resources and fierce competition for health care dollars, secure knowledge of one's financial status provides an edge. Financial survival depends on knowing

- what the clinical staff does
- how much it costs
- how the budget is spent
- how to obtain other monies
- how to inform administrators and other staff

A food and dietetic services department has an average budget of 1.5 percent of the total hospital budget. Clinical dietetic budgets vary, but are often in the range of 10 percent of the food service budget. The food service budget is generally based on an estimated number of patient days and/or a factor for the number of patient meals served. The department receives a set reimbursement rate per patient meal; clinical dietetics receives a portion of this fee or may generate a separate charge.

Each clinical dietetic manager needs to know the monies available for clinical services and whether these monies meet the needs of clinical dietetics. Basic dollars available are based on the reimbursement rate per meal and the patient occupancy rate. For example, if the food and dietetic services department received $25.00 per patient per day and clinical dietetics represents 10 percent of this amount, then clinical dietetics receives $2.50 per patient per day. If the institution has 300 beds and an occupancy rate of 90 percent, this would amount to $300 \times 2.50 \times 0.90 = \$675$ per day or a budget of $246,375 per year ($675 \times 365$ days). To meet needs much higher than this would require revenue generation from sources other than patient meals, such as extra fees for comprehensive nutrition services.

A delineation of what services are provided in the clinical budget as opposed to the food service budget is essential to the determination of what percentage of the total budget is clinical. Nutrition assessment, monitoring, follow-up, and counseling are obviously clinical dietetic budget items. Meal rounds, menu selection, diet calculations, and many technician and dietetic assistant functions could be part of either the clinical budget or the food service budget. Each institution needs to decide, based on its organizational structure and lines of authority, which services are provided by which section of the budget. After determination of the services provided by the budgetary unit, a cost per service is needed. The productivity data in Chapter 11 provide the means of determining cost per dietetic service. Different approaches can be used to determine whether the clinical dietetic service can operate optimally within its budget and how to align the budget and the services. One approach is outlined below.

Each direct care patient service has a typical time span; for example, an initial screening may take 15 minutes, and a comprehensive assessment may take 30 minutes. Once a time frame is determined for each service the estimated cost per service can be established based on the level of personnel who performs the service. Information shown in Exhibit 12-1 needs to be determined for each specific department. A definition of what is included in each service is essential. Appendix C provides some definitions recommended by the American Dietetic Association, or the unit may adopt its own definitions.

FEE-FOR-SERVICE

Once the time per service and the level of personnel are identified, the cost per minute for the employee must be determined. This figure is based on actual salaries, the cost of benefits, and overhead costs. In addition, the percentage of time spent in direct patient services as listed in Table 12-1 needs to be determined.

Table 12-1 shows how to convert time (minutes) to money. Actual salaries should be based on the midpoint of the range for the position. The cost of benefits can be obtained from the human resources department; it is often 20 to 35 percent of salaries. Overhead costs can vary significantly by department. The first decision is what to include in overhead costs. The example given includes cost for space, supplies, secretarial support, managerial costs, etc. It takes the entire budget and divides noncoverable costs across services that could be billable.

Once the cost per employee is known, the amount of productive work time per year needs to be determined. Institutional formulas are often available based on number of vacation days, holidays, average sick time used, and hour worked per day. Once the cost per employee is known and the minutes worked are known, the cost per minute can be determined. However, this cost per minute is based on each minute being utilized productively. This is unrealistic. How one determines productive time (see Chapter 11) and whether the clinical manager charges for a service determine whether an estimate of billable or productive time per dietetic service is needed. Time studies can determine the amount of time spent in direct patient care, and job descriptions and goals and objectives for each position can assist in setting optimal times for direct patient care. These may be different for each position.

Once the percentage of time for billable services is determined, an estimate of the charge per minute for the service can be determined. If only 25 percent of time is spent in billable services, the charge per minute must be

Exhibit 12-1 Estimated Time Needed for Each Clinical Service

Service	Time Needed by Each Level of Dietetic Personnel			
	Assistant	Technician	Dietitian	Specialist
Initial screening				
Basic assessment				
Comprehensive assessment				
Follow-up assessment				
Routine follow-up				
Nutrient analysis				
Diet instruction				
Comprehensive counseling				
Group Education				
Other				

Table 12-1 Estimation of Cost Per Minute for Clinical Dietetic Staff*

	Assistant	Technician	Dietitian	Specialist
Midpoint of salary range	20,000	25,000	32,000	40,000
Estimate of cost of benefits (25% of salaries) (usually % of salary)	5,000	6,750	8,000	10,000
Overhead costs (40% of salaries) (based on supply, space, management, etc.)	8,000	10,000	12,800	16,000
Cost per employee	33,000	41,750	52,800	66,000
Productive time per year estimated days worked per year† (260 days—vacation—sick—holidays) Hours of work per day†	225 7	225 7	225 7	225 7
Hours per year	1,575	1,575	1,575	1,575
Minutes per year (hrs/yr × 60 minutes)	94,500	94,500	94,500	94,500
Cost/employee/minute per year = total cost per minute	$ 0.35	$ 0.44	$ 0.56	$ .70
% of time in billable services	50%	50%	50%	30%‡
Minute cost per billable service to balance actual cost	$ .70	$ .88	$ 1.12	$ 2.10

*Actual dollars per institution need to be inserted.
†Actual days and hours are specific to the individual institution.
‡Allows specialist additional time for research and education; varies by institution.

four times higher than the actual cost to break even. If 50 percent of the employees' time is spent in billable services as in Table 12-1, the charge per minute must be twice the actual cost per minute to break even. Revenue generation means generating funds above this cost. Independent of whether the clinical dietetic service is revenue generating, costs per service need to be considered.

COST OF SERVICES

Evaluation of services by the minute and by the level of personnel shows that the cost of dietetic services can be reduced substantially whenever lower-level personnel can perform the task at the same rate and whenever procedures can be streamlined to reduce the time per procedure. The greater the amount of time in direct billable services, the lower the cost per service. Table 12-2 combines the information in Exhibit 12-1 and Table 12-1 to enable the estimation of cost by intensity of service. It suggests that cost per diagnosis can be determined when the service provided by diagnosis is known.

Time is money: therefore, the clinical dietetic manager must ensure that time is utilized well. A staff meeting of four dietitians and four technicians costs $4.00 per minute (.56 × 4 and .44 × 4); a 1-hour meeting or inservice costs $240. Whereas the use of billable time rather than straight-time encompasses this indirect cost, it is still an amount of time that must be used wisely. Often 80 to 90 percent of the clinical budget is for salaries; inappropriate use of staff time will result in insufficient services for the budgeted dollar.

BUDGET FOR CLINICAL DIETETIC SERVICES

The clinical dietetic services budget has four basic areas: salaries of dietetic staff, overhead, supplies, and professional development. Most institutions have a budgetary worksheet to categorize costs. There are three major categories of costs:

- fixed costs that do not vary based on output, such as salaries
- variable costs that change depending on output, such as educational materials
- opportunity costs that are realized if resources have been allocated to other services

Exhibit 12-2 is a worksheet to estimate expenditures per year. Often budget projections are compared to the previous year, and substantive changes

Table 12-2 Cost by Level of Service or by Diagnosis

Service	Cost Per Billable Minute*	No. of Minutes†	Cost/Procedure
Nutrition screening (by assistant)	$ .70	10	$ 7.00
Basic assessment (by technician)	$ .88	15	$13.20
Comprehensive assessment (by dietitian)	$1.12	30	$33.60
Comprehensive assessment (by specialist)	$2.10	30	$63.00
Example: for typical cardiac bypass patient			
Basic assessment (by technician)	$ .88	15	$13.20
Follow-up by technician	$ .88	15	$13.20
Comprehensive counseling by RD	$1.12	45	$50.40
Total Cost of Care to Bypass Patient			$76.80

*Actual cost needs to be determined by institution.
† Based on minutes per service determined by time study.

Exhibit 12-2 Budget Projection Worksheet

Clinical Dietetic Services

Year _____

	Actual Year	Request for Next Year	Amount Approved
SALARY			
Manager			
Specialist(s)			
Dietitians			
Technicians			
Secretaries			
Overtime			
Benefits			
Incentives			
Merits			
MATERIALS AND SUPPLIES			
Space/Utilities			
Office/Computer/Supplies			
Photocopying			
Material Development			
Entertainment/Production Catering			
Telephone			
Advertising/Recruitment			
Parking Fees			

PROFESSIONAL EDUCATION
Books/Periodicals
Computer Searches
Travel
Inservices
Tuition Reimbursement

RECURRING CHARGES
Computer Maintenance
Equipment

must be justified. Budgets are traditionally planned 2 to 6 months in advance. Major budgetary change projections are determined 1 to 5 years ahead. Predicting future budgets requires knowledge of projected expansion and shifts in number and types of patients and must be in concert with a departmental strategic plan.

The monthly or yearly budget needs to identify short-term budgetary alterations, such as the need for overtime to cover peak periods, personnel changes including recruitment; occupancy rate and patient loads and their effect on revenue projects; and changes in the expenses for office management, including equipment, purchases of services, and supplies. Some institutions use a factor of 5 to 10 percent to allow for unexpected expenses or inflation.

Salaries are affected by the local labor market. Periodically, a comparison of salaries should be made within the area and in similar types of institutions. An internal comparison to positions in other departments with similar job functions and responsibilities should also be considered. Dietitians need to be paid commensurate with their responsibilities. The time of budget projections is often a good time to review salaries.

If expenditures are projected above anticipated cost per patient meal allotment, income/revenues from other sources must be identified. Possible sources of revenue include hosting a workshop for professionals or the public, applying for educational or research grants, or establishing a fee-for-service clinic. See Exhibit 12-3 for some additional ideas. The budget and public relations department can assist with procedures and methods to generate revenue. When setting charges it is important to consider billable hours and start-up costs and to establish a timeline for when the service should be cost-recoverable.

When proposing a venture or new operation, be sure to analyze costs in detail. Identify volume projections for a 1- to 5-year period. Consider the price of similar services when setting up the service and developing fees for procedures and times for each procedure. A detailed and realistic financial forecast is essential.

BUDGET REDUCTIONS

With cost containment the key to survival in this decade, the clinical dietetic manager must justify services. A clear indication of how monies are spent is the first step. The next step is a contingency plan for budget reductions. If a decreased volume of patients reduces revenue, can the clinical dietetic manager cut salaries by reducing total personnel costs? This can be done by offering part-time hours to interested staff or not filling vacancies.

Exhibit 12-3 Ways to Generate Revenue

Inpatient	Outpatient
Fee for service	Fee for service
Grants/funding	Grants/funding
Physician support for travel	Special product sales
Education lunch for MDs/RNs	Weight loss contest
Diet manuals	Patient education materials
Enteral/parenteral product charges	Community catering service
Nutrition support consults	Computer nutrient analysis
Newsletters	Newsletters
Kilocalorie counts	Referral procedure incentives
Tubefeedings, pumps and administration sets	Consults in physicians' offices
Promotional mailings	Wellness program
	Home visits

Can procedures be re-examined to decrease the time per procedure and level of care? Can the staff spend more time in direct patient care? Can services be minimized on a specific unit? If reductions cannot be made without compromising patient care, proposals can be written and presented on the outcome of reduced service or nutrition intervention. Other departments, such as obstetrics or pediatrics, may be willing to augment the clinical budget to maintain service on a particular unit, or administration may be convinced of the cost utility of the service in relation to patient care, thereby sparing the budget reduction.

The clinical dietetic manager leads the staff in documenting the demand for and the impact of services provided for selected groups of patients. Cost-effectiveness and cost-benefit studies of dietetic services will assist in budget maintenance and growth.

SUGGESTED READINGS

Adamow, Christine L., and Andrew J. Clipper. 1985. Is prospective payment inhibiting the use of nutrition support services? Discussion and research implications. *J. Am. Dietet. Assoc.* 85(12):1616–19.

Campbell, Chelene. 1985. The enhanced productivity program. *J. Am. Dietet. Assoc.* 85(11):1479–82.

Finn. Susan Calvert. 1988. The value of cost benefit analysis in marketing nutrition services. *Clin. Man.* 4(2):5–8.

Jurdi-Haldeman, Dalal. 1988. Enhancing revenue producing activities and visibility of nutrition services. *Clin. Man.* 4(7):21–24.

Lowery, Eve, and Mary Abbott Hess. 1987. Starting a business on a shoestring. *Clin. Man.* 3(5):17–20.

Stokes, Judy, ed. 1986. Getting your worth in money. *Clin. Man.* 2(6):21–24.

Scott, Evalena. 1987. NSPS: Strategies for success. *Clin. Man.* 3(12):44–47.

Stokes, Judy. 1985. *Cost effective quality food service: An institutional guide.* Gaithersburg, Md.: Aspen Publishers, Inc.

Chapter 13

Decisions Regarding Equipment and Technology

Clinical managers separated themselves from the production and purchasing of foods by the mid-1950s. However, by the 1980s they were back into business and production. This time, however, the products include enteral and parenteral nutrition feedings, computer software and hardware, and equipment for nutritional assessment: body composition devices, computers for nutrient analyses, and direct calorimetry machines. This chapter identifies some important factors that should be considered before investing in products and new technology. Specific products are not discussed or recommended because information is outdated quickly.

Technological advances have been key determinants of both the quality and cost of health care. What was once extraordinary is now ordinary care due to these advances. The cost of health care could be curtailed if it was based more on science, rather than changing common practice prematurely to take advantage of new technology. This is also true in nutrition. Hopping on the bandwagon for each new piece of equipment or product is not cost effective. Careful consideration is needed. Although clinical dietetic managers are obliged to maintain appropriate standards of practice, new is not always better.

Clinical dietetic managers must exercise judgment on the extent and types of technology appropriate for good clinical care. What is the effect of the nutritional procedures on patient care or medical outcome? What tests are needed to confirm a nutritional status of malnutrition? For example, prealbumin levels in the blood illustrate acute protein depletion better than serum albumin levels. However, for the routine client this additional test does not alter nutritional care or medical outcome. The clinical manager needs to reexamine the concept of appropriateness of care. In medicine, this is called "technology assessment" (Schaffarzick 1985).

TECHNOLOGY ASSESSMENT

Technology assessment is the process of appraising the true value of a specified device or procedure in a structured way. The evaluation can be detailed or simple based on the cost of the technology, its maintenance, the manpower needed to operate the technology, and the mission of the institution. The process is similar to other assessment procedures. First, data on the subject are collected. When research data are unavailable, consensus opinions are formed on the value of the technology. Will the device be used for research or become an important component of nutritional care? Has the procedure been shown to be valuable, or is it still in the investigational phase?

Third-party payers base the evaluation of technology on certain criteria: its relative safety, the sensitivity or specificity of the procedure, its cost-effectiveness, patient selection and provider criteria (Schaffarzick 1985). Because available funds in nutritional services are finite, technology decisions must include a consideration of their impact on all areas, but especially those that will have reduced coverage or growth because of the new technology. Schaffarzick (1985, 224) suggests that an attempt be made to determine the "margin of clinical profit" or the "degree to which a new procedure improves clinical outcomes." Many technological advances improve precision, but not patient outcome or institutional cost containment.

The clinical manager must evaluate a broad array of technologies. Should recommendations be made to use new laboratory procedures, equipment to measure the metabolic rate or monitor dietary compliance/acceptance, automation to improve food/nutrient delivery, or interactive communication systems for counseling and education? The list goes on and on. To make such decisions effectively the clinical manager needs to utilize consultants efficiently, both internal and external, and read published reports carefully.

Since enteral nutrition is such an important dimension of clinical nutrition, this chapter focuses on a few areas of technology related to it. The discussion is divided into two sections: establishment of a formulary and selection of enteral equipment. Selection of other technologies is also considered. Parenteral equipment is not discussed because of the limited number of clinical managers responsible for its purchase.

ESTABLISHMENT OF A FORMULARY

The number of enteral nutrition products has grown from a half-dozen in the 1960s and early 1970s to well over 50 commercial formulas in the early 1990s. Once it became impossible to stock every product, a system needed to be developed to determine which products were essential to a specific department or institution. Generally, a group of dietitians and other health professionals set up a formulary committee to develop such a system. Such a committee established a method for product review and made recommendations to the clinical dietetic manager or institutional nutrition committee. When a product was added to the formulary an inventory level par and purchasing information were provided to the purchasing agent in the institution.

The goals of formulary development are to reduce duplication and excess costs and minimize the purchase of low-usage items while still meeting the needs of the patients within the institution. To accomplish these goals, enteral products are categorized into subsets, such as lactose-free, chemically defined, isotonic, nutrient-dense, and specialty and modular formulas. Criteria for product evaluation are set, including such items as palatability for oral feedings, product availability, micro- and macronutrient composition, size and available packaging, osmolality, and fiber. Patient acceptance is a critical factor; one institution found 40 percent of oral products were refused by patients (Quinn 1988). Records of taste tests may indicate preferences in certain subsets of patients; for example, oncology patients prefer products that are less sweet. Figure 13-1 illustrates a decision tree for client use of modular products. Decision trees facilitate the development of quality product use. Using firm procedures for product evaluation will reduce the number of enteral supplements from over 50 to less than a dozen.

A joint pharmacy/dietary committee can set up guidelines for a multivitamin and mineral formulary (Raatz and Jolowsky 1987). Limiting the number of vitamin and mineral supplements can reduce storage and monitoring costs. Selection of supplements for the formulary should be based on the Recommended Dietary Allowances, guidelines established by the Department of Foods and Nutrition of the American Medical Association, and any institutional policies.

Competitiveness of pricing, discounts for large orders, and the time span between ordering and delivery should also be considered when selecting vitamin and mineral supplements. If the product meets the criteria, then patient tolerance or preference is an essential consideration. It can be evaluated by a taste panel, monitoring of tolerance over time, and previous experiences with products from specific manufacturers. If the product meets departmental needs and is tolerated by the patients, then cost considerations come into play. The final decision on the formulary may rest either with the clinical dietetic manager or a nutrition committee.

Once the formulary is established, a maintenance program must be established. When will new products be evaluated? By whom? A regular update, at least annually, is recommended.

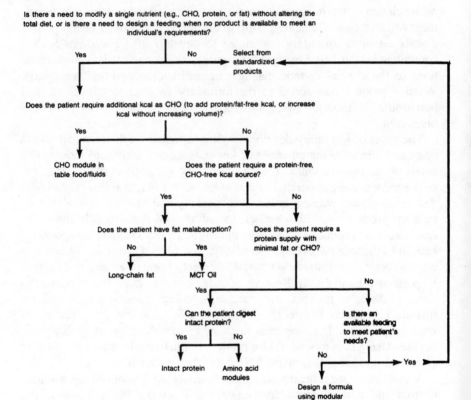

Is there a need to modify a single nutrient (e.g., CHO, protein, or fat) without altering the total diet, or is there a need to design a feeding when no product is available to meet an individual's requirements?

Yes / No → Select from standardized products

Does the patient require additional kcal as CHO (to add protein/fat-free kcal, or increase kcal without increasing volume)?

Yes → CHO module in table food/fluids

No → Does the patient require a protein-free, CHO-free kcal source?

Yes → Does the patient have fat malabsorption?
No → Long-chain fat
Yes → MCT Oil

No → Does the patient require a protein supply with minimal fat or CHO?

Can the patient digest intact protein?
Yes → Intact protein
No → Amino acid modules

Is there an available feeding to meet patient's needs?
No → Design a formula using modular ingredients
Yes

Figure 13-1 Modular Feeding Decision Tree. *Source:* Adapted from *Programmed Instruction Guide: Enteral Feedings* by Riva Touger-Decker, 1989.

SELECTION OF ENTERAL EQUIPMENT

Enteral tubes vary in length, diameter, and construction. The length varies from 30 to 36 inches for gastric administration and 42 to 45 inches for duodenal administration. The diameter varies from a 5 French (FR) to an 18 FR, which is equal to 0.96 to 2.64 millimeters in diameter. The tube diameter decreases with the size of the tube. The viscosity of the tubefeedings used within the institution dictates whether a large tube is needed. An 8 FR tube is usually considered comfortable for nasal feedings. Large-bore tubes may be uncomfortable and may increase the risk of aspiration and esophageal irritation.

Tubes are generally made of silicone, polyurethane, or polyvinyl chloride. The different materials have varying levels of pliability and durability, composition of tips, and use of stylets or wire. Each component should be included in the cost. Feeding tubes may be purchased separately or as a package with the pump. Often, samples may be obtained to allow testing of new equipment.

Tubefeedings may be administered via the drip method, by pump, or by gravity. The number of patients on tubefeedings and the criticality of slow or consistent administration of feedings determine the number of pumps essential for good practice within the facility. An estimate of the number of pumps needed can be ascertained through a retrospective review of the number of tubefeedings provided in a typical week, a count of the number of tubefeeding orders that are provided at a slow administration rate, and a discussion with the clinical practitioners on the number of tubefeeding complications that could be minimized by use of a pump.

SELECTION OF OTHER EQUIPMENT

Growth of computer applications for clinical dietetics has been slower than anticipated, but may increase in the future. In medicine, computer systems are called "medical decision-support systems" (Shortliffe 1987). These systems are further divided into three types of support: information management tools, such as bibliographic retrieval; key-finding systems, such as systems that flag abnormal laboratory tests or drug interactions; and systems that give patient-specific consultations. Although computers cannot replace the judgment of a competent dietitian, a computer system can use assessment parameters to provide an algorithm for making decisions. These decision-support systems can facilitate both the diagnosis and therapy of patients. Much of the software available is institution specific both in terms of equipment availability and the particular parameters used in assessment. As more standards of nutritional assessment are adopted and hospitals standardize their computer systems, the use of computers in clinical dietetics should increase. Exhibit 13-1 is an overview of computer usage in dietetics.

Hand-held computers and programmable calculators are decreasing in cost, save time, and can improve the accuracy of diet calculations. They have the potential to alter menu selection and diet order procedures. In the future, computerized communication systems will instantly inform the kitchen of missing items or the need for a tray. Calorie counts will be done in seconds if menu selection and intake evaluation are available within the same computer

Exhibit 13-1 Overview of Computer Uses in the Nutrition Field

1. Education
   a. Computer-assisted instruction, continuing education
   b. Assist consumer with food shopping, menus, recipes
2. Record-keeping jobs
   a. Personnel records, payroll, accounting
   b. Inventory and purchasing systems
   c. Spreadsheets, financial reports
   d. Menu rotation and recipe adjustments
   e. Ingredient control, work schedules, cost analysis
   f. Patient food item requirements
3. Diagnosis
   a. Diet (history, record, recall) analysis
   b. Exercise prescription
   c. Medical records
   d. Computer-assisted medical decision for diagnosis
   e. Record hospital procedures (clinical or other) to evaluate safety, efficacy
4. Information retrieval and storage
   a. Sending messages, electronic mail, electronic bulletin boards
   b. Access data bases, such as journal literature, government surveys, nutrient data bases
   c. Teleshopping, home banking
5. Predictions and forecasts
   a. Enter statistics on health care facilities, population growth, disease to predict needs
   b. As above factors change, the program predicts results and suggests action
6. Graphics
   a. Information display by graphs or charts
   b. Visual display of proposed component changes in laboratory, kitchen, room for better efficiency.
7. Robotics
   a. Robot carriers deliver meals, linens, medical supplies, mail, lab specimens
   b. Mechanical arm can guide a surgeon's probe directly to a brain lesion
   c. Robots can contribute to patient care. A voice-controlled mechanical arm can perform vocational tasks, such as turning a page, getting a drink of water, serving a bowl
8. Teletex and videotex
9. Interactive compact disc
10. Videodisc

Source: Reprinted from "The Nutrition Message and the Medium" by Sarah H. Short and William R. Short in *Food and Nutrition News,* Vol. 58, No. 5, p. 31, with permission of the National Live Stock and Meat Board, © 1986.

system. Exhibit 13-2 illustrates the variety of computer applications in food services.

Before deciding what computer usage to employ, the clinical dietetic manager should conduct a needs assessment. Detailed specifications are vital. What are the anticipated outcomes of the computer? Which parameters are needed for nutrition assessment? Are there specific institutional guidelines for drug-nutrient interactions? Once the desired output is known, a comparison can be made within the marketplace to decide which systems best meet the needs within a certain price range.

The skills of the staff also influence the selection of computer programs. The more personnel who will utilize the program, the more user friendly the computer and its program need to be. Training costs should be considered in the initial costs. The more intricate the computer system, the greater the time investment in the system and the longer the adjustment period. Will the vendor provide training, at what cost, and for how long? Is there a "hotline" for problems? How often are the programs upgraded? What is the cost of upgrading? Exhibit 13-3 provides a list of questions to consider when selecting a nutrition analysis system.

Exhibit 13-2 Computer Applications in Food Management and Nutrition Services

MENU MANAGEMENT
Maintaining menu data base
On-line menu updating
Printing master menu
Reporting nutrient composition
Printing production worksheet
Integrating menus with food-production control system
Desktop menu printing
Printing patient menus
Planning and costing of menus
Printing menu worksheet
Menu engineering for profitability and labor requirements
Automatic implementing of holiday menus
Tallying menus

FORECASTING, MATERIALS-REQUIREMENTS PLANNING, AND PRODUCTION
Maintaining recipe data base
Recosting recipes
Cross-referencing recipes and ingredients
Cross-referencing recipes and nutrient data bases
On-line adjusting of recipes
Adjusting recipe yields
Printing ingredient labels
Storeroom requisitioning
Printing freezer-withdrawal list
Printing advanced-preparation list
Printing consolidated grocery list
Integrating menu-management system to production planning
Scheduling food production
Analyzing food production
Forecasting demand
Forecasting daily food purchases
Forecasting daily sales
Printing recipe worksheet
Reviewing recipes
Analyzing waste
Managing commissary
Costing tubefeedings and nourishments, printing labels, and scheduling production

Exhibit 13-2 continued

INVENTORY AND PURCHASING

Maintaining food-item data base
Maintaining medical-nutritional-product
 data base
Maintaining perpetual inventory
Maintaining periodic inventory
Printing recommended-purchases list
Reporting daily purchases and issues
Reporting purchases per vendor
Reporting purchases per category
Reporting food and supplies issues per
 category
Reporting food and supplies issues per
 cost center
Ordering food and supplies based on
 forecasts
Listing foods and supplies ordered in
 quantities less than forecasted amount
Requisitioning purchases (generated by
 computer)
Posting automatic purchases
Reporting inventory discrepancies
Updating prices
Computing recommended maximum
 stock levels
Updating stock levels
Reporting monthly purchases and issues
Reporting year-to-date purchases and
 issues
Printing food-item syllabus
On-line entering of data
On-line inquiries
On-line updating of food-item file
Analyzing bids and group purchasing
Printing purchase orders
Printing ingredient labels
Printing shelf labels
Controlling invoices
Reporting shrinkage
Reporting vendor data
Printing physical inventory recording
 form
Printing par stock order worksheet
Just-in-time ordering

SERVICE

Assembling trays
Printing menu tickets
Printing distribution lists

Entering orders
Processing orders
Reporting banquet and catering data
Reporting home-delivery data
Printing host/hostess table-seating/
 waiting list
Printing tubefeeding and nourishment
 labels

FOOD-COST AND SALES ACCOUNTING

Costing issued foods, medical nutritional
 products, and supplies
Projecting selling prices
Maintaining ledgers
Reporting daily food costs for cost centers
Reporting month- and year-to-date
 summaries
Comparing costs to budget
Reporting costs per meal and per patient
 day
Reporting average-check costs
Counting customers
Computing meal equivalents
Computing food-cost percentages
On-line entering of data
On-line inquiries
Looking up prices
On-line generating of reports
Accounting and reporting beverage
 dispensing
Reporting sales
Analyzing checks
Reporting check activity
Reporting open-check and split-check
 data
Reporting variable costs
Point-of-sale reporting
Cashier reporting
Analyzing costs
Analyzing food and beverage sales
Reporting hourly sales
Totaling carry-out sales
Payment-system reporting
Analyzing revenues
Reporting taxes
Costing events (catering, special dietary
 requirements, and outpatient meals)

Exhibit 13-2 continued

Analyzing menu-item and nourishment-item costs
Analyzing items and categories
Comparing food costs to menu prices
Comparing store-by-store data
USDA reporting
Reporting Type A meals and USDA free/reduced prices
Reporting school-foodservice participation
Analyzing break-even data
General-ledger functioning
Reporting fixed assets
Reporting accounts-receivable and accounts-payable data
Recognizing and authorizing credit cards
Bookkeeping
Budgeting
Printing financial statements
Reporting profits and losses
Writing checks

PERSONNEL, PAYROLL, AND LABOR-COST ACCOUNTING
Maintaining personnel master data base
Maintaining personnel history data base
Filing attendance
Reporting absenteeism
Seniority reporting
Turnover reporting
Payroll reporting
Labor-cost reporting
Scheduling employees and students
Planning weekly schedules
Reporting vacation, sick leave, and holidays
Linking time clock and personal computers
Employee timekeeping
Totaling individual servers
Recording in-service training
Reporting tips
Computing labor requirements based on menu, nutrition-care tasks, and patient census

PRODUCTIVITY
Reporting labor productivity
Reporting hourly time data on server activity

Reporting meals per hour
Reporting minutes per meal and nutrition-care task
Reporting nutrition interventions per patient
Reporting patient activity

PATIENT CARE AND CLIENT SUPPORT
Maintaining nutrient data base
Analyzing nutrient intake
Comparing intakes to standards
On-line profiling patient nutrition
Entering diet orders
On-line reporting admissions, discharges, and transfers
On-line reporting meal and nourishment roster
On-line reporting diet-order histories
On-line inquiries into patient data base
On-line inquiries into operating-room schedule
Printing nourishment labels
Filing nutrition-education information
Tracking and notifying consultants
Scheduling outpatients
Reporting diet-order census
Computing basal energy expenditure
Computing required caloric intake
Assessing nutritional status
Scheduling weight loss and gain
Reporting nutritional high-risk census
Printing clinical dietitian's worksheet
Capturing charges for dietetics services

COMMUNICATIONS
Communicating diet orders from nursing station
Sending messages and data in and between departments
Maintaining order link to distributor
Maintaining data links to vendors, corporate headquarters, other organizations, and personal computers within the organization
Sending mail electronically

CUSTOMER SUPPORT
Providing demonstration disk
Providing initial data bases

Exhibit 13-2 continued

Customizing data bases
Training and tutoring (computer-assisted)
Providing management-tailored help
  screens
Providing a "help hotline"
24-hour servicing and supporting
Remote diagnosing via telephone lines
Providing directory of software that
  works with the system
Offering regional and national users-
  group meetings
Providing user newsletter or magazine

MISCELLANEOUS FEATURES
Entering touch-screen orders
Controlling security access

Security reporting
Exporting purchase-order data into data
  base
Routing and scheduling vehicles
Providing facility information
Managing vending operations
Formatting checks
Printing mailing lists
Loading data to spreadsheets
Downloading data to other software
  systems
On-demand reporting
Writing special reports
Word processing and spreadsheet
  functioning
Customizing programs

Source: L. Hoover, *Computer Technology Applications to Food Management and Nutrition Services.* Columbus, Ohio, Ross Laboratories, 1990, pp. 14–16.

Exhibit 13-3 Questions to Ask When Considering Computer Diet Analysis

1. Can you justify the cost?
2. Do you have hardware and software specialists? Do you have time to become both?
3. Will the program you buy work on your equipment?
4. How large is the data base of foods and nutrients that you are considering? Large enough for your purposes (research? education?) Will it fit your assigned storage space?
5. Will the program allow information updates? Frequently?
6. Are the holes (information lacks) in the data base identified?
7. Where did the data base information originate? USDA?
8. What is the turnaround time between input and results?
9. Is it easy to code and input your equipment?
10. Are your hardware (computer) and software (program) user-friendly?
11. Can you add more foods or nutrients to the data base?
12. How are the results formatted?
13. Is there quality control? Have values been checked? By different users?
14. Will you be able to have a hard copy (paper) printout of the diet analysis quickly? A fleeting look at it on a screen is of little use.

Source: Reprinted from "The Nutrition Message and the Medium" by Sarah H. Short and William R. Short in *Food and Nutrition News,* Vol. 58, No. 5, p. 30, with permission of the National Live Stock and Meat Board, © 1986.

Often, dietary census data and diet changes are the first systems to be computerized. This information can be used to produce statistical reports on diets used, duration of diet, and number of diet changes by disease entity or location. Census data may also be useful in identifying new patients and earmarking patients for referral to the dietetic assistant, technician, dietitian, or dietetic specialist. Taken a step further, census data can be used to identify patients admitted over a specific number of days or on a diet for a specific time span. If the census sheets can be sorted by different columns, then patients can be listed by diagnosis, thereby identifying patients for a specialist's assessment or for education or instruction. Ford (1987) found that the number of patients receiving nothing by mouth dropped by 23.6 percent in her institution and the number of tubefeedings increased by 28.6 percent through close monitoring of patient care.

Suggested data that can be collected are the method of patient referral, diet order recommendations by the dietitian, level of nutritional risk, and services provided by the dietitian or dietetic technician according to length of stay or diagnosis.

Technology can go a step further. Closed circuit television can be used as a method of basic diet education to save dietetic practitioner time.

Computer automation may revolutionize dietetic care. However, the price of complex computer systems is high; therefore, the institution must be committed to system development and maintenance. Automation will alter the skills needed to be an effective manager.

Finally, technology has altered the food supply. Determining value of new food substances in patient care will require participation of the clinical dietetic manager in product review.

REFERENCES

Ford, Margaret. 1987. The computer as an aid in clinical management. *J. Am. Dietet. Assoc.* 87(4):497–500.

Quinn, Eileen. 1988. Enteral product evaluation form: A tool for formulary decision-making. *Nutr. Supp. Serv.* 8(9):10–11.

Raatz, Susan, and Christine M. Jolowsky. 1987. Multivitamin/mineral formulary development. *J. Am. Dietet. Assoc.* 87(6):777–78.

Schaffarzick, Ralph W. 1985. Technology assessment and health benefits determination. *Qual. Rev. Bull.* 11(7):222–25.

Shortliffe, Edward. 1987. Computer programs to support clinical decision making. *JAMA* 258(1):61–66.

SUGGESTED READINGS

Backas, Nancy, Beth Gotschall, and Rob Townsend. 1989. The shape of things to come. *Restaurants Institutions* (April 17):49–52, 60, 66, 70, 74, 78.

Bunton, Peggy W. 1986. Using the computer as a referral source to find the patient at nutritional risk. *J. Am. Dietet. Assoc.* 86(9):1232-333.

DiPrete, Henry. 1986. Health care in an era of change. *Health Care Strat. Man.* (December):29-32.

Ford, Denise B., S. L. Bergerson, and P. Henderson. 1989. Establishing an enteral product formulary. *J. Am. Dietet. Assoc.* 89(5):681-83.

Frank, Gail C. 1986. Guidelines for selecting a dietary analysis system. *J. Am. Dietet. Assoc.* 86(1):72-75.

Gussler, Judith, ed. 1990. *Computers in food and nutrition services: Promises and prospects.* Columbus, Ohio: Ross Laboratories.

Hayes, Robert H., and Ramchandram Jaikumar. 1988. Manufacturing's crisis: New technologies, obsolete organizations. *Harvard Bus. Rev.* (September-October):77-85.

Karkeck, Joan. 1985. Computer applications in clinical nutrition. *J. Can. Dietet. Assoc.* 46(2):41-43.

Rohde, Cynthia L., and Terri M. Braun. 1986. *Home enteral/parenteral nutrition therapy: A practitioner's guide.* Chicago: American Dietetic Association.

Short, Sarah H., and William R. Short. 1986. The nutrition message and the medium. *Food Nutr. News* 58(5):29-32.

Stephens, Gregory, and Alger Waller. 1989. How to decide on which computer and when. *Provider* 15(7):18-20.

Stokes, Judy, ed. 1986. Beyond formula: Tube feeding equipment. *Clin. Man.* 2(11):1-4.

Stokes, Judy, ed. 1987. Computer guide for the techno-peasant. *Clin. Man.* 3(6):1-4.

Vailas, Laura, et al. 1987. A computerized quantitative food frequency analysis for the clinical setting: Use in documentation and counseling. *J. Am. Dietet. Assoc.* 87(11):1539-43.

Chapter 14

Managing Patient Nutrition Education

Patient counseling and nutrition education demand a portion of the dietitian's time in the clinical setting. Nutrition education uses basic educational techniques and methods to translate the complex concepts of nutrition into terms understandable to patients. The clinical dietetic manager is responsible for orchestrating the extent of educational services and the development and use of appropriate materials. Educational goals are formulated and coordinated to meet the needs of patients and the requirements of the institution. The degree to which nutrition education is implemented depends on the institution's organizational structure, its philosophy, and available resources. Programs for patients and their families should focus on educational goals and have a well-organized schedule of learning activities. Patients should have opportunities to begin counseling as inpatients and to receive adequate follow-up information and education as outpatients.

Before planning nutrition education one should ask these six questions:

1. What education is necessary?
2. For whom will it be offered?
3. Where will it be given?
4. Who will conduct the education?
5. How will it be implemented?
6. What type of evaluation will be done?

The most effective nutrition education is consistent with client needs and stated goals, is well planned, targets specific audiences, and has an evaluation component.

As counselors, nutrition professionals offer dietary guidance in the hopes of influencing patients' food behaviors. Nutrition counseling is a long-term process done after hospital discharge in a private practice or ambulatory care setting.

DEVELOPMENT OF A PATIENT EDUCATION PROGRAM

The clinical dietetic manager is responsible for managing patient nutrition counseling and education in the institution. Planning and coordination of patient education should be guided by departmental goals and objectives. The institution may also have a patient education committee that has promulgated specific guidelines for initiating any new programs. Departments often represented on this committee are biomedical communications, dietetic services, hospital administration, medicine, nursing, occupational therapy, patient representatives, outpatient services, pediatrics, pharmacy, psychiatry, public affairs, and social work. The members of the committee assist various departments in accomplishing their educational objectives and "helping the patient feel more positive about hospitalization and/or treatment, and less worried about leaving the hospital" (Patient Education Committee 1986). Cost-containment measures have encouraged greater attention to preventive care and marketing all patient services. The emphasis on patient education and the continuity of care is a priority for progressive institutions in the 1990s.

A major responsibility of the clinical manager is to review and approve appropriate educational programs and materials. Assistance may be available from the institution's communications/media department, the patient services administration, or the patient education committee.

Assessing Needs

The decision-making process in developing a patient education program involves several steps. The first step is identifying what is wanted and what is needed (Cox, 1989). The needs assessment can be done through interviews, surveys, or focus groups with patients and staff, or with community outreach. Reaching out to the community identifies potential clients and community groups interested in nutrition education and publicizes the services and resources of the institution.

The quickest way to conduct a needs assessment is to interview dietetic staff members, potential users, and other health care providers. The interview format encourages the generation of new ideas and provides immediate feedback. Scheduling and conducting the interviews can be time-consuming, so the interviewees should be carefully selected to represent all viewpoints. Taping interviews is helpful so that one can focus one's undivided attention on the interview.

Surveys or questionnaires can reach a wider audience than interviews, but take a longer time to develop and administer. They have the advantage of providing a large number of respondents and therefore a larger data base that help the clinical manager to justify the development of needed materials. However, a survey has to be pilot tested for clarity and comprehension, and its administration may require several weeks until an adequate response is received.

A focus group is a structured session with six to ten patients or staff members who have an interest in what type of education or materials are needed. During a 1- to 2-hour session, focus group members respond to a set of structured questions. Responses are summarized and analyzed for pertinent data.

During interviews and focus groups more information is obtained when questions are given to the participants before the sessions. Interviewers and group leaders should be sensitive to the participants' concerns and should pursue apparent gaps in nutrition knowledge. The use of open-ended questions may allow new ideas to emerge.

Once educational needs are determined, priorities are set in terms of staff and material resources, time, and budget. McCabe and her colleagues (1989) have developed a method for planning and preparing effective printed materials, including an analysis of needs, instructional and materials development, and evaluation.

Setting Priorities and Budgeting

When setting priorities for the educational materials budget, one should focus on these issues:

- What materials are essential for quality patient education?
- What is outdated and needs revision?
- What content adapts well to different styles and formats?
- What would enhance nutrition education in selected areas?
- What would be wonderful to have on an unlimited budget?

Usually priority setting is done on an annual basis to coincide with the fiscal year. However, the resourceful clinical manager should plan for a longer period—3 to 5 years. Budget decisions are made on the basis of projected usage and production costs. Sophisticated visuals, audio- and videotapes, and compact discs are more costly than most printed materials but may reach a wider audience and enable sales to other institutions, agencies, or individuals in private practice.

Even though sales may be a factor in gaining financial support for the budget, developing materials for too wide an audience may limit their usefulness. The patients and other audiences served by the dietetic services should be targeted first and remain the priority. Selling printed materials and media may happen, but only after several revisions and input from content experts and users.

Selecting Patient Education Materials

Patient education materials may be prepared by the department or purchased from outside vendors. In fact, outside referral agencies may recommend appropriate materials or educational programs that fit within local or state health initiatives. A review of such materials is particularly helpful when the departmental budget is limited. Private organizations and government agencies produce materials for wide-ranging audiences, which can be used selectively. However, some of these materials may be too closely identified with a particular product or agency. Nondietetic staff members sometimes question the value of materials from outside food companies or private organizations that advertise specific commercial products. Testing commercial publications with a sample of the intended audience is a helpful tool for decision making and may help determine the degree of institutional support for those materials.

Some advantages may accrue to purchasing nutrition education programs that have been designed, pretested, and used in other parts of the country. Doing so saves the costs of development. Implementation is easier because of the experiences shared by other individuals and centers. For example, prepackaged weight loss programs have already established goals and objectives of the education program and developed the supporting materials.

Selection of the appropriate prepackaged nutrition education program depends on whether the center is for-profit or not-for-profit. For-profit centers must consider the real costs of operation based on dietitians' salaries and compensation, materials, space, equipment, a marketing allowance and secretarial assistance. Selection is based on the size of the market, requirements for equipment, space and overhead, and immediate and long-term planning and budgetary considerations. One must also consider the practical aspects of packaging, implementing, storing, and updating the program and the situations in which the program will be used, presented, and expanded.

Examination of the strengths and limitations of patient literature can be done by the clinical manager or interested clinical staff or dietetic students. Use the checklist in Exhibit 14-1 to evaluate patient literature and to decide whether to prepare institution-specific materials or to purchase them from outside vendors.

Exhibit 14-1 Checklist for Nutrition Education Programs/Materials

Title _____
Primary Audience: _____ Other Uses: _____
Date Initiated: _____ Date Completed: _____
Use: Assessment _____ or Evaluation _____

	Plans and Accomplishments	
Needs assessment		
Overall goal		
Determination of learning objectives		
Measurement of learning Objectives		
Process for medium selection		
Content review: accuracy, flow of material, readability		
Pretesting with _____		
Implementation plan		
Impact on the institution		
Evaluation of effectiveness		

Types of Media

Selection of the most effective medium for presenting information and achieving the desired educational outcome is determined by the following factors:

- size of the audience
- the budget, both immediate and long term
- equipment requirements and maintenance
- practical aspects of packaging, implementation, and storage
- ability to update the context in which the material will be used

Audiocassettes and videotapes/discs are growing in popularity, but they are costly to produce. The institution's communications department or other media experts should be consulted before embarking on a multimedia venture. Automatic slide presentations and filmstrips have been used most successfully in clinics to augment discussion groups and food demonstrations. Videotapes of food demonstrations can be used for inpatient cable television viewing. Displays at health and nutrition fairs may employ interactive computer programs to attract and teach the public about nutrition and se-lected nutrients.

Despite advances in technology, the printed word is still used in many instances as the sole educational medium or as an adjunct to visuals and media productions. Printed materials are effective in reinforcing face-to-face discussions and counseling sessions. They are easier to prepare, modify, update, package, and distribute than multimedia materials.

Setting Timelines

Once decisions have been made about the focus, medium, and content of the nutrition education programs, realistic timelines are needed to ensure that the products or outcomes are finished when needed. Evaluation also is im-portant to determine how the goals and objectives have been met. Monitoring of the steps taken and timing helps facilitate prompt completion. The clinical manager or nutrition education committee should adhere to the timeline, although some delays or unexpected interruptions may occur. However, rushing to meet a production deadline may diminish the effectiveness of the finished product. If delays occur, they should be analyzed so as to prevent them in future projects and to assess their impact on the quality of the finished product.

Securing Approvals and Evaluation

Institutional approvals of patient education materials are necessary, gener-ally from a patient education committee, department director, and hospital administrator, and, in some instances, the medical director, the inter-disciplinary nutrition committee, or the board of trustees. Appropriate word-ing, logos, and visual impact can be reviewed and changed during the ap-proval process. Implementation and evaluation can proceed after all approvals are obtained.

Evaluation is the process that examines whether or not the educational objectives of the material or the program have been met. It determines the impact of the medium, what has been successful, and what needs revision or clarification to improve its usefulness. Whatever method is used to evaluate learning—whether checklists, self-administered tests, problem-solving tasks, observations of behavioral change, or interviews—documentation is vital for planning future projects. An evaluation checklist for the clinical manager is shown in Exhibit 14-2 and can be used for preplanning and as a final evalua-tion tool.

Exhibit 14-2 Questions for Developing Nutrition Education Materials

AUDIENCE

1. What is the primary purpose of the educational material?
2. Who is/are the targeted audience(s)?
3. Will it be available for both inpatients and outpatients?
4. Will other health professionals be able to instruct patients with the material?
5. What is the appropriate reading level?

USAGE

6. How will it be used by patients and others?
7. Will it supplement other materials or be incorporated into nutrition classes?
8. Will it be used as a comprehensive information piece or require verbal instructions?
9. Will it provide reference or referral information for the users?
10. What type of artwork will be needed? Drawings? Tables? Graphs? Pictures?
11. Will it be typeset? What size print will be used, including headings, italics, and underlining?
12. What color or colors will be used for the background and the print?
13. Will there be any highlighted areas with arrows, bullets, boxed displays, boldface, or shading?
14. Will this publication be part of a series with similar design, color, ink, or placement?
15. Is there a logo or institutional insignia available or required on the publication?
16. Will the department's name be displayed?
17. Whose name(s) will appear for identifying a contact, dating of the publication, and credits or initials?

PREPARATION

18. Is there someone who can assist with technical production?
19. Should someone check it for technical accuracy and ease of understanding the information?
20. Will the material be folded, stapled, glued, bound, or perforated?
21. Will one side be used for mailing or adding written instructions?
22. Can information be put on the word processor and the diskette given to the printer?
23. Will printing be done on-site or outside?
24. What weight of paper will be best for its intended use?
25. Will the paper be textured, coated, or uncoated?
26. Who will proofread the draft?
27. Will a committee or sample of users test out a draft?
28. Will galleys be prepared and who will proofread them?

IMPLEMENTATION

29. How will usage be monitored?
30. How many copies are necessary for a first printing?
31. How soon before the material will be outdated?
32. Are there institutional restrictions on monitoring or revising printed materials?

A system needs to be established to monitor and evaluate patient education materials in the department. Exhibit 14-3 suggests how to evaluate purchasing/printing needs, distribution systems, and the usefulness of the product to the patient or client.

PREPARING PRINTED MATERIALS

The appearance of handout materials may either promote or diminish the image of the dietetic services department. Materials should be legible and attract the reader. Budgetary constraints may preclude a four-color glossy brochure, but faded photocopies will not encourage compliance from patients. Diet counseling materials should be eye-catching and easy to use—the content should be learner-focused and proceed in a logical sequence—an important marketing tool for dietetic services. Handouts may be in any of these forms:

- leaflet—one sheet of printed matter folded once or more
- pamphlet—small, unbound publication up to 15 pages

Exhibit 14-3 Model of Evaluation Procedures for Patient Education Materials

	Input	*Process*	*Outcome*
Monitor	How many materials are in stock?	How many materials were distributed to patients this month/year?	Do materials meet individual needs of patients?
	What materials are free and for which are there charges?	What is the distribution profile of the materials?	How much income is derived from sale of materials?
	What unavailable materials have been requested?	How are materials adapted to meet individual patient needs?	How much income is lost from unavailable materials?
Compare	Do materials meet established criteria?	Which patients received materials with instruction?	Is the patient education budget in line?
	How does usage compare with last month/year?	Do patients take materials home?	Do patients call asking for further assistance? (if a desired outcome)

- booklet—unbound or softbound publication over 15 pages
- manual—similar to booklet or a small book that is a quick reference or guide on one topic
- book—soft or hardbound publication protected by copyright

As with any publication, levels of reading and comprehension should be directed to the educational background and ages of the group. Selected formulas, such as the Fog Index, Fry Readability Graph, SMOG Readability Formula, and Raygor Readability Estimate, as well as software programs are available for assessing readability levels (Alldredge 1959; Fry 1968; Hess 1986; Raygor 1977). Caution should be exercised, however, in relying too heavily on readability formulas as the sole criterion for designing printed materials (McCabe 1989). Low literacy materials should only include essential information, positive rather than negative statements, and short and familiar words and sentences.

To encourage use of the materials, follow these suggestions:

- Descriptions of nutritional concepts and medical terms are explained carefully.
- Length of the material is brief, although it can be longer for healthy individuals than for patients who are ill.
- Selected, up-to-date references can direct the reader to other sources of information.
- Language is simplified and major points reiterated in concluding statements or call-outs (phrases taken from the text, typed in larger print, and boxed or lined).
- Numbers and data are listed or displayed accurately and reinforced in the text discussion.
- Writing can incorporate the second person, you, and contractions for a conversational, informal style.
- Figures of speech, examples, and questions are employed for personalizing the text.
- Controversial information or research is in a separate section or paragraph for easy revision.
- Pretesting with a small group of users will improve the presentation, especially its clarity, relevancy, and attainment of the educational objectives (Smith and Alford 1988).

Permissions for using illustrations, models, data, or substantial quotations (a page or longer) should be received from the owner of the copyright.

Copyright ownership is cited in the beginning of a book or journal. Sometimes the publisher will also require approval of the author. A letter requesting permission should include the following:

- exact title, author, and edition of the material to be cited
- intent for using the information or data
- exact paragraphs or pages in the publication
- any adaptation(s) of the model(s) for review and approval
- anticipated circulation and distribution
- number of copies to be printed and planned reprinting

The usefulness of newsletters as an informal, short source of current information is not to be underestimated. Typeset copy and desktop publishing offer a polished appearance and make possible a very creative layout, which can be a powerful means of communication on its own. Using a variety of typestyles adds interest and more copy to a page. However, typesetting does require professional operators and sophisticated equipment, two factors that increase costs. Desktop publishing may be available in the hospital's communications department. Overdesigning is sometimes a problem so pretesting copy with a sample of readers is a good idea. Evaluation is the last component to assess whether the message reaches the readership. The appearance of the final product relies on careful planning and creativity.

Writing for publication can be a frightening experience. Many authors begin by writing for newletters or doing poster sessions with peers at local, state, or national meetings. Poster sessions can give an indication of colleagues' interest in your ideas. A sample format for poster sessions is depicted in Exhibit 14-4. Sometimes in poster sessions suggestions are made to publish the data or expand the topic to reach a wider audience.

Journals provide opportunities to write short focused articles, commentary, or research reports. Some journals are peer reviewed and, although the review process may be sometimes discouraging to first-time authors, it may provide valuable criticism that enriches the manuscript. Practice-oriented articles enable dietitians to share ideas, findings, and new information and advance the profession of dietetics.

DEVELOPING VISUALS

Pictures, posters, graphs, slides, and transparencies are used in oral presentations to reinforce ideas, keep the audience interested, and clarify major points. Visuals also can identify specific steps in a process.

Exhibit 14-4 Guidelines for Poster Sessions

All illustrations—figures, charts, tables, graphs, photos, etc.—needed for your presentation must be readable from a distance of 3 feet or more. Regular typewriter type is not appropriate in size. Illustrations may be in color, and should be a minimum of 9" x 12". Keep all illustrations simple.

   a. Typed material should be prepared on BULLETIN typewriters, larger than orator type. It may also be typed double-spaced with large type (orator) on a regular typewriter in black carbon ribbon and photographically enlarged from an 8½" x 11" paper to 14" x 17" or larger.

> Orator on 8½" x 11" enlarged to 14" x 17".

   b. Hand lettering should be at least ½" high and in bold characters.
   c. Photographs should be a minimum of 8" x 10".
Be sure that your presentation material can be mounted with thumb tacks or stickpins. Do not mount illustrations on thick cardboard because these may be difficult to tack into position on the posterboard.
Any background covering as noted above.

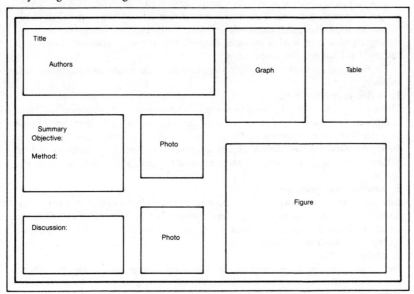

If you have any questions, please contact Bernice Meager, Abstract Coordinator, at the Society for Nutrition Office, (415) 444-7133.

Source: Poster Guidelines Chart: Society for Nutrition Education, Annual Meeting Poster Guidelines 1990.

Visuals help emphasize major concepts—the one or two important facts that should be remembered by the audience. By highlighting the key information, visuals differentiate it from nonessential facts. A general guideline is that about four to six concepts can be assimilated by an audience in an hour.

The simplest way to get an idea across is to draw pictures in the mind. Pictographs are effective for retaining a concept, particularly for slides. For example, a graph about the increased use of a fast-food salad bar or an overlay of numbers on a booklet can show a rise of consumer interest in nutrition transposed on a picture of a healthful market basket.

Slide presentations have the advantage of being reusable for a variety of classes, particularly when food pictures or slides of important words are available. Other practical guidelines for slides are shown in Exhibit 14-5.

Exhibit 14-5 Slide Shows Made Easy

How many times have you become bored and lost interest in a meeting that seemed to drag on and on? And, how many times have you had to present a program filled with information, charts, and graphs too complicated to describe in words alone?

Slides are an excellent technique for stimulating your audience's attention and helping you get your message across. A good slide presentation can add "zip," as well as clarity to your message. And, slides also help you keep "on the track" during your delivery. Putting together a good slide show is easy—if you are well-organized, know your audience, and follow a few simple rules.

The following are some hints to help you plan and produce your own successful slide shows:

1. Define your objectives.

The first step is to establish your objective(s). What do you want to accomplish? What changes do you want to take place in the attitude or behavior of the members of your audience? Do you want them to perform a task? Recall some information? Or express a feeling or attitude? A well-defined objective is specific and includes a description of the behavior you expect, as well as a statement about the quality of performance you will accept.

2. Analyze your audience.

How much does your audience know about your topic? What are their ages and educational backgrounds? Are they fifth graders? College students? Or skilled technicians in the field? The more you know about the audience, the easier it will be to plan the appropriate content of your program.

3. Make an outline.

Prepare an outline of the material you want to cover in your presentation. It is a good rule to keep your outline simple and limit it to a concise summary of those major points and supporting facts that will help your audience attain your objective(s). In organizing this outline, you will want to plan the logical "flow," as well as the content of your major points.

4. Review your progress.

It is much easier and more economical to review what you have done so far and make changes during early stages, rather than later during production.

Exhibit 14-5 continued

5. Identify an overall treatment plan.

Make a decision about the prevailing mood and overall treatment of the content. Do you want a humorous treatment using cartoons and a light, comic narration? Or maybe a more serious, informative treatment is appropriate? The way you treat your content will greatly influence the effectiveness of your presentation.

6. Write a script.

This step is optional. Some people prefer to deliver their presentation directly from their outline. Others like to prepare a full script that includes everything they want to say. If you decide to write a script, you can follow your outline as you do your writing. Remember to keep your script simple, well-organized, and not too long. Your audience's attention span is limited. Therefore, your goal is to keep their attention without boring them with unnecessary facts and details.

7. Plan your slides.

Now you are ready to develop your visual ideas. Your outline and script will be your guide for deciding how many and what kind of slides you will need. As you plan your slides, keep in mind the following rules-of-thumb:

- **Use the horizontal format.** The standard 2:3 ratio in the horizontal format will always result in a larger effective viewing area for your slides. Vertical slides do not work well in filmstrips, videotape, and certain screen situations.

ARTWORK FORMAT GUIDE

Exhibit 14-5 continued

- **Prepare artwork using a 6 x 9 inch "critical working area."** This maintains the 2:3 ratio for slides, and makes it easy to photograph the art. The 6 x 9 inch "critical working area" is the portion of the frame that will be projected. Extend your art to a 10 x 12 inch "safe edge." The 10 x 12 inch "safe edge" is used when the artwork is photographed.

- **Keep all copy and symbols simple and legible.** Eliminate small type, thin lines, and poor color contrasts. Adequate spaces should be left between words. Light-colored type should be used against dark-colored backgrounds. White and light-colored backgrounds show dust and dirt, as well as creating a harsh distracting glare.

- **Make all copy (word) slides short and concise.** A slide should never be cluttered with too much copy. If a slide is to contain only copy, try not to use more than 15 words. (An effective highway billboard uses only 5 words!)

- **Keep your slides simple and bold.** Limit each slide to one main idea. Use two or more simple slides, rather than one complicated slide. There is nothing that "turns off" an audience faster than visuals that are complex and confusing.

- **Use charts and graphs rather than tables to display your facts and figures.** Visual comparisons can be made more quickly and easily with a graph. Tables tend to look complicated and confusing.

- **Use a 3 x 4½ inch template for typewritten copy slides.** The template will help you keep your copy within the "critical working area" for copy produced on a typewriter. The typewriter is a convenient tool for producing quick, inexpensive copy slides.

- **Keep your photographs uncluttered and plan your scenes carefully.** Many times, a close-up showing details is more effective than an overall view. Effective lighting is also important. Your audience needs enough time to see and read the slide at a comfortable rate.

- **Never leave a slide on the screen for too short or too long a length of time.** The pacing of your slides is important. Your audience needs enough time to see and read the slide at a comfortable rate. Remember you are using slides to supplement and support your oral presentation.

8. Make sure all slides are legible.
Throughout production, you will want to check all slides for legibility. This means all elements of a slide are sufficiently large and sharp enough to be seen and read by everyone in your audience, including the people in the last row. Just because a graph or chart is legible in a book or magazine doesn't mean it will be legible in a slide.

Legibility is also affected by the lighting conditions in the presentation room, the projected image size, the viewer's distance from the projected image, and the amount of time the image will appear on the screen.

9. Edit your slide presentation.
When the production of your slides is completed, it is time for you to put your presentation together and edit your work. Your outline will be helpful during this process. You will want to check your slides and script for sequencing and to see how adequately you have covered each point. When editing, ask yourself the following questions:

- Have you covered all of the major points in your outline?

Exhibit 14-5 continued

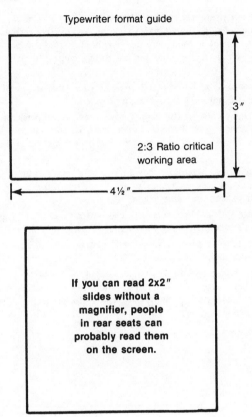

Typewriter format guide

- Does the content of each slide fit the content of the narration?
- Are your slides legible?
- Are the colors in your slides bold and effective?
- Does each slide depict one clear idea?
- Is there good continuity from one slide to the next?
- Do all of the slides together add up to form a visually coherent and pleasing presentation?

10. Prepare for a smooth presentation.
After the final touches have been completed on your script and slides, you are ready to prepare for your presentation. The following are some suggestions to help your presentation go smoothly:

- **Never carry your slides in your baggage when you are traveling.** If you lose your bags, you will have nothing to show at your presentation.

Exhibit 14-5 continued

- **Rehearse your presentation many times.** You can never rehearse too much. You should be completely familiar with your script and the sequence and timing of your slides. Make a mark at each place on your script where you want to advance to the next slide. Avoid reading your script—reading can be boring for you and your audience.
- **Visit the room in which you will present your slide show.** Make sure it is an appropriate size and adequate lighting is provided.
- **Make arrangements for the proper equipment to be available.** Request a projector with remote control so you can control your slide changes from the lectern. Always have a spare bulb on hand. Obtain a pointer and tape recorder if you need them.
- **Check your slides.** Make sure they are numbered and properly placed in the tray. To avoid spills, do not remove the ring from the top of the tray. Always store your tray in a box to keep your slides clean.
- **Project your slides.** Make sure they can be seen and read by everyone in your audience under the conditions provided in the presentation room.
- **On the day of your presentation—arrive early.** Allow yourself enough time to make sure your equipment is working properly.

The preceding points won't make you an expert on the first try, but they will help you put together a successful slide presentation. Just remember—organization, simplicity, clarity, and legibility are the key elements for producing a good script and an effective slide show.

Source: Courtesy of Visual Horizons, Rochester, NY.

REFERENCES

Alldredge,Everett O. 1959. Improving your writing ability. *J. Am. Dietet. Assoc.* 35:1037–40.

Cox, Barbara G. 1989. The art of writing patient education materials. *Am. Med. Writers Assoc. J.* 1:11–14.

Fry, Edward. 1968. A readability formula that saves time. *J. Reading* 11:513–16, 575–78.

Hess, Mary Abbott. 1986. Writing for the general public. In *Communicating as professionals,* edited by Ronni Chernoff. Chicago: The American Dietetic Association.

McCabe, Beverly J., et al. 1989. A strategy for designing effective patient education materials. *J. Am. Dietet. Assoc.* 89(9):1290–95.

Patient Education Committee, Memorial Sloan Kettering Cancer Center. 1986. *Patient education booklet.* New York: Sloan Kettering.

Raygor, Alton. 1977. The Raygor readability estimate: A quick way to determine difficulty. In *Reading: Theory, research and practice,* edited by P. Pearson. Clemson, S.C.: National Reading Conference.

Smith, Suzanne B., and Betty J. Alford. 1988. Literate and semi-literate audiences: Tips for effective teaching. *J. Natr. Ed.* 20:238B–8C.

SUGGESTED READINGS

Allensworth, Diane DeMuth, and Cynthia R. Luther. 1986. Evaluating printed materials. *Nurse Educator* 11(2):18–22.

Boles, Kaye. 1968. Writing a policies and procedures manual for the dietary department. *Hospitals, JAHA* (November 1):86–90.

Foltz, Mary Beth, ed. 1987. *Workbook in communications: How to tell the WIC success story.* Columbus, Ohio: Ross Laboratories.

Hestwood, Thomas M. 1988. Making policy manuals useful and relevant. *Personnel J.* 67:43–46.

Improving employee-management communication in hospitals: A special study in management practices and problems. 1965. New York: United Hospital Fund of New York.

McConnell, Charles R. 1982. *The effective healthcare supervisor.* Gaithersburg, Md.: Aspen Publishers, Inc.

Roswell, Charles G. 1959. Making your reports more meaningful. *J. Am. Dietet. Assoc.* 35:351–53.

Skipper, Annalynn. 1981. Effective communication: A powerful tool for dietitians. *Dietet. Curr.* 13(4):17–20.

Smith, Judson. 1981. Writing for the eye and ear. *Training/HRD* (March):65–70.

Steinbaugh, Maria. 1986. Writing technical reports. In *Communicating as professionals,* edited by Ronni Chernoff. Chicago: The American Dietetic Association.

U.S. Department of Health and Human Services. 1984. *Building nutrition counseling skills. II. Workshop resource manual.* Washington, D.C.: U.S. Government Printing Office.

Chapter 15

Health Promotion and Marketing Plans

Health promotion activities began in the early 1970s and have since become a viable way to market nutrition services. A sound marketing plan can convince consumers that nutrition services are needed as part of a health promotion program. This chapter describes the use of marketing techniques to extend inpatient services to promote the health and well-being of employees and consumers. It also includes guidelines on instituting a preventive nutrition initiative in an acute care institution.

HEALTH PROMOTION AND DISEASE PREVENTION

Over the past decade the pattern of diseases has shifted from acute to chronic, with cardiovascular heart disease, cancer, and accidents accounting for 75 percent of all deaths (Adams 1985). Research studies have demonstrated the relationship between lifestyle and illness.

Prevention is broadly defined as health maintenance and health improvement of a non-crisis nature. Its primary goal is to reduce health risks and prevent disease or handicapping conditions from occurring prematurely. Education on preventive health care increases awareness and an understanding of the interrelationship between nutrition and health. Its central theme is that the individual takes responsibility for changing behavior and the health setting provides a framework for change (Donato 1988).

Preventive health programs aim to reduce significantly the negative impact of lifestyle-related diseases on individuals, curtail rising health costs, and promote healthy aging. Such programs include immunizations and visual, dental, diabetes, and hypertension screening (Green 1985).

Screening is often incorporated into preventive health programs to identify those at risk for developing chronic diseases. It applies simple and accurate tests or measurements to an asymptomatic population to identify those likely to manifest the problems in question. Screening tests are not diagnostic;

suspect results require a diagnostic evaluation to confirm a problem. Not every condition lends itself to screening. For the most effective use of screening, the optimal time to begin intervention must be during the asymptomatic period, and the screening test must identify suspected cases before the optimal treatment time. Given our current state of practice and knowledge, certain diseases will occur even with the best of primary prevention. Therefore, a major component of health prevention must be secondary prevention. Its purpose is to facilitate the early diagnosis and treatment of risk factors and symptoms and to improve the ultimate outcome.

Health promotion is any combination of health, education, and related organizational, environmental, and economic interventions that will promote wellness according to a fixed plan, as in the *1990s Objectives for the Nation.* It begins with people who are basically healthy and fosters the development of lifestyles to maintain and enhance health at all stages of the life-span. Examples of healthy behaviors are smoking cessation, reducing the misuse of drugs and alcohol, exercise and fitness, improved nutrition and stress management. Wellness, a popularly used term in connection with health promotion, refers to a redefinition of health not as the mere absence of disease but as the existence of a positive state of emotional, physical, and mental well-being of the whole person (Douglas 1986).

Health promotion initiatives began in earnest with the publication of *Healthy People* (U.S. Health and Human Services 1979). Five broad health goals and 15 priority areas were introduced for various stages of the lifespan. From this framework, the Public Health Service established working groups that identified 227 health objectives, 17 focusing on nutrition, which were embodied in *Health Objectives for the Nation* (Sorenson et al. 1987). Progress toward accomplishing these objectives is being assessed by the Office of Health Promotion and Disease Prevention, and new objectives have been devised for the year 2000. The objectives for *Healthy People 2000* (U.S. Department of Health and Human Services 1990) are more realistic and quantifiable and do not differ significantly from the previous ones.

The potential to reduce health care costs by the adoption of healthier lifestyles has attracted the interest of government and industry in health promotion activities (Califano 1987). Recent reports from the Surgeon General's Office and the National Research Council (U.S. Department of Health and Human Services 1988; National Research Council 1989) underscore the message of the *Health Objectives for the Nation.* The stage is set for consumers, food companies, government officials, and health care administrators to become more responsive to nutrition education and health promotion. Achieving the nutrition objectives has been slower than some of the other health objectives because of insufficient baseline data to track progress and the multifaceted nature of some nutrition conditions.

The definition of health promotion has expanded to include an emphasis on the value of supportive environments to influence permanent changes. Health protection encompasses environmental measures taken by governmental agencies, industries, and communities to safeguard people from harm. Originally, health promotion was defined as "the science and art of helping individuals change their lifestyle to move toward a state of optimal health" (O'Donnell 1989, 5). The expanded definition is as follows:

> Optimal health is defined as a balance of physical, emotional, social, spiritual and intellectual health. Lifestyle change can be facilitated through a combination of efforts to enhance awareness, change behavior, and create environments that support good health practices. (O'Donnell 1989, 5).

ROLE OF THE DIETITIAN IN HEALTH PROMOTION

Dietetics is the profession that should supply responsible leadership in providing preventive nutrition care services to individuals and groups. A systematic, assertive approach should be taken to implement an institution-wide pervasive philosophy of preventive nutrition care that involves all employees, technical, and professional staff. The focus of dietitians in preventive health care is to increase the awareness of the interrelationship between nutrition and healthy behaviors and to motivate clients to adopt healthy behaviors.

Both the clinical dietetic manager and the teaching dietitians have unique roles in preventive health care. The clinical manager should be responsible for administration and communication. Administration involves the facilitation of resources to meet organizational and programmatic goals through planning, organizing, actuating, evaluating and controlling the program. The communication function involves sharing knowledge and information with the community and, internally, with administrators, public relations, and other health care providers. Teaching dietitians can do group sessions and refer clients for individualized nutritional care and counseling. In addition, they can motivate clients to adopt or maintain positive behaviors, prepare and promote education materials for the public, and conduct staff development and inservice training.

DIETETIC MARKETING

Marketing in dietetics involves promoting and developing products or professional services and then convincing clients of their need for that service. For the clinical dietetic manager, marketing is a consumer- or patient-based approach to management that fits into the objectives of the institution and the department. Accurate analysis of consumer needs and wants and the environmental climate facilitates the planning, implementation, and control of a carefully designed program (Eisenberg 1986; Kotler 1982). The four Ps of achieving a successful marketing program are

1. product (nutrition services)
2. price (actual or potential professional fees or program cost)
3. place (the site)
4. promotion (advertising, publicity, and public relations methods)(Ward 1984)

Marketing clinical dietetic services has two primary targets: (1) patients and (2) health care system coordinators, administrators, and health planners. With the changes in health care delivery and reimbursement systems, the clinical nutrition manager has to work hard to market services that generate revenue and provide visibility for the institution or department (Egan and Kaufman 1985). He or she must set goals based on a needs assessment, target a market segment, define the plans, and provide the resources to accomplish the goals. Marketing efforts can reposition the department as not only focusing on illness and treatment but also on health and prevention.

Marketing Plans

Because registered dietitians provide services rather than a tangible product, marketing should be consumer-oriented, not producer-oriented (Parks and Moody 1986). Each new program should have a targeted group or groups and a marketing plan before it is delivered to clients. The plan should be designed to achieve these marketing goals:

- develop a profile of the potential participants based on community health care needs and available outpatient records or employee surveys
- evaluate interest in an institution-based health promotion program
- examine competition for the program
- establish an ongoing evaluation process for the program to facilitate changes and increase participant satisfaction
- make the intangible product desirable to the consumers

The written document outlining the marketing plan has four sections:

1. a mission statement stating the overall purpose of the plan
2. a ranking of target segments and rationale

3. an analysis of recommendations for the marketing plan
4. a detailed zero-based budget

Exhibit 15-1 shows how to market and develop a hospital-based health promotion program that serves the needs of employees and the community. Its premise is that staff involvement will generate a sense of enthusiasm and employee commitment that will interest patients and potential clients in the program. A good guide to use for the program content is *Worksite Nutrition: A Decision-Maker's Guide,* jointly prepared by the American Dietetic Association and the Society for Nutrition Education (1986).

Selling the Department

The three types of communication most frequently used to promote services are personal communication, public relations, and advertising. Word of mouth is also a very effective means of communication (MacStravic 1985). Public relations expertise is often available in hospitals that compete for patients. The purpose of public relations is to promote a favorable image to consumers. A hospital starting a new health promotion program can receive publicity through interviews with dietitians, administrators, physicians, and patients. In addition, an advertising budget sometimes exists to communicate with potential clients via electronic and print media.

The clinical dietetic manager must make the department as visible as possible, both internally and externally. Professional publications, presentations, and poster sessions are some of the most common and least costly methods of external publicity. Internally, newsletters and patient literature offer valuable opportunities to publicize the department.

Exhibit 15-1 How to Develop and Market a Preventive Nutrition Program

---

1. Develop a philosophy of health promotion and disease prevention for nutrition.
   - Read background material, *Healthy People 2000, Health Objectives for the Nation,* and the *Surgeon General's Report on Nutrition and Health and Diet and Health.*
   - Determine personal philosophy and philosophy for reaching and treating clients.
   - Rank program priorities.
   - Achieve consensus among dietitians and other team members.
   - Consider current consumer demands for preventive care.
2. Identify needs of the population to be served.
   - Do a health needs assessment.
     - facts and statistics from medical records
     - extrapolation of national data to local situation

Exhibit 15-1 continued

- local health status indicators
- patient/client profile to include community and facility characteristics descriptors
- trends and forecasts
- social, cultural, psychological, economic, and geographical factors

3. Establish a preventive nutrition committee and work with other disciplines.
   - Establish a working group to identify the continuum of care.
   - Examine the role of nutrition in total preventive health services.
   - Consult other disciplines/departments:

medicine	public relations
nursing	patient education
exercise physiology	external affairs
pharmacy	community outreach
physical therapy	employee benefits

   - Obtain level of administrative support.

4. Designate an individual or individuals to plan, organize, and implement the nutrition program.
   - Assign sole or shared responsibility for
     - program development
     - client-managed care
     - staff liaison and resource person
   - Write job descriptions, based on these functions:
     - administrative
     - educational
     - communication
     - clinical/counseling
   - If necessary, restructure the outpatient nutrition component to maximize its effectiveness.
   - Assess all possible resources for providing a preventive nutrition program
     - adequacy of funds
     - time available
     - level of administrative support
     - facilities/space for groups and individuals within the institution
     - outside community services
     - need for staff training and orientation sessions for employees, staff
     - public relations efforts
     - employee assistance program with potential for preventive nutrition
     - drug and medical equipment companies

5. Set program goals and objectives that make nutritional care an integral part of health maintenance.
   - Develop broad goal statements based on background reading, philosophy, and profile.
   - Set measurable and feasible objectives:
     - short-term results (1 year)
     - long-term results (5 years)
   - Do priority ranking to address risk factors:
     - impact (morbidity, mortality)
     - size and nature (how many and who affected)
     - staff and funds available

Exhibit 15-1 continued

- effect of intervention on prevention or reduction of problems
- Consider alternative ways to meet objectives.
6. Coordinate nutrition goals with the other preventive health services being provided.
   - Examine the existing continuum of care and extent of nutrition referrals.
   - Assess internal and external health promotion ventures.
   - Integrate goals into total program.
   - Coordinate with outpatient services and specialized programs, i.e., cardiac or alcohol rehabilitation or geriatric medicine.
   - Examine roles and responsibilities of preventive health staff.
7. Determine policies and procedures for program implementation.
   - Develop guidelines and standards of preventive care, based on the following:
     - extent of services
     - team and client accountability
     - policies for program participation
     - methods for recording and retrieving nutrition data
   - Establish mechanism for referring clients
8. Devise a budget for proposed nutrition services.
   - Calculate the projected costs of program
   - Examine the need for revenue-generating services.
   - Calculate ancillary vs. routine charges.
   - Justify program expenses and benefits to the facility.
   - Calculate cost savings of possible reduced hospitalization.
9. Develop a screeing mechanism and ways to refer clients.
   - Institute a screening system to find clients requiring in-depth counseling by other dietetic specialists.
   - Develop referral criteria for counseling, program participation, and referral to outside programs.
   - Train staff in early identification of nutrition risk factors.
   - Contact external organizations to develop continuity of preventive nutrition care, such as worksite wellness, schools, unions, rehabilitation facilities, and private and government-supported programs.
10. Plan health risk reduction and educational content of the program
    - Develop action plan and activities.
    - Develop program design based on the following:
      - nutrition
      - smoking cessation
      - fitness
      - drug and alcohol use
      - weight reduction/control
      - stress management
      - safety and accident prevention
      - reduced exposure to environmental toxins
      - education for self-improvement
      - appropriate use of medical services
    - Designate level of client responsibility to be achieved.
    - Develop nutritional concepts, activities, behavioral objectives, and evaluation of knowledge.
11. Present the educational component of the preventive nutrition program.
    - Develop and select instructional materials and audiovisual aids.

Exhibit 15-1 continued

- Organize and group classes for clients and employees.
- Participate in training of students and allied health personnel.
- Provide expert technical assistance and preventive nutrition consultant for staff.
- Integrate recent research findings and implications for preventive care.
- Do self-awareness health screen:
  - selected lab values
  - food patterns
  - height, weight
- Develop preventive nutrition topics:
  - nutrition and dental health
  - the fat/cholesterol conundrum
  - hypertension and minerals (Na,Ca)
  - diabetes
  - U.S. dietary guidelines and consumption patterns
  - "at risk" nutrients
  - nutrition and physical activity
  - weight control
  - food and drug interactions
  - nutrition and cancer guidelines
12. Establish a documentation system to compare objectives with outcomes.
    - Select type of reports (monthly/quarterly/annually).
    - Implement quality assurance methods.
    - Develop means of communication and documentation of nutrition risk intervention.
    - Monitor to assess effectiveness and efficiency of procedures.
    - Design flow sheets to reveal: changes in risk factors, behavioral objectives, and lifestyle adaptations.
13. Market the program to potential clients and technical and professional staff.
    - Develop screening/health assessment questionnaire or inservice classes.
    - Conduct employee awareness campaign, i.e., notice in paycheck.
    - Develop advertising and promotional strategies for specific disease conditions.
    - Provide selected outreach programs for the community.
    - Act as liaison with personnel department to reach new employees regarding preventive nutrition activities.
    - Write news releases and contact public relations department.
    - Achieve wide dissemination of materials through internal information channels.
    - Coordinate with food services to promote nutrition and encourage appropriate food selections in dining areas.
    - Develop resource center for nutrition-related consumer information.
14. Conduct biennial or annual evaluation.
    - Develop plan for comprehensive evaluation of all preventive services.
    - Determine prevention nutrition program progress toward measurable objectives.
    - Compare program outcomes to government initiatives and studies.
    - Assess adequacy of surveillance system to monitor quality of care.
    - Revise goals, action plans, and timetable to achieve goals if necessary.
    - Develop productivity measures for staff to refine services.
    - Provide justification data for review.

REFERENCES

Adams, Simone O. 1985. Dietitians at the worksite: A new role. *J. Health Promotion* 2(1):2–3.

American Dietetic Association. 1986. *Worksite nutrition: A decision-maker's guide.* Chicago: American Dietetic Association.

Califano, Joseph A. 1987. America's health care revolution: Health promotion and disease prevention. *J. Am. Dietet. Assoc.* 87(4):437–40.

Donato, Donna. 1988. New opportunities to expand the role of the dietitian: Can we meet the challenge? *J. Am. Dietet. Assoc.* 88(11):1369–71.

Douglas, Priscilla D. 1986. Are dietitians ready for the wellness movement? *J. Am. Dietet. Assoc.* 86(1):92–93.

Egan, Mary C., and Mildred Kaufman. 1985. Financing nutrition services in a competitive market. *J. Am. Dietet. Assoc.* 85(2):210–14.

Eisenberg, Joni G. 1986. Marketing the professional services of the dietitian. *J. Can. Dietet. Assoc.* 47(2):92–95.

Green, Karen. 1985. Health promotion: Its terminology, concepts and modes of practice. *Health Promotion* 9(3):8–14.

Kotler, Philip. 1982. *Marketing for non-profit organizations.* 2nd ed. Englewood Cliffs, N.J.: Prentice-Hall.

MacStravic, Robin Scott. 1985. Word-of-mouth communications in health care marketing. *Health Progr.* (October):25–29.

National Research Council. 1989. *Diet and health.* Washington, D.C.: National Academy Press.

O'Donnell, Michael P. 1989. Definition of health promotion. III. Expanding the definition. *Am. J. Health Promotion* 3(3):5.

Parks, Sara C., and Debra L. Moody. 1986. Marketing: A survival tool for dietetic professionals in the 1990s. II. *J. Am. Dietet. Assoc.* 86(1):33–36.

Parks, Sara C., and Debra L. Moody. 1986. Part II. A marketing model: Applications for dietetic professionals. *J. Am. Dietet. Assoc.* 86(1):37–40.

Sorenson, Ann W., Joel Kavel, and Marilyn G. Stephenson. 1987. Health objectives for the nation: Moving toward the 1990s. *J. Am. Dietet. Assoc.* 87:920–925.

U.S. Department of Health and Human Services. 1979. *Healthy people.* Washington, D.C.: U.S. Government Printing Office.

U.S. Department of Health and Human Services, Public Health Service Division. 1990. *Healthy people 2000: National health promotion and disease prevention Objectives Summary.* Washington, D.C.: U.S. Department of Health and Human Services.

U.S. Department of Health and Human Services. 1988. *The Surgeon General's report on nutrition and health.* Washington, D.C: U.S. Government Printing Office.

Ward, Marcia. 1984. *Marketing strategies.* Johnson City, N.Y.: Niles and Phipps.

Chapter 16

Managing Continuity of Care

Until the 1980s nearly all the responsibilities of the clinical dietetic manager revolved around the provision of services to hospitalized patients. The clinical manager's role has now been expanded outside the hospital setting to include home health care, including home-delivered nutrition services.

DISCHARGE PLANNING AND REFERRAL SYSTEMS

Dietitians should be involved in planning appropriate follow-up nutritional care when hospital discharge is imminent, particularly for patients at potential nutritional risk. As a matter of policy, dietitians ought to participate in discharge planning for patients who meet any of the following criteria:

- more than 20 percent above optimal body weight
- more than 15 percent below optimal body weight
- medical conditions or surgical procedures requiring nutritional care
- eating disorders or inability to eat
- high-risk pregnancy
- high-dose or extended radiation or chemotherapy
- disabilities or handicapping conditions

Discharge plans are designed to help meet the nutritional needs of individual patients. In some cases, an innovative dietetic staff may wish to develop programs or contract with other agencies to provide services to patients at home or in the community. Techniques for writing such proposals are discussed in this chapter. In other cases, referrals are made to existing community services using such a form as in Exhibit 16-1.

Exhibit 16-1 Discharge Nutrition Summary

Directions

1. Complete for all items.
2. Complete the form for transfer of patients from Interhospital Nursing Home, Rehabilitation Units or other facility.

Admitting DX: _____
PMH*: _____
Surgery: _____

Admitting Status

1. Diet PTA**: _____
   Supplements: _____
2. Instructed on Diet: Yes   No
   Comprehension: G   F   P
3. Food Allergies: Yes   No
   Food Intolerance: Yes   No
4. Feeds: Self-independent
            with Assistance
5. Ht _____ Wt _____
   WT Loss PTA _____ MOS
6. Appetite   G   F   P
7. Dentition   G   F   P
   Ill fitting: Yes   No
   Edentulous   Yes   No

Noted Occurrences During Admission

1. Diet: _____
   Supplements: _____
2. Instructed on Diet: Yes   No
   Comprehension: G   F   P
3. Food Allergies: Yes   No
   Food Intolerance: Yes   No
4. Feeds: Self-independent
            with Assistance
5. Ht _____ Wt _____
   WT Loss PTA _____ MOS
6. Appetite   G   F   P
7. Dentition   G   F   P
   Ill fitting: Yes   No
   Edentulous   Yes   No

Discharge Status

1. Diet: _____
   Supplements: _____
2. Instructed on Diet: Yes   No
   Comprehension: G   F   P
3. Food Allergies: Yes   No
   Food Intolerance: Yes   No
4. Feeds: Self-independent
            with Assistance
5. Ht _____ Wt _____
   WT Loss PTA _____ MOS
6. Appetite   G   F   P
7. Dentition   G   F   P
   Ill fitting: Yes   No
   Edentulous   Yes   No

	Yes	No			Yes	No
8. Constipation:	Yes	No	8. Constipation:		Yes	No
9. Diarrhea:	Yes	No	9. Diarrhea:		Yes	No
10. Nausea:	Yes	No	10. Nausea:		Yes	No
11. Vomiting:	Yes	No	11. Vomiting:		Yes	No
12. Dysphagia:	Yes	No	12. Dysphagia:		Yes	No
13. Stomatitis:	Yes	No	13. Stomatitis:		Yes	No
14. Decubiti:	Yes	No	14. Decubiti:		Yes	No
15. Significant Medications: ___			15. Significant Medications: ___			

16. Disabling conditions:

	Yes	No			Yes	No
16. Disabling conditions:			16. Disabling conditions:			
Hearing Impairment:	Yes	No	Hearing Impairment:		Yes	No
Visual Impairment	Yes	No	Visual Impairment		Yes	No
Paralysis	Yes	No	Paralysis		Yes	No
Mentation ___			Mentation ___			

NURSING: *Please forward this form with RN Discharge Summary. This should then be forwarded to dietary.*

*Prior Medical History   **Prior to Admission

Exhibit 16-1 continued

Admission	Hospitalization	Discharge
Date of Lab _____	Date of Lab _____	Date of Lab _____
Gluc _____	Gluc _____	Gluc _____
BUN _____	BUN _____	BUN _____
Creat _____	Creat _____	Creat _____
K⁺ _____	K⁺ _____	K⁺ _____
ALB _____	ALB _____	ALB _____
TLC _____	TLC _____	TLC _____
Other _____	Other _____	Other _____

List Food Allergies: _____

List Food Intolerances: _____

Plan / Suggestions / Meal Pattern / Patient Accomplishments, Goals / Other:

USUAL MEAL PATTERN

Exchanges	B	L	S	D	HS
Meat					
Bread					
Milk					
Fruit					
Fat					
Vegetable					

Date _____

Dietitian _____

Phone _____

Institution _____

Source: Reprinted with permission from *Dietitians in Nutrition Support*, September 1987.

Discharge plans may include one or more of the following services:

- arrangements for supplements, enteral formulas, or total parenteral nutrition
- provision of written diet instructions or nutrition education materials
- limited diet counseling
- comprehensive diet counseling
- referral to ambulatory care services for classes or counseling
- referral to a dietitian who provides nutrition services at a nursing home, extended care facility, or residential setting
- referral to a hospice dietitian
- referral to various government programs for food assistance
- referral to local programs for home-delivered meals or shopping services

A study at Cleveland Metropolitan General Hospital showed that a significant percentage (43 percent) of patients in the outpatient clinic needed nutritional services but that most of these patients were not referred to dietetic personnel (Walters et al. 1972). The study resulted in the following recommendations for improving nutritional services for ambulatory patients:

- Expansion of referral systems to include, in addition to physician referrals, those from periodic screening of charts by the dietitian, other health professionals, team conferences, patients' requests, and other health care institutions
- Active dietitian participation in medical nutrition education to help physicians recognize patient nutritional needs and increase awareness of services provided
- Education and use of technical level personnel to assist in delivery of nutrition services
- Design and use of effective methods for documenting and communicating nutritional information
- Inclusion of nutrition in the centralized appointment system

Another study found that 15 percent of discharged patients had problems following a prescribed diet at home (Bell 1981). Most (86.5 percent) patients wished to be contacted by a dietitian, yet they did not initiate calls to the hospital, even though a telephone number had been provided.

Criteria for nutrition referrals can be distributed hospital-wide to promote referral of patients who would benefit from the professional services of the dietitian. Posters, such as the one shown in Exhibit 16-2, can be displayed,

Exhibit 16-2 Display Poster to Encourage Referrals

Frustrated with your diet?

We can help! Ask us to:

- fit your diet to your lifestyle
- calculate your nutrient needs
- suggest good substitutes for your favorite foods that are not allowed on your present diet
- suggest tasty recipes and cooking methods
- help you deal with anorexia, weight loss, or taste changes that may accompany medical treatment

Call (123) 456-7890 for an appointment or ask your physician for a referral.

Helping you cope with your diet is our specialty. Services offered include:

- Personalized diet plans
- Computerized dietary assessments
- Individual nutrition counseling
- Group supermarket classes
- Cooking classes
- Creative ideas for dealing with your dietary problems

Fees may be covered by your medical insurance.

encouraging patients to seek nutritional counseling or to ask their physician for a referral.

AMBULATORY CARE

Ambulatory care is provided in a noninstitutional setting and includes routine maintenance of functional status, treatment of chronic diseases, and health and nutrition education. Ambulatory care patients are usually referred to as "outpatients," denoting the same institutional affiliation or, more broadly, as "clients" and the dietitian as the "nutritionist."

Ambulatory care may be given in hospital clinics or through private practices or health maintenance organizations (HMOs). Hospital clinics may be organized according to the segment of population served—prenatal, pediatric, family planning, adult maintenance, or geriatric; may be discipline-specific, such as medicine, nutrition, or mental health; or may be disease-specific, such as diabetes, hypertension, obesity, or cardiovascular disease. Outpatient services in private practices have trendier titles, such as cardiofitness, sports medicine, and health promotion. The ambulatory care nutritionist may work within an interdisciplinary framework or on a specific team. Duties and responsibilities are dictated by the setting.

The clientele for ambulatory services may include patients discharged from the hospital, other clinic and outpatients, HMO participants, self-referred clients, primary care patients, or others who seek nutrition information or services.

The growing number of dietitians in private practice suggests an increased demand for nutritional services outside of institutional settings. Experience shows the need for consultation and counseling to address a wide variety of nutritional problems (Shovic et al. 1988).

Early hospital discharge enhances the need for referral services. In the past most diet counseling could be started during hospitalization. With the advent of prospective payment systems, however, there is often insufficient time to prepare a hospitalized patient to receive more than minimal instruction, let alone the skills and resources needed to follow a complex dietary regimen at home.

Outside the institutional setting, dietitians are responsible for assessing and monitoring the nutritional needs of individuals served. In-depth counseling regarding dietary requirements and/or changes is provided to individual patients and their families. To help preserve health and prevent future health problems, regularly scheduled nutrition education classes can be offered to impart knowledge about food composition, food preparation, and eating habits. Clients may need referral to food assistance programs that provide food or the ability to obtain food. Exhibit 16-3 lists resources for nutrition counseling, nutrition education, and food assistance programs.

Establishing Outpatient Nutrition Services

The clinical manager may be instrumental in establishing nutrition services in an outpatient clinic. To justify the establishment of an outpatient nutrition service, a brief summary should be compiled on patients requiring follow-up nutrition care and time factors and barriers for adequate education. A proposal to initiate outpatient nutrition care could include a survey of current inpatient needs and retrospective data on patients needing education and counseling and readmissions for inadequate monitoring. Certain diseases, such as diabetes mellitus and cardiac conditions, can be targeted because nutrition counseling has been effective in modifying the health status of individuals with these conditions.

A written proposal requesting an outpatient nutrition service should include the need for services; the role of outpatient care in relation to inpatient care; the available resources; and the benefits to the institution in terms of improved patient care, increased services to the community, and cost effectiveness of prevention. Another benefit is the increased awareness within the hospital and the community of the importance of nutrition in improving health status.

Outpatient nutrition care can generate revenue for inpatient services. A separate cost center should be established to distinguish revenue from direct patient care and from nutrition education and materials and how they contribute to the budget. The budget should project revenues and expenses for a 3- to 5-year period. That time period allows sufficient time to recoup start-up costs, reach a breakeven point, and begin to show a profit. Salaries are a major portion of clinic expenses. Additional expenses include capital expenditures, materials and supplies, marketing and promotion costs, and overhead—usually space, equipment, and administrative fees.

To determine charges per patient visit, estimate the number of patients to be served. Once the program is in full operation, each dietitian may be able to see patients for 5 to 6 hours a day. Costs of group classes should be calculated on a different basis depending on the philosophy of the institution. Other budgetary considerations are similar to those for inpatient services, as discussed in chapters 11 and 12.

Reimbursement for Ambulatory Services

Individual patient counseling can be part of ambulatory services or be under separate contract with an HMO affiliated with the acute care institu-

Exhibit 16-3 Nutrition Resources

NUTRITION COUNSELING RESOURCES

- dietitians in private practice
- family practice clinic
- local health department
- home health agencies
- hospitals
- Maternal and Infant Care Project
- medical clinics
- nursing homes
- Planned Parenthood
- Visiting Nurses' Association
- Women, Infants, and Children (WIC) Program
- faculty practice units

NUTRITION EDUCATION RESOURCES

- adult day care
- American Cancer Society
- American Diabetes Association
- American Heart Association
- American Institute for Cancer Research
- American Red Cross
- Arthritis Foundation
- child day care
- community action agency or community center
- county extension service
- Dairy and Nutrition Council
- Dial-A-Dietitian
- local dietetic associations
- Head Start program
- local/state health department
- Kidney Foundation

Exhibit 16-3 continued

- Laleche League
- Lamaze—prepared childbirth
- March of Dimes
- medical clinics
- National Cancer Institute
- Nutrition Education and Training Program
- Planned Parenthood
- schools and universities
- U.S. Department of Agriculture
- U.S. Food and Drug Administration
- U.S. Department of Health and Human Services
- Women, Infants, and Children (WIC) Program
- YMCA/YWCA/YMHA

FOOD ASSISTANCE RESOURCES

- adult day care
- American Red Cross
- Church- or synagogue-sponsored food pantry or program
- community center
- congregate meal program for the elderly
- food commodities distribution
- food bank
- Food Stamp program
- local health department
- home enteral and parenteral nutrition services
- Meals on Wheels
- school lunch program
- welfare program
- Women, Infants, and Children (WIC) program

Source: Adapted from Boussos, Deborah B. and Virginia Jorstad. 1985. The role of the registered dietitian in discharge planning. *Discharge Planning Update* 5(2) (Winter):12–18.

tion. Reimbursement for nutrition counseling varies depending on the care structure and patient's diagnosis. The first step in establishing a fee-for-service for nutrition counseling is to examine the policies and procedures used in other departments and to consult the hospital finance department for submitting a proposal that establishes fees for nutrition services.

Health Maintenance Organizations

When HMOs were established in 1974 through federal legislation, there were no provisions for nutrition services. A revision of the laws in 1980 included reference to "nutrition education and counseling," without defining the types of nutrition services to be provided or the qualifications of the provider (Wegman et al. 1983). However, results of a 1983 survey indicated that 80 percent of federally funded HMOs provided nutrition education (Wegman et al. 1983) to both outpatients and inpatients. Nutrition educators even visited HMO clients in the hospital to provide diet counseling, although they were not members of the hospital staff. Nearly 60 percent of these HMO nutritionists developed their own patient literature with a great reliance on outside materials; 78 percent used government publications, and 94 percent used materials from private associations and companies. Sixty-one percent had diet manuals for their clientele. In addition to teaching patient classes, three-quarters gave inservice training classes to physicians, nurses and other support staff (Wegmen et al. 1983).

HOME CARE

Consumers and health care providers alike share a marked increased of interest in home health care and adult day care sparked by several factors. They include the growing numbers of early hospital discharges, the greater number and proportion of chronically ill elderly in the population, increased costs of inpatient hospital services, and the increased consumer demand for alternative modes of health care.

The benefits of home care are increased patient satisfaction, improved care, and financial savings. The average monthly cost for hospital care in 1986 was $10,050 compared to $1500/month in a skilled nursing facility and only $1050/month for home care (Hinton 1986). Patients received the benefits of interdisciplinary health care in all three settings.

Cooperative care—home care in an institutional setting—has gained popularity as well (Grieco 1988). Cooperative care or step-down (from hospitalization) units are institutions where patients manage their own care and medications, as well as attend classes and therapy sessions. Patients are aided by health care teams who provide education and evaluation. Cooperative care combines family involvement, shared responsibility, and service partnerships between health care professionals and family members. Such programs are especially beneficial to ease the transition of complex medical cases from hospital to home care.

Home health care is profoundly influenced by government policy. Eligibility and benefit structures, established by the major public programs that fund home care, largely determine both the type of services and the recipients of care. Home health care often is limited to services that are financially reimbursed by government and insurance programs.

The key deterrent to involvement of dietitians as home care providers is the lack of reimbursement by Medicare, Medicaid, and other third-party payers. Many organizations are advocating new reimbursement legislation. Changes in payment systems, including reimbursement for nutrition services, will contribute to the feasibility of extending dietetic services to primary care, cooperative care, and home settings.

Dietitians are not often viewed by the public as a group of professionals involved in the planning or delivery of home health care (Koteski and McKinney 1988). However, recent data show that more than half the patients referred to home health care needed dietary modifications; many of these patients could benefit from home-delivered dietetic services (Gaffney and Singer 1985).

Five major types of home nutrition care can be identified: (1) hospital-based continuing care programs, (2) services of a home health agency, (3) home nutrition support, (4) home-delivered meals, and (5) hospice care.

Hospital-Based Continuing Care Services

Hospital readmissions can result from poor discharge planning and follow-up, which cause treatment complications or exacerbation of chronic disease. To alleviate this problem some hospitals have developed continuing care services (Goodhue et al. 1976).

These services are designed to increase the ability of patients to follow medical therapy after hospital discharge in an environment most conducive to their needs. The continuing care interdisciplinary team, often consisting of a physician, nurse, social worker, dietitian, and occupational therapist, works with the patient at home or serves as a liaison with extended care facilities.

Working with clinical dietitians, the continuing care dietitian makes sure the patient's diet is practical for nonhospital circumstances. Suggestions are offered for menu planning, shopping, or the use of community nutrition resources. Regular meetings of continuing care and staff dietitians are needed to communicate a patient's nutritional status, food preferences, and usual dietary habits that may affect meal patterns, dietary needs, and, ultimately, patient outcome.

The Veterans Hospital in Indianapolis conducts a hospital-based home care program that involves staff dietitians (Birge and Maxwell 1979). During hospitalization dietitians assess patients' nutritional status, need for prosthetic feeding devices, and appropriateness of the dietary prescription. Changes are recommended as necessary, and patients are counseled regarding dietary modifications, nutritional guidelines for meal planning, and the importance of adequate fiber and fluid intakes. Shortly after discharge, a 1-hour home visit is conducted to observe dietary practices and assess the home situation. One or more home visits are scheduled if needed, depending on the situation and patient response to treatment. When predetermined goals have been achieved, patients are discharged from home care.

Home Health Agencies

For the most part, nutrition services offered by home health agencies are delivered by nurses (Malloy and Hartshorn 1989, 259–313). In a survey of Ohio home health agencies, Arnold found that most home health nurses conduct nutritional assessments, but 88 percent of respondents said they would consult a dietitian if confronted with a health condition necessitating a therapeutic diet prescription (Arnold 1985, 147). Conditions for which nurses would most often seek assistance from a dietitian included congestive heart failure, uncontrolled diabetes, cachexia, obesity ($>30\%$ optimal body weight), chronic renal failure, and food-drug interactions (Arnold 1985, 118).

Clinical dietetic managers should explore the establishment of ties with one or more home health programs or agencies, at least to provide consultation and referral services. Such initiatives can be justified by cost savings and the benefits of nutritional intervention in home care.

Home Nutrition Support

Both the American Dietetic Association (1989) and the American Society for Parenteral and Enteral Nutrition (1988) offer guidelines for specialized nutrition support of patients at home. Each of these professional groups emphasizes the role of registered dietitians in the organization, delivery, monitoring, and evaluation of these services.

Many hospital nutrition support teams offer specialized home nutrition support services either under the auspices of the hospital or through a separate corporation. Dietitian involvement in such programs is important for assessment, formula progression, and follow-up. Yet, because dietetic services often are not reimbursed, dietitians are frequently excluded from the team. In response, some entrepreneurial dietitians have established their own home health agencies, employing nurses for tube insertion and maintenance; dietitians can then make home visits and include nutrition assessment and evaluation as part of service delivery (Hinton 1986).

If dietitians are not included in hospital-based home nutrition support programs, the clinical dietetic manager may use this situation to investigate dietitian performance. Such a situation may indicate a need for better collaboration, improved human relations, open communication, continuing education, or other enhancements in the unit.

When one or more clinical dietetic staff members serve on a home nutrition support service, their responsibilities and relationships should be delineated clearly. All policies and procedures should be in writing, and care should be taken to document nutritional care services. Also, written financial arrangements should ensure appropriate reimbursement for the department. The clinical dietetic manager's supervisory role in home nutrition support services should be spelled out and the same care given to these responsibilities as those conducted within the hospital.

Home-Delivered Meals

Many elderly recipients of home-delivered meals use this service for short periods of time after hospital discharge (Frongillo et al. 1987). Dietitians are encouraged to refer patients for home-delivered meals when it is apparent that this service will enhance patient independence and avoid the need for institutionalization after hospital discharge.

Some hospitals hold the contract for home-delivered meals in the community. If no such service exists in the area, establishing such a program may be a practical method of extending services to the community and providing a source of revenue for the department.

Hospice Care

Although dietitians can play an important role in hospice care, results of a 1982 study revealed that only 12.5 percent of hospice programs included a dietitian (Ott 1985). Responsibilities of the hospice dietitian may include nutritional assessments; development of individualized therapeutic care plans; monitoring for food acceptance and correction of such complications as anorexia, constipation, diarrhea, early satiety, fatigue, food aversions, etc.; suggestions for food preparation and presentation; and recommendations for family members who need to cope with dietary problems, time pressures, and psychosocial aspects of food and eating.

In hospital-sponsored hospice programs, staff dietitians often serve as consultants. Independent hospice programs benefit from outreach efforts by nutrition services personnel and dietetic students. Dietetic services may include direct care for patients, consultation to program personnel, inservice education programs for staff, and nutrition guidance for family members.

DEVELOPING CONTINUING CARE PROGRAMS

Using a business plan to develop a continuing care program makes good sense. It helps focus planning activities, ensures that all steps are completed in a logical fashion, provides a framework for problem solving and anticipating future needs, and serves as a logical presentation for administrative approval. Keep the plan confidential so that others do not take the idea and implement it first. A business plan should include the following components:

- overview
- description of services
- market analysis
- advantages of proposed service
- marketing strategy
- structure
- time line
- financial projections
- exhibits or appendixes

Proposal Summary

Begin with a two- to three-page overview of the plan. Although this section comes first, it is written last. It provides key highlights of the entire business plan.

Description of Current Nutrition Services

Begin the proposal with a description of the unit and the services currently provided. State the numbers of patients receiving quantifiable nutrition services, income from continuing care services, and numbers of patients who would benefit from home services. Describe successful initiatives in the unit, highlight important achievements of staff members, and demonstrate the capability to mount successful continuing care services.

Market Analysis

This section describes the need for nonhospital nutrition services in the area and indicates that the proposed program will meet those needs and those people will buy your services, resulting in a profit. Information needs to be provided about potential customers, market size and trends, and competition.

Potential Users

Draw on your hospital experience to create a profile of who might use your service. For example, report the numbers of patients discharged on enteral or parenteral feedings or having other major nutritional problems. Obtain data from local home health agencies on the numbers of patients with special dietary needs. Report experiences of others who have successful counseling practices or home nutrition programs.

This section should answer these questions:

- What is the current health care profile of potential clients?
- How often are they hospitalized?
- Is hospitalization related to nutritional complications?
- What will induce clients to buy your services? Value? Expertise? Convenience?
- What kind of quality, price, and service do customers expect from you?
- How will they pay for services? Personal income? Insurance? Government programs?

Market Size and Trends

This component of the marketing analysis should address these questions:

- Are there sufficient nutritional problems to warrant the development of new services?
- How large is the geographic area to be served?
- Is the population increasing or decreasing?
- What are the current and potential age profiles in the area?
- What is the expected growth of users in 5 years, 10 years?

- Are patient/client needs likely to change over time?
- What market factors in the region have an impact on your potential client pool?

Competition

In this section it is important to show that your program has the best opportunity to satisfy patient needs. What community nutrition programs or home health agencies exist in the area? Does any other group offer the nutrition services you are proposing? How successful have they been? What has contributed to their success or failure?

Describe how the proposed program compares with others in terms of services offered, price, quality, convenience, and professional expertise. What are the competition's strengths and weaknesses? A matrix or chart is a good way to present this information.

Advantages of Proposed Services

In this section describe the plan for expanded nutrition services. Show what distinguishes the proposed services from others offered in the community and how they can offer a competitive advantage.

Description of Services

Describe the proposed services clearly. Answer such questions as

- What services will be offered?
- What personnel will be involved?
- What locations will be used?
- When (hours) will services be provided?
- What is the plan for documentation and record keeping?
- What facilities and equipment are needed? How will these be provided?
- How will clients contact the service? Who will take appointments?
- How will patients be billed? What is the fee schedule? Will insurance cover any of the services?

Regulatory Requirements

In some cases a state license may be required to establish a program. The plan should describe steps for obtaining the necessary regulatory approvals.

Program Evaluation and Termination

The business plan should contain a method for determining the program's success or failure. Will success be measured in numbers served? Net income? Patient satisfaction? Also, there should be a plan for terminating the program if it is unsuccessful. Who will assume the loss? What will happen to the equipment purchased?

Marketing Strategy

This section of the plan identifies target markets and strategies for promoting service usage. Include the following information:

- Analyze market segmentation: newly discharged patients, those on home nutrition support, hospital employees, families of former patients, patients obtained through outreach efforts, women and/or mothers, homebound elderly, etc.
- Estimate the number of patients expected in the next 2, 3, or 5 years.
- Give pricing schedules and show how these compare with the competition. Describe how price schedules will enable market penetration, increased market share, and profit margins.
- Describe the plan for promotion. How will potential clients find out about your service? Will advertising, public relations, promotional literature, or incentives be used? How much will they cost?

Management and Organization

In this section, describe who will manage the venture and how it will relate to current nutrition service operations. What is the role of the clinical dietetic manager? Who will be involved in this venture and what role will each play? The description should elaborate on organizational structure, assigned responsibilities of staff members, corporate relationship within the hospital, physician involvement (titles, roles, relationships), and legal considerations, if applicable.

Timeline

Prepare a schedule of activities showing major events over the next several years. Include such activities as writing policies and procedures, recruitment and employment of staff, identification and preparation of space, purchase of equipment, promotional activities, pilot testing, and full-scale delivery of services.

Financial Information and Cost Projections

Prepare a financial statement covering the next 3 to 5 years. Include projected operations, cash flow projections, and anticipated balance sheets. These should be computerized to illustrate managerial expertise and to facilitate development of breakeven models.

Administrators will want to know how much money is needed now, as well as anticipated needs over the next 3 to 5 years. Indicate distribution plans for the initial funds and how cost underestimates will be handled.

Exhibits and Appendixes

Append to the proposal additional information that will help tell the story. Include such elements as marketing studies, photographs of dietitians in action, and resumes of key personnel.

REFERENCES

American Dietetic Association. 1989. Nutrition monitoring of the home parenteral and enteral patient. *J. Am. Dietet. Assoc.* 89(2):263–65.

American Society for Parenteral and Enteral Nutrition. 1988. Standards for home nutrition support. *Nutr. Clin. Pract.* 3(5):202–05.

Arnold, Susan E. 1985. Descriptive analysis of nutritional care processes by community health nurses in Ohio certified home health care agencies. Master's thesis, The Ohio State University, Columbus, Ohio.

Bell, Donna M. 1981. Patient nutrition education follow-up in the hospital setting. *J. Am. Dietet. Assoc.* 79(3):309–10.

Birge, Kristine R., and Douglas R. Maxwell. 1979. Home health care: The dietitian's role. *J. Am. Diet. Assoc.* 74(1):47–49.

Frongillo, Edward A., et al. 1987. Continuance of elderly on home-delivered meals programs. *Am. J. Public Health* 77(9):1176–79.

Gaffney, Joan T., and Gloria R. Singer. 1985. Diet needs of patients referred to home health. *J. Am. Dietet. Assoc.* 85(2):198–202.

Goodhue, Phyllis J., Mary Ellen Collins, and Susan Baumgarten. 1976. Continuing nutritional care for the discharged patient. *Dietetic Curr.* 3(1):1–4.

Grieco, Anthony J. 1988. Home care/hospital care/cooperative care, options for the practice of medicine. *Bull. NY Acad. Med.* 64(4):318–26.

Hinton, Agnes W. 1986. Home health: Trend to the future. *Clin. Man.* 2(1):1–4.

Koteski, Dorothy R., and Shortie McKinney. 1988. Who does the public think should perform health care tasks? *J. Am. Dietet. Assoc.* 88(10):1281–83.

Malloy, Catherine, and Jeanette Hartshorn, eds. 1989. *Acute care nursing in the home: A holistic approach.* Philadelphia: J. B. Lippincott Company.

Ott, Dana B. 1985. Hospice care: An opportunity for dietetic services. *J. Am. Dietet. Assoc.* 85(2):223–25.

Shovic, Anne C., Susan Adams, and Melody Anacker. 1988. Client profile assessment of a private nutrition practice. *J. Am. Dietet. Assoc.* 88(10):1279–80.

Walters, Farah M., Carolynn Onetto, and Patricia A. Jerman. 1972. Nutritional needs of the out-patient—an overview. *J. Am. Dietet. Assoc.* 61(2):170–72.

Wegman, Judith A., Rebecca J. Dunn, and Christina F. Coleman. 1983. HMO nutrition educators: Qualifications and roles. *Journal of the American Dietetic Association* 83(3):327–29.

SUGGESTED READINGS

American Dietetic Association Committee on Dietary Services for the Chronically Ill and Aging. 1968. Opportunities in home health services. *J. Am. Dietet. Assoc.* 52(5):381–86.

American Dietetic Association Committee on the Development of an Integrated Manpower Policy for Primary Care. 1977. The dietitian in primary health care. *J. Am. Dietet. Assoc.* 70(6):587–90.

Ernst and Whinney. 1986. *Preparing a business plan—a guide for the emerging company.* Los Angeles: Ernst and Whinney.

Goodspeed, Scott W. 1985. How to write a business plan for a new venture. *Health Care Strat. Man.* 3(5):11–13.

Hermann-Ziadens, Mindy, and Riva Touger-Decker, eds. 1989. *Nutrition support in home health.* Gaithersburg; Md.: Aspen Publishers, Inc.

McCrae, Jo Ann D., and Nancy H. Hall. 1989. Current practices for home enteral nutrition. *J. Am. Dietet. Assoc.* 89(2):233–40.

Suski, Nancy S. 1981. The dietitian makes home visits. *J. Am. Dietet. Assoc.* 79(9):311–12.

Part IV

Professional Skills Development

Chapter 17

Communications

Managers spend a majority of their time communicating with others through many channels: verbal, pictorial, electronic, actions, gestures, facial expression, stance, and the written word. The effectiveness of both nutrition services and dietetic personnel is often judged by the quality of verbal communication and written documentation. This chapter includes guidelines for oral communication, conducting meetings, and improving written communication in such forms as memos and letters, manuals, newsletters, reports, and medical records.

ORAL COMMUNICATIONS

Many undergraduate curricula include at least one course in oral communication. However, it is often assumed that the principles of public speaking learned in such courses apply primarily to formal presentations. Yet, these same principles also apply to routine encounters between the clinical dietetic manager and staff dietitians, administrators, patients, physicians, health care team members, and numerous other individuals met in the round of daily contacts.

Verbal communication should be characterized by SEVEN Cs. For greatest effectiveness, one should speak with

1. Clarity: Do not mumble. Use simple language; avoid complex words that may be misinterpreted. Speak slowly enough for others to understand your message easily but not so slowly that they lose interest.
2. Conviction: Use the positive approach, stating things in the affirmative. Avoid the use of phrases that imply a lack of importance for nutrition and dietetics.

3. Coherence: A logical flow of thought is critical to clear communication. Do not confuse others by interjecting meaningless information where it does not belong. Provide adequate data to support a point or show the connection between one point and another.
4. Caution: Hold your tongue when angry to avoid making accusations that are better left unsaid. Keep confidential information secret. Do not be a source of gossip or tale-bearing.
5. Confidence: Speak with a modulated tone, a low pitch, and a strong voice. A whiny, high-pitched voice often conveys a complaining, negative attitude. Use eye contact to enhance the value of well-spoken words.
6. Correctness: Use correct grammar and word pronunciation. Lack of attention to proper word usage detracts from a positive professional image.
7. Consideration: Give others a chance to speak. Do not monopolize the conversation. Listen with attentiveness.

Verbal communication is an essential component of both face-to-face encounters and telephone conversations. Yet, adequate attention to these skills is often lacking, especially among new practitioners. Clinical dietetic managers should work with their staff to improve these skills where necessary. A demonstrated support and respect for other health care professionals, a clearer definition of the dietitian's role, and recognition of the dietitian's nutritional expertise can improve communication with physicians and nurses (Skipper 1986).

To improve their own skills in this area, managers can first compare their speaking styles to those of others who demonstrate optimal oral communication skills. If disparities are apparent, seek out mentors or colleagues who can identify problem areas and illustrate specific instances where improvements would enhance your management and leadership potential.

EFFECTIVE MEETING MANAGEMENT

Meetings consume a substantial portion of the clinical dietetic manager's time. They are often an effective means to obtain or provide information, solve problems, motivate staff, develop new ideas, or make announcements (Berryman-Fink 1989). The judicious use of meetings requires care in planning and conducting them, as well as paying attention to follow-up procedures to ensure appropriate implementation of ideas suggested during the meeting.

Planning the Meeting

Every meeting should have a defined purpose, whether information sharing, decision making, or team building. The planning process should follow these steps.

- Define the purpose of the meeting.
- Determine who should attend.
- Plan the agenda, including the amount of time expected for each agenda item.
- Make arrangements for the meeting space and refreshments, and send announcements including the agenda well in advance of the meeting date.
- If appropriate, plan the process to be used for problem identification, decision making, or consensus building.
- Arrange for any needed resources, such as reports, documents, visual displays, etc.
- Anticipate conflicts or disruptions that might occur and consider how these can best be handled to achieve desired outcomes.

Conducting the Meeting

The success of a meeting usually rests with the chairperson. These techniques can be used to foster productive meetings.

- Start on time and end at or before the designated hour. Be sure someone has been designated to keep minutes of the meeting.
- At the beginning, state the purpose of the meeting and review the agenda. Stick to the agenda: cover all items, but do not allow discussion of extraneous items—save them for another meeting.
- Select processes congruent with the purpose of the meeting. Use brainstorming for idea generation. Use a problem-solving approach to clarify and deal with situations that need changing. Follow the decision-making process for participative management when there are several alternatives from which to choose.
- Use constructive group processes skills: keep the atmosphere open and positive, involve all participants in the discussion, do not allow a few individuals to dominate the meeting, do not squelch ideas or dampen enthusiasm, and strive for consensus and strong support of decisions.

- Let the meeting center on its participants. Encourage debate, constructive criticism, and friendly disagreements, but steer away from confrontation and pointless arguments. The chairperson should remain neutral. Do not begin by stating your position lest others assume a decision has been made and that further discussion is useless.
- Keep control of discussions. Put an end to side conversations tactfully. Do not let the comments of one person stop others from voicing their opinions. Guide the discussion by summarizing issues and directing questions to move the agenda forward.
- Conclude discussion on an item with a summary of comments, conclusions, follow-up actions as warranted, and assignment of tasks as necessary.
- End the meeting on a positive note. Offer thanks for attendance and give praise for group participation and work accomplished. Set the stage for follow-up activities and summarize what should be accomplished before the next meeting.

Meeting Follow-Up

After the meeting minutes should be prepared and distributed to participants and others who should be kept informed of ongoing activities. Minutes should include the meeting time and place, attendees, agenda items and how each was concluded, decisions reached, action to be taken, assignments and deadlines, and plans for subsequent meetings.

A method should be in place to ensure that decisions are implemented and that participants are held accountable for their assignments. Subsequent meetings can include a report of progress and outcomes of previous assignments. This is one simple way to monitor activities related to previous decisions and to keep everyone informed of movement within the department.

Meeting Effectiveness

On occasion the chairperson ought to assess the effectiveness of the meetings he or she runs. This can be done by soliciting opinions from participants regarding such key characteristics as adequate planning and preparation by the chairperson and participants, problem-solving and decision-making processes, group dynamics, meeting times and space, adequacy and openness of discussions before decisions are reached, and the psychosocial atmosphere of meetings.

Such a review and evaluation may point out some common problems often associated with meetings (Berryman-Fink 1989):

- failure to define clearly the purpose of meetings
- lack of a detailed agenda and sufficient time for participants to prepare adequately for meetings
- inability of the chairperson to control the meeting, allowing diversions from the agenda and failure to reach decisions on key items
- frustration over long, boring meetings in which time limits are not maintained, discussions ramble, and conclusions are shared by only a small minority of participants
- domination by the chairperson or other individuals, curtailing involvement by other participants, which can easily divert attention from the agenda and deter productive work by interested attendees

POLICY AND PROCEDURE MANUALS

Operations manuals set forth the mission, goals, policies, and key practices of an organization. At the departmental level these manuals serve these purposes:

- serve as reference books
- ensure consistency in decision making
- orient new employees
- inform personnel of changes in policy or practices
- prevent misinformation or unanswered questions
- provide common ground for problem solving

Exhibit 17-1 illustrates the variety of manuals, files, and notebooks used to record the status of present operations and help assure quality control.

Several techniques can be used to ensure the readability and thus the effectiveness of these manuals (Hestwood 1988; IEC 1965).

- Computerize manuals to facilitate their organization and updating.
- Bind departmental manuals in loose-leaf notebooks or folders to facilitate additions and revisions.
- Create and use a logical, comprehensive numbering system with capacity for subsystems. Give each policy a number and date. For replacement purposes, note the policy superseded and its date of issue.

Exhibit 17-1 Recommended Files or Manuals for Clinical Nutrition Services

Annual reports and goals	Patient education materials
Diet manual	Policy and procedure manual
Employee manuals	Position descriptions
Equipment maintenance manuals	Quality assessment/quality control
Financial reports and budgets	procedures, standards, and reports
Inservice manual	Research studies
Meeting minutes file	State inspection standards and survey
Nutrition committee minutes	results
On-the-job training manual	

- Organize materials and develop a table of contents according to your established numbering system. Paginate section-by-section, rather than from cover to cover, to facilitate replacement of outdated material.
- To make procedure manuals more readable, aim for a comprehension level equivalent to that of the service-level employees. Examine procedure statements to be sure each is clear, concise, and easy to read.

When disseminating a new or revised procedure, link it with the policy from which it stems. Doing so accents the existing policy and demonstrates that the new procedure is derived from established policy. Periodically (every 2 to 5 years), evaluate the effectiveness of manuals. One method of evaluation is a simple questionnaire to the target audience containing such questions as "How often do you use the manual?," "How can it be improved?," or "What policies or procedures have caused the greatest problems of interpretation or implementation?" Provide training for supervisors on new policies. Both new and existing policies and practices can be presented at departmental inservice meetings, highlighted in newsletters, and posted on bulletin boards. Repetition and reinforcement help employees understand and value the importance of the material.

DIET AND NUTRITION MANUALS

Diet and nutrition manuals guide clinical dietetic services for the entire institution and, as such, need to be updated continually, with input from pertinent members of the health care team. Usually diet manual generation and update are coordinated by the clinical dietetic manager in conjunction with the nutrition committee at the facility or a similar committee that reports to the medical board.

The function of the diet manual has expanded with the increasing responsibilities of clinical departments of dietetics. Institutional manuals should include descriptions of all aspects of nutrition care: screening protocols, definitions of malnutrition, documentation policies, consultation and referral systems, standards of care for major conditions, and, of course, dietary modifications used at the facility. The manual should be a readable tool of communication for all other health professionals as it is the only required dietetic services document in each medical/nursing unit.

Contents of the diet or nutrition manual should be realistic for the setting. All practices and diets served at the institution should be consistent with policies and specifications written in the diet manual. The manual also may be used as the document to explain or justify services provided.

Smaller institutions may want to combine forces and write a cooperative diet manual (Signore 1982). Many facilities, especially specialty hospitals, may wish to develop a comprehensive diet manual concentrating on the major conditions seen within the facility.

Departments may consider the adoption and use of a published diet manual, such as the Mayo Clinic Diet Manual or the ADA Manual of Clinical Dietetics. These manuals may contain sufficient guidance for diet prescriptions and modification, but may lack certain guidelines or protocols desired at a specific hospital. If an outside manual is adopted, departmental policies and procedures should reflect the adoption and should be expanded to include any desired policies or procedures not contained in the diet manual. When the decision is made to adopt a commercial diet manual, the institutional nutrition committee may review several manuals and select the one best suited to the particular hospital.

SHORT MEMOS AND LETTERS

Written communication has the disadvantage of delayed feedback, but can augment oral communication. Dellinger and Deane (1980, 224–25) suggest the following five justifications for putting a message in writing:

1. When a written record is needed to prevent misunderstandings. Topics dealing with patient care (medical or dietetic records, and advance directives), money, safety, and contracts should be put in writing.
2. When several people are informed at the same time, multiple copies speed communication.
3. When a piece of information should be permanent and easily retrievable. Keep a copy, either on disk or in a file.
4. When the message is complex. Written materials allow slow and reflective analysis. It is more difficult to comprehend numerical data and

Exhibit 17-2 Sample Memo: Without Editing

TO: Sandra Nichols, MRA,
         Head, Medical Records Department
         Cork Medical Center

FROM: Cynthia Rogers, MA, RD, LD, CNSD
         Clinical Dietetic Manager

DATE: January 14, 1991

TOPIC: Documenting in Medical Record

New guidelines for documenting nutritional care in the medical record were discussed earlier this year at a meeting of the American Dietetic Association, attended by eight clinical dietitians from our department. After hearing about these guidelines, our staff held several meetings to discuss options and develop new procedures for us to use when charting nutritional care information in the medical record.

We have finished writing a draft of our new policy and we would like your comments on the draft before submitting it to the Hospital Nutrition Committee for their review and approval.

If possible, please review the document and send me your comments before February 15, 1991 so we can move forward with the approval process in a timely manner. I and my staff deeply appreciate your assistance in this matter.

---

complicated ideas by listening. The opportunity to reread and study material facilitates understanding.

5. When clarification of thinking is necessary. While organizing thoughts for a presentation to others, a clearer picture of the issues may emerge to the writer.

Memoranda (memos) and letters are the backbones of business communications. Successful memos follow basic rules of composition. Exhibit 17-2 shows the result of ignoring these suggestions: an unnecessarily wordy memo in which the desired action is buried in the text. In contrast, Exhibit 17-3 is simple and to the point, eliminates unnecessary words, and is directed to the reader. The date and assignment are highlighted clearly at the beginning of the memo.

Distribution of Memos

Using these recommended practices can ensure that the information is received by those who require it.

- Have important messages hand-delivered or placed in payroll envelopes, increasing the chances of immediate and undivided attention.

Exhibit 17-3 Sample Memo: After Editing

TO: Sandra Nichols, MRA,
Head, Medical Records Department

FROM: Cynthia Rogers, MA, RD, LD, CNSD
Clinical Dietetic Manager

DATE: January 15, 1991

TOPIC: Draft Policy—Please comment by February 15, 1991

The Department of Clinical Dietetic Services has revised a policy on charting. These changes are based on the new guidelines for documenting nutrition care published by the American Dietetic Association. Your comments are appreciated by February 15. We plan to submit the policy to the Hospital Nutrition Committee in March.

Thank you for your assistance.

- Make follow-up phone calls to emphasize important details and encourage a timely response.
- Use preprinted routing slips, to be checked off as the material passes through designated hands.
- Direct memos and notices to a limited audience, pinpointing narrow interests of selected groups. For example, rather than writing to ''nursing personnel,'' target head nurses, primary nurses, nursing supervisors, or unit supervisors.
- Request supervisory personnel to schedule meetings for the purpose of discussing the content of important memos and notices.
- Post selected notices and memos on bulletin boards at the same time as they are placed in mail boxes. Doing so provides double exposure and may stimulate conversation, giving the topic greater attention.
- Give due dates at the top of the memo. Indicate that timely action will be taken and only those responses received by the deadline can be used.

Business Letters

An original letter addressed to one person attracts more attention than a memo directed to several individuals. When your message needs attention, send a letter. The letter may stand on its own, or it can follow an initial contact or phone call.

Keep letters short. Two or three paragraphs are usually sufficient to convey your message; letters should rarely exceed one page. McConnell (1988,

p. 250) suggests that most business correspondence contains from 25 to 100 percent more words than are needed for effective communication. Unneeded words lead to both misunderstandings and frustration.

To draw immediate attention to the topic, insert a teaser just below the inside address. Reference headlines (''RE'') should be short and to the point. For example, a letter to the chief of staff might include the reference headline, ''RE: Introduction of new diet manual.''

REPORTS AND PROPOSALS

Clinical dietetic managers need to keep top management informed and seek administrative approval for their program initiatives. This is often accomplished through reports, performance analyses, business plans, or written proposals, which are major forms of upward communication.

Many reports provide financial or statistical data: budgets, labor turnover, overtime coverage, absenteeism, accidents, occupancy, and productivity. For these reports, take clues from management by providing the desired information in the format requested. For general assistance in preparing such reports, read articles on the topic, such as ''Writing Technical Reports'' by M. Steinbaugh (1986) or ''Making Your Reports More Meaningful'' by C. G. Roswell (1959).

To improve the effectiveness of written reports, follow these guidelines (Roswell 1959):

- Keep reports short and concise. Do not overload them with too much information.
- Present material in a clear and meaningful form.
- Design the report to serve the specific needs and interests of its reader(s). Do not write one report to serve many purposes.
- Use charts and graphs to illustrate quantitative data, rather than filling the report with detailed tabulations. Figure 17-1 shows how a graph can enable trends in productivity measures for the previous year to be identified quickly. Such charts can be computer generated.
- Simplify and interpret data presented; highlight the relevance of information.
- Differentiate ''controllable'' matters from those over which there is limited control. Focus on solutions, not on problems outside your scope of responsibility.
- Keep reports timely. Reports used primarily for planning, monitoring, coordinating, and controlling activities need to be submitted while the

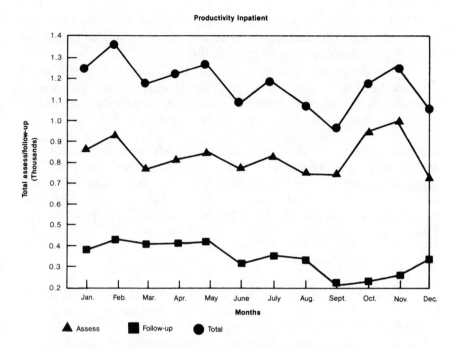

Figure 17-1 A Computer-Generated Chart to Enhance a Report or Proposal

topic is "hot," not after the administrator makes judgments or decisions on the topic.

When preparing your report, outline it carefully and organize its content to maximize its impact. Be sure to include an executive summary at the beginning of the report or proposal. This orients the reader and accents key points, even if the entire document is not read.

MENU MINDERS

Menus can be an excellent means of educating patients about good nutrition or motivating them to make healthy food choices. To enhance the effective use of menus as an educational tool, follow these suggestions:

- Write crisp narratives on the back of daily menu sheets. Focus the message; target one concept at a time. Consider using a different feature each day of the week. Have dietary personnel discuss with patients the day's lesson.

- Make cryptic points on the day's menu. For example, ask, "Did you select a well-balanced meal?" Or state, "The National Cancer Institute recommends eating 20 to 30 grams of fiber per day."
- Provide nutrient information on specific menu items. Rotate nutrients to vary the focus on kilocalories, cholesterol, sodium, fiber, vitamins, or minerals. Do not offer information about all nutrients at the same time or try to provide an analysis of all items on the menu.

Regardless of the method, communicate effectively. Pinpoint the message. Do not overwhelm the patient with too much data. Use short words and simple sentences. Be colorful and creative in word usage. Leave plenty of white space. Draw attention to points through headlines or bullets. Tie nutrition to recovery and good health. Make the message direct, personal, and interesting.

MEDICAL RECORDS

Legal dimensions of charting in the medical record are considered in Chapter 9. This section deals with documentation as a form of communication.

Clinical dietetic managers have overall responsibility for dietetic documentation in the medical record. To assess the effectiveness of communication with physicians and other health care professionals, conduct an occasional audit of medical record notations. Exhibit 17-4 provides a checklist for such an audit. Pay especial attention to the following:

- Notations should be written according to institutional policy: location in the medical record, screening and assessment information, note(s) on each patient hospitalized for more than 48 hours, signature and date.
- Documentation should be brief, clear, and precise without redundancy. The use of problem-oriented medical records ensures pertinence, but requires the repetition of information. Consider revising policies to achieve more informative, readable, and salient documentation. For example, adopt the Plan, Intervention, Evaluation (PIE) system for progress notes (O'Sullivan Maillet 1989; Siegrist et al. 1985) as illustrated in Exhibit 17-5.
- Jargon may confuse other care providers. Use only institutionally approved standard abbreviations; write out nutrition terms that may be unfamiliar to the medical team.
- Recommendations should be straightforward and definitive. Soft-pedaled suggestions are less likely to be followed than those stated with authority and precision (Skipper 1986).

Exhibit 17-4 Checklist for Evaluating Medical Record Notes

Criteria	Sample 1	2	3	4	5	Comments
Format conforms to institutional policy						
Location is appropriate						
Patient's name appears on every page						
All entries signed and dated						
All entries are permanent; rules for correcting notes are followed						
Screening and assessment information given if patient hospitalized more than 48 hours						
Notes are brief, clear, and precise						
Only standard abbreviations used						
Accurate calculations; precise details are given when necessary						
Notes are legible						
Facts are given; generalizations and impressions avoided						
Patient education needs recorded						
Evaluation of care documented						
No extraneous remarks and criticisms						
Recommendations straightforward and definitive						
Dietitian's recommendations accepted; reflected in physician orders						
Countersignatures affixed as appropriate						
Referral and discharge needs indicated						

Y-Meets criteria; N-Does not meet criteria

Exhibit 17-5 Progress Notes Reflecting Patient Problems, Interventions, and Evaluations (P.I.E.)

Date	Remarks
9/1	Problem: Newly diagnosed diabetic; blood glucose 370.
	Intervention: Recommend 1500 kilocalorie diabetic diet: 50% CHO, 30% fat, 20% protein based on body weight and energy needs.
	Intervention: Plan to begin diet instructions when stabilized.
9/2	Problem: Blood glucose 200, needs education on diabetic diet.
	Evaluation: Responding to insulin and diet restrictions.
	Intervention: Meal pattern adjusted to meet food preferences. Evening snacks provided to cover PM intermediate insulin.
9/3	Intervention: Diabetic diet instructions initiated.
	Evaluation: Patient responded accurately to verbal questions testing knowledge of exchange lists.
9/5	Evaluation: Accurately followed meal pattern to complete selective menu.
	Intervention: Suggested attending inpatient diabetic classes.
	Gave expanded exchange lists; recommended cookbook for diabetics.

- Monitor the frequency of implementing the dietitian's recommendations. If implementation is rare, assess the adequacy of medical record communication or quality of the recommendation.

The image of a department rests, to a large extent, on written communication. Try improving both the quality and appearance of written materials to improve the status of the unit and of the personnel. Such a project may require long-term commitment, an integrated approach, and involvement of all professional staff.

REFERENCES

Berryman-Fink, Cynthia. 1989. *The manager's desk reference.* New York: American Management Association.

Dellinger, Susan, and Barbara Deane. 1980. *Communicating effectively: A complete guide for better managing.* Radnor, Penn: Chilton Book Co.

Hestwood, Thomas M. 1988. Making policy manuals useful and relevant. *Personnel J.* 67(4):43–46.

Improving employee-management communication in hospitals: A special study in management practices and problems. 1965. New York: United Hospital Fund of New York.

McConnell, Charles R. 1988. *The effective health care supervisor.* 2d ed. Gaithersburg, Md.: Aspen Publishers, Inc.

O'Sullivan Maillet, Julie. 1989. Improved documentation as easy as P.I.E. *Dietitians Nutr. Supp. Newsl.* 11(3):6–7.

Roswell, Charles G. 1959. Making your reports more meaningful. *J. Am. Dietet. Assoc.* 35(4):351–53.

Siegrist, Linda M., Ruth E. Dettor, and Barbara Stocks. 1985. The P.I.E. system: Complete planning and documentation of nursing care. *Qual. Rev. Bull.* 11(6):186–89.

Signore, Juliette. 1982. Some suggested "dos and don'ts" of cooperative diet manual ventures. *J. Am. Dietet. Assoc.* 81(3):280–83.

Skipper, Annalynn. 1986. Effective communication: A powerful tool for dietitians. *Dietet. Curr.* 13(4):17–20.

Steinbaugh, Maria. 1986. Writing technical reports. In *Communicating as professionals,* edited by Ronni Chernoff. Chicago: American Dietetic Association.

SUGGESTED READINGS

Alldredge, Everett O. 1959. Improving your writing ability. *J. Am. Dietet. Assoc.* 35(10):1037–1040.

Allensworth, Diane DeMuth, and Cynthia R. Luther. 1986. Evaluating printed materials. *Nurse Educator* 11(2):18–22.

Boles, Kaye. 1968. Writing a policies and procedures manual for the dietary department. *Hospitals, JAHA* 42(November 1):86–90.

Creighton, Helen. 1987. Legal implications of policy and procedure manual. I. *Nurs. Man.* 18(4):22–28.

Creighton, Helen. 1987. Legal implications of policy and procedure manual. II. *Nurs. Man.* 18(5):16–18.

Davidhizar, Ruth. 1985. Memorable memos. *Hosp. Topics* 63(2):34–37.

Dumaine, Deborah. 1983. *Write to the top.* New York: Random House, Inc.

Foltz, Mary Beth, ed. 1987. *Workbook in communications: How to tell the WIC success story.* Columbus, Ohio: Ross Laboratories.

Grindol, Mary A. 1984. A manager's guide to procedure manuals. *Nurs. Man.* 15(1):12–14.

Hess, Mary Abbott. 1986. Writing for the general public. In *Communicating as professionals,* edited by Ronni Chernoff. Chicago: American Dietetic Association.

Chapter 18

Research in Clinical Nutrition

Research can be an important dimension of the clinical manager's role. However, research generally has been limited in the clinical setting. This chapter clarifies the clinical dietetic manager's research role and delineates how managers can both lead and participate in the research process.

CURRENT STATUS OF RESEARCH

Research is gaining momentum in dietetic circles. Schiller (1988) found that about one-fourth of nutrition support dietitians were either principal or coinvestigators in various research studies. A surprising 80 percent of nutrition support dietitians wanted to devote more time to research. Jones, Bonner, and Stitt (1986) found that about one-third of nutrition support dietitians were engaged in research, whereas 70 percent perceived research to be an important part of their role.

To date dietitians have had little experience in collaborative research. Rinke and Berry (1987) noted that dietitians were involved in 68 percent of the 53 research articles published in the Journal of the American Dietetic Association during 1985. However, only six articles had been reported by a dietitian and physician team working in the practice setting.

Dietitians involved in clinical research need to participate in defining research questions, developing research designs, collecting and recording data, calculating and interpreting findings, discussing implications and applications of findings, publishing or presenting results, and raising questions for further study. Some individuals will engage in these activities concurrent with other service responsibilities.

IMPORTANCE OF RESEARCH IN THE PROFESSION

Research has been called the "backbone of our profession" (Smitherman and Wyse 1987). Some argue that it is essential for professional survival

(Hendricks and Sharp 1987). Research has been advocated in dietetics as a necessary basis for demonstrating professional legitimacy and advancing the profession (Hendricks and Sharp 1987; Rinke and Berry 1987). The lack of a strong research base now threatens the profession.

Research enhances professional image. Grady (1987) observed that the practitioner's activities, publications, expertise, and external recognition contribute to a composite professional image. Only when a profession's unique body of knowledge is founded on research can members claim the credibility and respect that they desire from society.

The Standards of Practice for the Profession of Dietieics (1985) emphasize that dietitians must engage in research to advance professional practice. Only through creative problem solving, assesssing new modes of service delivery, examining opinions and attitudes, testing new procedures, developing new methods, and exploring alternative ways to address daily problems will dietitians adapt to changing needs and circumstances in the field.

Clinical dietitians need to incorporate research findings into practice. Application to practice may be deterred by disagreement with the research findings, the perception that a new process is too expensive or too time consuming to implement (Charold 1986), lack of individual commitment to research, unsupportive organizational climate, and insufficient organizational and community resources (Oberst 1985).

RESEARCH ROLE OF THE CLINICAL DIETETIC MANAGER

The complexity of the clinical manager's research role is evident in both the multiplicity and diversity of his or her research activities. The role requires that one

- recognize the importance of using and conducting research in clinical nutrition
- function as an informed consumer of research and use research to advance dietetic practice
- create an environment conducive to research within the department
- promote research participation among staff dietitians
- engage in both independent and collaborative clinical management studies
- ensure that ethical procedures are followed
- disseminate results of research in clinical dietetic management or patient care
- arrange staff development opportunities in research methodology and applications

• hire staff members with a positive attitude toward the use of valid research to induce change and innovation

Creating a Research Environment

The challenge facing clinical dietetic managers is to create an environment that supports research involvement of all dietitians. Some ways that managers can meet this challenge are to

• establish research as a high priority in the department and include research in the evaluation process
• review and revise job descriptions to include research responsibilities
• make computer, statistical, and research design consultation available
• support small research studies by allocating some money for research in the budget
• recognize publicly the achievements of those who conduct research
• report research studies and findings at staff meetings and hospital committee meetings
• provide at least partial funding for dietitians to attend meetings to present research findings
• allow library time to conduct literature searches or write manuscripts
• provide funding for slides, graphics, and poster displays
• have a few current research methodology and statistics texts available in the department library
• encourage dietitians to present their research at local professional meetings and to submit abstracts for presentation at state and national meetings
• set annual research goals for the department
• assign routine nutritional care tasks to support personnel, giving dietitians time to engage in research activities
• arrange inservice programs on research methodology; provide time for dietitians to discuss potential collaborative research projects with each other
• develop liaisons between academic researchers and practitioners
• encourage dietitians to pursue graduate work and to focus their theses or dissertations on pertinent clinical problems
• engage institutional administrators in conversations regarding the value of research in the department

- encourage dietitians to involve students in research projects if the hospital offers a dietetic educational program
- realize that not all dietitians have an interest in conducting research; allow these staff members to contribute in other ways

There are several dimensions to the clinical nutrition manager's role of facilitating staff research efforts. Managers may provide consultation and guidance for specific projects. They may channel requests for research data to designated individuals and foward requests for proposals (RFP) or research grant applications to the staff. They can also facilitate multidisciplinary research teams associated with specific areas of practice. They play an important role in the review and approval process as shown in Figure 18-1.

Conducting Research in Daily Practice

There is an interactive relationship between practice and research (Rinke and Berry 1987). Research originates from questions generated in practice and results in new knowledge. This new knowledge is transmitted to students and current practitioners; new findings in the profession are then implemented to upgrade or improve practice. New questions arise, starting the cycle again. This model applies to both management and clinical practice.

Good documentation is fundamental to appropriate decision making and is at the heart of effective management. Operational research can be seen simply as a sophisticated method of reporting, a task required for accountability (Rose 1985).

Hinshaw and Smeltzer (1987) outlined several steps, basic to integrating nursing research and practice, that apply to dietetic settings as well.

First, define which management and clinical problems are researchable and which are not. Problems worth researching are repetitive, occur regularly in clinical units, can be tested empirically, and represent practices or policies for which accurate information or data will improve decision making.

Second, generate knowledge or build the theoretical base needed to guide practice and improve the quality of patient care. The role of research in the profession is to answer questions basic to the field as a whole. Institutional research, however, tends to focus on gathering information needed for onsite policy decisions and practice. Dietitians must balance the need for advancing knowledge in the profession with providing some institutional benefit in order to sustain research amidst the daily pressures of patient care and administration. The ideal is to satisfy both needs simultaneously.

Third, balance the institution's need for immediate information with scientific replication. There is always the danger that results of a single clinical study are biased by the unique conditions of the study. Replication of the

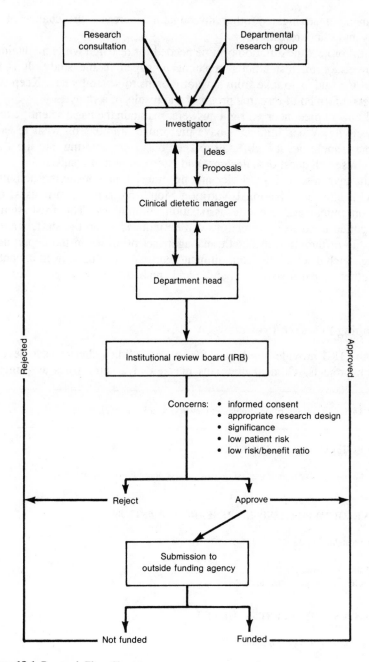

Figure 18-1 Research Flow Chart

work in other settings by other investigators increases the chance of reliability and standardization.

Fourth, protect the duration of time needed for research while maintaining high levels of interest among personnel engaged in the study. It is not unusual for studies to take from several months to several years. Keep staff members informed of research progress and results of a study.

Fifth, avoid preconceived right answers; maintain the basic scientific tenet of objectivity. When clinicians have preformed opinions on what research outcomes should be, it is difficult to keep bias from entering into the statement of research questions, designs, and interpretation of results.

Sixth, give research a priority among other, time-consuming activities, such as health fairs, National Nutrition Month projects, open houses, outreach programs, and dietetic association committees. The frustration of being pulled in so many directions can be reduced when the staff, with the leadership of the clinical dietetic manager, set priorities in the department. Through such discussions, commitment to research can be viewed in context with other departmental demands and realistic activity goals can be established.

Developing Research Projects

Exhibit 18-1 provides guidelines for assisting clinical dietetians to develop research projects. Clinical dietitians may either assume roles as principal

---

Exhibit 18-1 Clinical Nutrition Problems: Developing a Research Project

---

SELECT A CLINICAL PROBLEM

What hypothesis or research question can you ask about this problem?

DEVELOP HYPOTHESIS ON RESEARCH QUESTION

Is it a testable question?

1) Ethical consideration
2) Potential confounding variables

DESIGN STUDY OR EXPERIMENT

Does it accomplish your purpose?

1) Provide answers to your research question
2) Control variance

Exhibit 18-1 continued

PLAN STATISTICAL EVALUATION

How can you select the best statistical test for your question and design?

1) Sample size and selection procedures
2) Adequacy of measurement—validity and reliability
3) Selecting appropriate tests for design

DEVELOP PROTOCOL FOR DATA COLLECTION

Who, what, when and where will data be collected?

1) Potential error or bias
2) Completeness of data set (how will you handle missing data?)

DEVELOP PROTOCOL FOR DATA EVALUATION

How do you plan to process your data?

1) Data tabulation
   a) by hand
   b) computerized
2) Overview of tabulated data
   a) distribution curve
   b) assumptions required for some statistical tests
3) Statistic evaluation
   a) hand calculation
   b) computerized using standard statistical packages
   c) other

Source: Courtesy of Judith Wylie-Rosett, Albert Einstein Medical Center, Bronx, N.Y.

investigators for independent research studies or they may engage in collaborative studies. There are several models for collaborative associations. In some of the more common models, nutrition care dietitians or managers link with dietitians in the same institution, dietitians at other health care institutions, educators at academic institutions, and physicians or other multidisciplinary team members at the same institution. Most collaborative researchers join a team and stay with that group, rather than moving from one team to another or claiming to be a committed member of several groups.

There are both benefits and disadvantages of working with a collaborative research group. Among the benefits are

• complementary skills of team members
• broad-based expertise regarding a subject
• shared labor
• mutual encouragement and group motivation
• access to larger data pool
• expanded resources (Lenz 1987)

Collaborative work also has its drawbacks. Sometimes, group members fail to deliver their allotted work to the project on schedule. Disagreements may occur regarding the study design, requiring conflict resolution. Group meetings are time consuming, as more effort is needed to ensure that everybody is informed adequately about the progress of each component of the study. Mutual compatibility may be a problem in long-term studies or established research teams. Ownership of data or research reports (articles, presentations) may cause disharmony or tension in the group. However, many of these problems can be avoided by clear understandings at the outset regarding division of labor, authorships, time frames, and mutual expectations (Bergstrom et al 1984; Lenz 1987).

Managing Departmental Research

How does one find time to balance both patient care responsibilities and clinical research? The first step is to determine how much time one *ought* to spend on research. Schiller (1988) suggested that practitioners might begin by devoting a minimum of 4 hours per week to research, depending on the nature of the study. This figure gives a reasonable target for goal setting and personal time assessments. The clinical dietetic manager can hold dietitians accountable for research time and productivity.

Major teaching hospitals are most likely to have departmental philosophies and resources that support the conduct of scientific investigations. In these instances, research studies generally center around a focused research topic.

For example, one group of nurses selected patient problems with tubefeedings as their research topic. The research team, working at hospitals located in different geographic areas, met only two or three times each year to formulate new questions and assign research responsibilites. Over a period of 5 years the group published 29 articles and presented numerous papers related to their subject (Bergstrom et al. 1984).

Clustering research projects around a single topic area is a complex strategy, but very effective. Guidelines on the development, maintenance, coordination, and enhancement of such research groups have been published (Lenz 1987).

One decision facing clinical nutrition managers is whether to designate a research position in the department. Duties associated with such positions might include planning and writing grant proposals; implementing and reporting original research; coordinating collaborative research efforts of other dietitians; serving as a consultant for research design, data collection, statistics, or dissemination; and spearheading efforts to utilize research in the practice setting (Chance and Hinshaw 1980). The clinical dietetic specialist sometimes assumes major research responsibilities; others may play important roles, depending on how dietitians work with team members who initiate projects.

Making Research Cost Effective

Many dietitians claim that it is futile to attempt research initiatives in an extremely cost-sensitive health care environment. However, those cost constraints also make it essential to develop a sound research base for improved systems and modalities for quality care.

Managers must convince both clinical dietitians and administrators that departmental involvement in applied research is both essential and valuable. Cronewett (1987) suggested several ways by which managers can increase the cost effectiveness of research efforts.

- Give research assignments only to those who have the knowledge and experience to be effective and productive.
- Establish departmental research guidelines based on institutional policies and guidelines.
- Do not ask a new researcher to review research protocols for scientific merit; this causes much valuable time to be wasted in discussion, clarification, and negotiation.
- Define research expectations in written job descriptions; provide enough time to allow coordinating research projects.
- Protect the staff against spending time on poorly designed studies. Authorize only projects that ask pertinent questions and include sufficient subjects to predict relevant outcomes.
- Rather than paying large sums of money for outside research consultation or statistical services, consider hiring a research specialist to spearhead research efforts and provide research services within the department.

• If a position is created to develop research programs and obtain outside research support, take rigorous steps to ensure that the person employed can do the job well. The applicant chosen needs to have adequate research experience and publications necessary to secure external funding. Otherwise, large amounts of money will be spent on an unsuccessful research enterprise.

Managing Research Utilization

Every department, even the smallest, ought to aim toward changing practice to remain current with valid and reliable research findings. The first step requires continual scanning of the current literature. It is important for clinical dietitians to be familiar with pertinent research published in a variety of journals. Articles must be scrutinized to be certain that results are applicable for utilization in the clinical setting. Journal clubs can facilitate this activity.

Second, clinicians must determine whether the original study is consistent with the setting in which it is to be utilized and whether the findings provide a relevant basis for practice and are feasible in terms of a particular institution or agency. Not all research findings can be applied in every practice setting. An analysis to determine what is "good" for a specific department will help distinguish important from incidental research findings.

The third step entails integrating appropriate findings within the department. Impractical or inappropriate findings for a particular situation are disregarded. Applicable findings that merely add to the knowledge base may be presented at an inservice session. Findings that require action may necessitate a change in policies, standards of practice, or departmental procedures (Stetler and Marram, 1976).

TOPICS FOR CLINICAL RESEARCH

The ADA Council on Research defined five research focus areas unique to the profession and its future development:

1. cost-benefit data to document the cost of nutrition services relative to health, therapeutic, and financial benefits to target groups of clients in various settings
2. information regarding the public need for nutrition guidance in the appropriate selection of food
3. development of a research base to support the educational preparation and continuing competency of dietetic practitioners
4. creation of a data base to determine, obtain, and forecast information about the profession

5. improved understanding of processes for management and delivery of food and nutrition services (Wyse 1987)

Several publications in the nursing literature describe results of Delphi surveys to delineate clinical nursing research priorities (Brower and Crist 1985; Lewandowski and Kositsky 1983; Lindeman and Schantz 1982; Ventura and Waligora-Serafin 1980); Delphi studies to identify research topics require multiple rounds of input. In the first round each participant generates a list of important research topics. Results are collated and a second round is conducted to determine agreement with the comprehensive list of items. Results are again summarized and the list refined to clarify items and delete topics receiving little support. A third round is conducted to determine agreement with each item on the revised list. Items receiving strong support are designated as high priority research topics. Such studies are valuable because topics are generated by practicing professionals and because consensus opinions generally receive broad support within the field. Delphi studies could be conducted to develop a list of research priorities in clinical dietetics.

In the meantime studies can be done in clinical dietetics to answer such questions as the following:

• What are the effects of various nutrition modalities on patient comfort and prevention of complications?
• Does timing of nutritional supplement ingestion alter intakes of supplements or meals?
• Does frequency of dietetic team interaction with a patient alter food intake or patient satisfaction?
• Does long-term comprehensive diet counseling result in positive changes in knowledge, attitude, behavior, or outcome of patients?
• Does nutritional screening result in improved evaluation of nutritional status?
• Do certified dietetic specialists improve the quality of nutritional care and increase the dietitian's job satisfaction (Lewandowski and Kositsky 1983)?

A national Delphi study was conducted to identify nursing administration research priorities (Brown and Henry 1987). Among the research topics (translated into dietetic terms) identified were

• What are the philosophies, nutritional care models, and administrative behaviors used by dietitians in units that deliver high-quality care?

- What environmental, organizational, technological, and individual criteria are best used to evaluate the overall effectiveness of nutrition service units?
- What impact will the increase in outpatient services have on employment and management?
- How does patient education affect the quality of patient care, length of patient stay, need for health services, and health care costs?

RESEARCH RESOURCES

Several books, articles, and mongraphs are available to guide the research endeavors of both beginning and veteran researchers (see Suggested Readings).

Dietitians in clinical settings are encouraged to join forces with academicians in the research process. Educators have both research skills and interests that can be very beneficial in the clinical setting. Most educators are flattered to have a practitioner invite them to collaborate on research studies. Educators may focus their research on a single theme to gain recognition and expertise in a focused area of study.

Many hospitals employ statisticians who may be consulted on research design and data analysis. Some institutions also have data processors who enter raw data into the computer and run statistical tests for investigators.

Institutional research departments and committees can be invaluable resources for clinical dietetic managers. They can provide guidelines and funding information, assist in development of studies, administer research budgets, and offer secretarial support for grant proposals.

Human subjects review committees offer guidelines to protect both human and animal rights. It is important to work through these committees to ensure compliance with rules for expedited reviews, exemptions, and informed consent.

Much has been written about grantsmanship (Schiller 1986) and sources of funding for research in nutrition and dietetics (Crouch 1987). Research, however, can be conducted without the aid of outside funding. A lack of money should not be used as an excuse for ignoring research responsibilities.

RESEARCH ETHICS

Ethical dimensions of research concern the following:

- protection of subjects from pain, suffering, undue risk, unauthorized experimentation, or breach of confidentiality

* compliance with institutional review committes and policies for informed consent, privacy, and anonymity
* complete and accurate reporting and interpretation of methodologies, results, and statistical analysis
* acknowledgment of citations, findings, and the products of the works of others

The International Committee of Medical Journal Editors (1985) developed these guidelines for authors:

Each author shall have participated sufficiently in the work to take public responsibility for its content. This participation must include: (a) conception or design, or analysis or interpretation of data, or both; (b) drafting the article or revising it for critically important intellectual content; and (c) final approval of the version to be published. Participation solely in the collection of data does not justify authorship.

The guidelines also specify that those who give advice, collect data, or assist in pilot studies may be listed under "acknowledgments" in a category separate from authors. Such persons must have given their permission to be named. Sources of funding must also be acknowledged.

REFERENCES

Bergstrom, Nancy et al. 1984. Collaborative nursing research: Anatomy of a successful consortium. *Nurs. Res.* 33(1):20–25.

Brower, Terri H., and Mary Ann Crist. 1985. Research priorities in gerontologic nursing for long-term care. *J. Nurs. Scholarship* 7(1):22–27.

Brown, Barbara, and Beverly Henry. 1987. Nursing education administration, practice, and research. In *Health care administration: Principles and practices,* edited by Lawrence F. Wolper and Jesus H. Pena, 317–57. Gaithersburg, Md.: Aspen Publishers, Inc.

Chance, Helen C., and Ada Sue Hinshaw. 1980. Strategies for initiating a research program. *J. Nurs. Admin.* 10(3):32–39.

Charold, L. 1986. Nursing research: Sacred cow or fatted calf? *Holistic Nurs. Pract.* 1(1):8–20.

Cronewett, Linda R. 1987. Increasing the cost-effectiveness of research in clinical setting. *J. Nurs. Admin.* 17(5):4–5.

Crouch, Jean Baker. 1987. Grant support for clinical nutrition research. *Dietitians Nutr. Supp. Newsl.* 4(1):4,9.

Grady, Ann P. 1987. Research: Its role in enhancing the professional image. *Am. J. Occup. Ther.* 41(6):347–49.

Hendricks, Suzanne, and Marsha Sharp. 1987. Research as a priority for the dietetic profession. *J. Can. Dietet. Assoc.* 48(2):69–70.

Hinshaw, Ada Sue, and Carolyn H. Smeltzer. 1987. Research challenges and programs for practice settings. *J. Nurs. Admin.* 17(7,8):20–26.

International Committee of Medical Journal Editors. 1985. Guidelines on authorship. *Br. Med. J.* 291(6497):722.

Jones, Mary G., Judith L. Bonner, and Kathleen R. Stitt. 1986. Nutrition support service: Role of the clinical dietitian. *J. Am. Dietet. Assoc.* 86(1)68–71.

Lenz, Elizabeth R. 1987. Developing a focused research effort. *Nurs. Outlook* 35(2):60–64.

Lewandowski, Linda A., and Ann M. Kositsky. 1983. Research priorities for critical care nursing: A study by the American Association of Critical-Care Nurses. *Heart Lung* 12(1):35–44.

Lindeman, Carol A., and Donna Schantz. 1982. The research question *J. Nurs. Admin.* 12(1):6–10.

Oberst, Marilyn T. 1985. Integrating research and clinical practice roles. *Topics Clin. Nurs.* 7(2):45–53.

Rinke, Wolf J., and Michelle W. Berry. 1987. Integrating research into clinical practice: A model and call for action. *J. Am. Dietet. Assoc.* 87(2):159–61.

Rose, James. 1985. Research or practice. *J. Am. Dietet. Assoc.* 85(1):797.

Schiller, M. Rosita. 1986. Developing and writing project grant proposals. In *Communicating as Professionals*, edited by Ronni Chernoff, 15–21. Chicago: The American Dietetic Association.

———. 1988. Research activities and research skill needs of nutrition support dietitians. *J. Am. Dietet. Assoc.* 88(3):345–46.

Smitherman, Alice L, and Bonita W. Wyse. 1987. The backbone of our profession. *J. Am. Dietet. Assoc.* 87(10):1394–96.

Standards of practice for the profession of dietetics. 1985. *J. Am. Dietet. Assoc.* 85(6):723–26.

Stetler, Cheryl, and Gwen Marram. 1976. Evaluating research findings for applicability in practice. *Nurs. Outlook* 24(9):559–63.

Ventura, Marlene R., and Barbara Waligora-Serafin. 1980. Study priorities identified by nurses in mental health settings. *Int. J. Nurs. Stud.* 18(1):41–46.

Wyse, Bonita W. 1987. Your foundation and its support for research. *J. Am. Dietet. Assoc.* 87(1):90–91.

SUGGESTED READINGS

Broski, David C. 1980. *Self instructional modules. Area IV: Research.* Columbus, Ohio: School of Allied Medical Professions, The Ohio State University.

Feitelson, Marion. 1987. Integrating research into clinical dietetic practice. *Dietitians Nutr. Supp. Newsl.* 4(1):4.

Gordon, M. J. 1978. Research workbook: A guide for initial planning of clinical, social, and behavioral research projects. *J. Fam. Pract.* 7(1):95–110.

Hefferin, Elizabeth A., Jo Anne Horsley, and Marlene R. Ventura. 1982. Promoting research-based nursing: The nurse administrator's role. *J. Nurs. Admin.* 12(5):34–40.

Hulley, Stephen B., and Steven R. Cummings. 1988. *Designing clinical research.* Baltimore: Williams and Wilkins.

Krathwohl, D. R. 1977. *How to prepare a research proposal.* 2d ed. Syracuse, NY: Syracuse University.

Leedy, Paul D. 1980. *Practical research : Planning and design.* 2d ed. New York: Macmillan Publishing Co., Inc.

Levine, Robert, J. 1986. *Ethics and regulation of clinical research.* 2d ed. Baltimore and Munich: Urban and Schwarzenberg.

Lewis, Mary E., ed. 1987. Proceedings from the leading edge in nutrition education: Research enhancing practice. *J. Am. Dietet. Assoc.* 87(9): suppl.

Lindeman, Carol A. 1975. Delphi survey of priorities in clinical nursing research. *Nurs. Res.* 24(6):434–41.

Lindeman, Carol A., and Donna Schantz. 1982. The research question. *J. Nurs. Admin.* 12(1):6–10.

Monsen, Elaine. R., and Carrie L. Cheney. 1988. Research methods in nutrition and dietetics: Design, data analysis and presentation. *J. Am. Dietet. Assoc.* 88(9):1047–65.

Padilla, Geraldine V. 1979. Incorporating research in service setting. *J. Nurs. Admin.* 9(1):44–49.

Polit, D., and B. Hungler. 1987. *Nursing research: Principles and methods.* 3d ed. Philadelphia: J. B. Lippincott, Co.

Satter, Ellyn. 1987. Relating research to practice. *Nutr. News* 50(1):1–4.

Schantz, Donna, and Carol A. Lindeman. 1982a. Reading a research article. *J. Nurs. Admin.* 12(3): 30–33.

Schantz, Donna, and Carol A. Lindeman. 1982b. The research design. *J. Nurs. Admin.* 12(2):35–38.

Schiller, M. Rosita, and Maureen Geraghty. 1987. Dietitians' involvement in research and publication. *J. Am. Dietet. Assoc.* 87(12):1709.

Schiller, M. Rosita. 1988. Research activities and interests of dietitians. *JPEN* 12(1):1–7.

Twomey, Pat. 1981 *Getting started in clinical research.* Washington, D. C.: American Society for Parenteral and Enteral Nutrition.

Verhonick, Phyllis J., and Catherine C. Seaman. 1978. *Research methods for undergraduate students in nursing.* New York: Appleton-Century-Crofts.

Chapter 19

Responsibilities in Professional Education

Dietitians are involved in educating both dietetic students and other health professionals. Clinical education, team teaching, and collaboration between educators and practitioners help prepare students to become providers and leaders in the delivery of nutrition care.

COMPONENTS OF PROFESSIONAL EDUCATION

Professional education is the process by which knowledge, skills, and values are developed in order to become a qualified or more proficient dietetic professional. Its three components are preprofessional, collegial, and continuing education. A professional is committed to lifelong education and the future competence of the profession.

In allied health, as in other aspects of education, controversy exists on the distinction between education and training. Education is the process of developing knowledge, mind, and character. In contrast, training is instruction to become qualified or more competent in a specific area that involves "learning by doing." According to Ralph Waldo Emerson and John Dewey: "A thinking, balanced truly educated individual is one of action, a person growing through empirical experiences—not just storing facts but one acting on and with them to develop better processes to examine ideas and solve problems" (Canizaro 1986). Using this definition, education and training are not distinct, but simply range along a continuum of personal and professional development. Critical thinking skills are also inherent to education and training. Critical thinking is the ability to define and analyze problems, make inferences, and determine solutions with logic and creativity.

Today's clinical training programs combine the learning of factual information with the affective and psychomotor domains. Professional education in clinical nutrition primarily focuses on the training of future practitioners according to guidelines set by the American Dietetic Association. (Exhibit 19-1). It should provide experience in clinical dietetics, community nutrition, and food service systems management. The educational programs for dietitians are based on the Standards of Education (American Dietetic Association 1987), which provides a framework for academic and supervised practice settings and a peer review system. They must meet these five standards:

- program goals and objectives
- adequate organizational structure and resources

Exhibit 19-1 Dietetic Education Programs of the American Dietetic Association

Approved academic program that meets the knowledge requirements of the Standards of Education
    Four-year baccalaureate degree
    Plan V, formerly Plan IV
    Plan IV will be valid until 12/31/99

Programs that combine knowledge and performance requirements of the Standards of Education
    1. Technician 2-year associate degree
        Practice component—minimum of 450 hours
        Completion allows registration eligibility for DTR
    2. Coordinated program* at undergraduate or graduate levels
        Academic component—minimum of baccalaureate degree
        Practice component— > 900 hours of supervised practice

Supervised practice programs that meet performance requirements of the Standards of Education
    1. Dietetic internship*
        Follows completion of Plan IV/V and baccalaureate degree
        Full-time > 900 hours of supervised practice
    2. Approved preprofessional practice program (AP4)
        Follows completion of Plan IV/V and baccalaureate degree
        Full-time or part-time > 900 hours of supervised practice

Programs must comply with the Standards of Education in the *Accreditation/ Approval Manual for Dietetic Education Programs*. Approval includes a self-analysis process and peer review by the Council on Education's Division of Accreditation/ Approval.

*Accredited programs meet the above requirements plus they are required to have an on-site evaluation visit by a team of professional peers.

• curriculum design
• accountability to students
• evaluation

The development of collegial and continuing education is more institutionally based and under the purview of the program designers. Collegial education is characterized by shared responsibility and informal and formal instruction. Continuing education should be a synonym for self-styled life-long education; however, professional associations and certifying agencies often dictate minimum requirements.

Requirements to maintain professional certification are more flexible than preprofessional education standards. A dietitian may develop his or her own continuing education plan for maintaining certification. For example, a clinical dietetic manager may decide to initiate research activities in the department after establishing a learning plan. The annual plan may include formal continuing education (CE hours) from the *Journal of the American Dietetic Association,* attendance at symposia research lectures in the medical center, participation in a workshop, library reading, and self-directed learning on protocol development with a staff investigator.

Practice-oriented learning emphasizes basic, repetitive, and observable tasks. Since dietetic care has an essential performance aspect, the use of "experiential" applies to those activities assigned or performed outside the classroom. The term "supervised practice" refers to the involvement of students in dietetic practice experiences under the guidance and supervision of clinical preceptors. The supervised practice or preprofessional experience is completed in three ways: dietetic internship, coordinated program, and approved preprofessional practice program (AP4).

Every institution has its own unique resources for the provision of dietetic training. One institution may be the sponsor for an approved program, such as an AP4 or a dietetic technician program. The sponsoring site may also provide activities in a variety of settings that give baccalaureate students or those enrolled in clinical programs elsewhere a broad exposure to dietetic practice. For example, students or interns may be at the hospital for a brief exposure to pediatric services, metabolic research, a renal dialysis unit, or other specialized experiences.

A reciprocal sharing of responsibility can be instituted between health care and educational institutions. Both academic faculties and dietetic staffs can benefit from a collaboration involving practice-based research, mutual planning of learning activities, open discussion of problems and solutions, and recruitment of students to fill staff vacancies. Cooperating institutions benefit from having students as trainees, and dietetic staff members often enjoy the challenge of working with them. Also, many academic programs give courtesy faculty appointments to clinical dietitians, enhancing their professionalism and giving them access to numerous college/university benefits.

FRAMEWORK FOR CLINICAL INSTRUCTION

The clinical dietetic manager often serves as the departmental coordinator for the clinical instruction of preprofessional students. Affiliation agreements should be made between the university and the hospital, outlining the responsibilities of both parties. The clinical manager, as coordinator, usually arranges assignments and rotations, reviews assignments, observes and critiques performance, and evaluates the students.

Clinical instruction is essential to the emergence of a professional person. If only the acquisition of facts were necessary to enter dietetic practice, clinical education would be unnecessary. It expands theoretical concepts of dietetic practice. Practice-oriented situations allow the formation of sound judgment and accountability for the demonstration of professional skills. Clinical education enables students to:

- develop and defend their positions on patient care
- select and apply appropriate intervention strategies
- confront ethical decision making
- make choices on alternative therapies based on costs and benefits
- clarify attitudes and values based on professional performance

Students develop preprofessional attitudes by observing dietitians perform their responsibilities, especially making decisions and seeing how the results of these decisions affect patient care.

Practice theory is introduced in the academic setting, but is developed more fully in the clinical program. A clinical learning environment allows students to see the complex interrelationships of patient problems, alternate approaches to intervention, and institutional operations. Sometimes referred to as reality-based education, clinical students learn their responsibility as professionals to individual patients or clients, to a code of ethics, and to society.

Several skills can be enhanced in the clinical environment. Technical skills—applying assessment, evaluative, and treatment techniques to achieve the desired results—are learned in the clinical setting. Doing diet calculations is one example of a technical skill. The application of appropriate techniques requires effective management of oneself, patient care, time, and other resources.

Interpersonal relations and communication skills are strengthened in clinical programs. Interactions occur with a wide range of people, including patients and their families, other health professionals, dietetic support staff, business personnel, administrators, visitors, and students. In addition to informal conversation and listening techniques, three other important communication skills are interviewing, information giving, and counseling.

Teaching, managerial, and research skills are also emphasized in clinical training. Students have various opportunities to teach food service classes, nursing and medical students, and patient seminars while learning various approaches to use with each group. Managerial expertise is observed by watching staff manage resources and time as students improve their abilities to organize and implement workable solutions. Research skills are developed through participation in clinical trials, scientific studies, and audits or formulating a project and then collecting and analyzing data.

Close supervision in clinical education provides an opportunity for students to develop a professional philosophy and expand abilities from previous learning.

TEACHING RESPONSIBILITIES

The teaching role of clinical dietetic managers and clinical dietitians requires managing resources of the learning environment, planning established learning objectives, and ensuring the appropriate continuity, integration, and sequencing of learning activities. The learning resources must be organized, beginning with basic patient care and progressing to complex cases and specialty practice. Controls must be in place to determine whether the students are successful in meeting objectives. Students in the clinical setting must have knowledge of what is expected of them and should learn to establish priorities of care (Huyck 1986).

In several practice programs students develop their own personal goals during their experiences. The clinical dietetic manager and preceptors should encourage students to share ideas, thoughts, values, and perceptions and to exercise self-direction. As the student progresses through the program, transfer of information and clinical reasoning should be observed and fostered.

Planning a supervised practice program takes considerable preparation. Any approved program requires a self-study, which takes 1 to 2 years to complete. An initial step, before preparing a self-study, is to secure support from the facility's administration. The program designer should also meet with the dietetic staff who will work with the program and who can contribute vital information for the proposal. Assistance of a consultant may be sought to provide guidance for doing the self-study. A comprehensive and persuasive document should be presented as a request for proposal (RFP) to the administration. The RFP should include the following:

- a needs assessment of the department
- estimated costs of the program
- tangible/intangible benefits of the program
- program rationale
- impact on patient care
- productivity analysis

The contributions of practicing dietitians who serve as coordinators and instructors are a major resource for any progressive teaching program. Dietitians who plan practicums must have these basic qualifications:

- commitment to the profession and to teaching others
- the ability to adopt the administrative framework of an institution
- flexibility in using professional and managerial skills
- knowledge that can be used to formulate major goals and performance objectives
- willingness to share knowledge, keep current, and inspire others
- skills to develop evaluation tools and encourage self-evaluation for students and staff
- ability to motivate staff and achieve administrative support (Schiller 1974)

When students learn in a practical setting, the dietetic staff and related professionals become both practitioners and teachers. They teach by presenting information, planning and guiding activities for students, and acting as role models to exemplify the skills to be learned. Usually all three methods are used in a practical teaching/learning setting.

With the cost-containment initiatives in health care today, some practitioners find it difficult to manage student learning and the performance of other responsibilities at the same time. One method of alleviating the teaching burden is team management of patient care (Wagstaff 1989). Three students work together in handling one patient with a team leader; one collects information and one observes and assesses the actions of the other two. This method has been effective in nursing education. In a pilot study in dietetics, teams were shown to decrease student-related staff time by one-half without sacrificing the quality of the learning experience (Wagstaff 1989).

The basis for a supervised practice program is a set of performance requirements that state the tasks and roles for practicing dietetics (American Dietitic Association 1987). Competency is defined as the minimum knowledge, skills, behavior, and judgment deemed essential for a professional person to function adequately in a specified position. For example, a competency in the area of nutrition care may be "develops a nutritional care plan for individual clients/patients." Competency also indicates a level of expertness and completeness: "develops a nutrition care plan for individual clients/patients which specifies short-term goals (e.g., food pattern based on diet prescription) and long-term goals, (e.g., eating behavior change based on counseling plans)."

ASSESSMENT OF PERFORMANCE

Assessment is a multidimensional process of judging the behavior and actions of individuals (Loacker et al. 1986). The dietetic preceptor should assess the extent to which the student can perform the behavior; that is, evaluate the accomplishment of the objectives of the learning experience. Assessment is an ongoing process; written evaluations should document the ongoing feedback.

Assessment of performance has two phases: the first involves the staff preceptors (teachers), and the second involves both the staff and student. The first phase provides the basis for the program, stating the minimum level that all students will achieve. The second phase allows for adaptation to individual student needs.

Program-Level Assessment

Program assessment has three major parts: setting performance statements, planning and implementing which activities accomplish which statements, and developing evaluation tools.

The performance statements in the Standards of Education, the Role Delineation Study, and the roles for dietetic practice in the institution, are used to determine the minimum capability (competence) that one would accept from a beginning practitioner. The statements should reflect essential components necessary for performing the position.

The next step is to determine which activities would facilitate learning these competencies at an acceptable level. The competencies are used to determine the program goals and learning objectives. In turn, the learning objectives and goals help determine the content, methods, and tools needed for the students to acquire and apply the skills. They should be stated in assessment and behavioral terms that

- identify the purpose of the learning experiences
- explain the behavior(s) for the teacher and the learner
- demonstrate the behavior(s)
- give the student the opportunity to practice the behavior
- present varied examples of the behavior(s) by the teacher and the student
- give feedback to the student on the performance of the behavior(s)

A rating system should assess student performance based on expected levels, that is, "performance appropriate for this point in the program." During a 900-hour program, student performance should not remain the same; what is considered satisfactory performance during the first month may only be considered marginal during the fourth month. Suggested levels of skill development are imitating, patterning, mastering, applying, and improvising.

Student-Level Assessment

Student evaluation has two primary purposes. Formative evaluation, occurring at designated points during the experience, provides continuing guidance in teaching and learning. Summative evaluation provides a basis for making a comprehensive judgment regarding the student's minimum competence at the end of an experience. Exhibit 19-2 gives an example of a summative evaluation form. A formative evaluation for individual rotations is provided in Exhibit 19-3.

Student performance is evaluated against a specific set of criteria or rating tools that assess how well the planned activities were accomplished. Performance criteria are standards external to the object of judgment (Loacker et al 1986) and can be applied easily, such as, "Follows the diet manual in planning nutrition intervention." Other criteria require more subjectivity, such as, "Exhibits appropriate use of patient instruction materials." Repeated samplings of performance provide a good composite picture of student abilities.

The role of assessment in a clinical setting is critical. Does it provide an opportunity to improve "now"? Is it based on problem solving and not on recall of "facts"? Does it indicate that the learning can be transferred to another situation? The more data used in assessment and the more evaluation, the more objective the judgment is. The evaluation is the basis for an action plan of additional activities to help the student meet the objectives and

Exhibit 19-2 Summative Evaluation for Students in Practice Programs

EVALUATION OF STUDENT IN _____
ROTATION/CLINICAL/COMMUNITY/MANAGEMENT

Evaluation Criteria	Pts Possible	NA Pts	Pts Earned	Comments
1. Assures that food service operations meet the food and nutrition needs of clients served and target markets.	5			
2. Utilizes food, nutrition, and social services in community programs.	5			
3. Provides nutritional care through systematic assessment planning, intervention, and evaluation for individuals and groups.	5			
4. Provides nutrition counseling and education to individuals and groups for health promotion, health maintenance, and rehabilitation.	5			
5. Applies current research information and methods to dietetic practice.	5			
6. Utilizes computer and other technology in the practice of dietetics.	5			
7. Integrates food and nutrition services in the health care delivery system.	5			
8. Promotes positive relationships with others who impact on dietetic service.	5			
9. Coordinates nutrition care with food service system.	5			
10. Participates in the management of cost-effective nutritional care systems.	5			
11. Utilizes menu as the focal point for control of the food service system.	5			
12. Participates in the management of food service systems, including procurement, food production, distribution, and service.	5			
13. Participates in the management of human, financial, material, physical, and operational resources.	5			

Exhibit 19-2 continued

Evaluation Criteria	Pts Possible	NA Pts	Pts Earned	Comments
14. Participates in the management of a Quality Assurance (QA) Program.	5			
15. Provides education and training to other professionals and supportive personnel.	5			
16. Engages in activities that promote improved nutrition status of the public and advance the profession of dietetics.	5			
17. Recognizes the impact of political, legislative, and economic factors on dietetic practice.	5			
18. Complies with the Standards of Professional Responsibility and Standards of Practice for the Profession of Dietetics.	5			
19. Utilizes effective communication skills in the practice of dietetics.	5			
20. Engages in a program of self-development and continuing education.	5			

Rating Scale: 2 = Unacceptable   3 = Needs Improvement   4 = Competent
5 = Exceptional   NA = Not Applicable to Rotation

Final Percentage Score = Points Earned divided by (100 − NA Pts) x 100

Note: Evaluation criteria are the performance requirements for entry-level dietitians (American Dietetic Association 1987).

Source: Courtesy of University of Utah, Division of Foods and Nutrition, Salt Lake City, Utah.

Exhibit 19-3 Formative Evaluation

EVALUATION OF ROTATION

What is your evaluation of your learning experience in this rotation? Check the appropriate column in each category and make comments.

Criteria	Exc*	Good	Sat*	Poor	Comments
1. *Objectives:* a. Clear					
b. Achievable					

2. *Learning Experiences*
  from:
  a. Objectives					

b. Literature					

c. Medical/
    management team/
    program staff					

d. Preceptor					

3. *Communication*
  between:
  a. Student and
    preceptor					

b. Student and staff					
c. Student and client					

What additional comments do you have?

_____

_____

_____

SIGNATURE AND DATE:

Dietetic student: _____ Date: _____

Preceptor: _____ Date: _____

  *Exc = excellent; Sat = satisfactory.

  Source: Courtesy of Judy Roundtree-Benedict, Internship Director, VA Medical Center, Salt Lake City, Utah.

---

performance outcomes desired. Such an action plan can incorporate activities into future rotations or extend the rotation time to allow the student to improve performance.

A student self-analysis provides a picture of the students' own view of their performance, achievement of competence, and areas needing improvement. This evaluation should also focus on strong and weak points and potential areas of improvement.

TEACHING OTHER HEALTH PROFESSIONALS

The educational role of clinical dietetic managers may be exercised in staff development and training other health professionals. Teaching strategies are similar for conducting continuing education for colleagues and other professional staff. Planning, instruction, and evaluation procedures are necessary for successful programs. The content and methods of teaching are similar, with information well-organized and specific to the audience. Colleagues usually want learning experiences to be meaningful, interesting, immediately practical, and with clear expectations of what is necessary for them to accomplish learning. Informal teaching may focus on guidance for selected procedures, introduction of new techniques, application of pertinent research, peer coaching, and mentoring.

Mentoring is particularly helpful for developing the skills of new staff members. It has been defined as "a set of behaviors applied to a relationship that provides guidance and support in career development" (Bunjes and Canter 1988). Mentoring seems to have as much value to the mentors as it does to the new staff members, providing both career opportunities and psychosocial rewards.

One extension of mentoring has been the establishment of residency and fellowship programs for registered dietitians seeking additional training. Teaching hospitals and medical centers have developed postregistration training in selected specialities, most commonly in nutrition support, pediatrics, and developmental disabilities. Dietetic educators and practitioners have also established professional development programs for educators to re-enter the practice arena and become familiar with changes in dietetic practice.

REFERENCES

American Dietetic Association. 1987. *Accreditation/approval manual for dietetic education program.* Chicago: American Dietetic Association.

Bunjes, Malinder, and Deborah D. Canter. 1988. Mentoring: Implications for career development. *J. Am. Dietet. Assoc.* 88(6):705-07.

Canizaro, Vincent J., Jr. 1986. Education represents learning by doing. *Am. Med. Writers Assoc. J.* 1(1):15–18.

Huyck, Norma. 1986. Teaching dietetic students in the clinical setting. *J. Am. Dietet. Assoc.* 86(2):234–36.

Loacker, Georgine, Lucy Cromwell, and Kathleen O'Brien. 1986. Assessment in higher education to serve the learner. In *Assessment in American higher education: Issues and contexts,* edited by C. Adelman. Washington, D.C.: Office of Educational Research and Improvement, U.S. Department of Education.

Schiller, Rosita M. 1974. Exploring the feasibility and planning traineeship in Michigan. *J. Am. Dietet. Assoc.* 62(4):512.

Wagstaff, Margene A. 1989. The team concept in supervised practice: Benefits for students and preceptors. *J. Am. Dietet. Assoc.* 89(1):78–81.

SUGGESTED READINGS

Doherty, Austin, Marcia M. Mentkowski, and Kelly Conrad. 1978. *New directions for experimental learning.* San Francisco: Jossey-Bass, Inc.

Kane, Michael, et al. 1990. Role delineation for dietetic practitioners: Empirical results. *J. Am. Dietet. Assoc.* 90:1124–33.

Oliver, Richard. 1986. Legal liability of students and residents in the health care setting. *J. Med. Educ.* 61(7):560–68.

Vickery, Connie E. 1989. Formative course evaluation: A positive student and faculty experience. *J. Am. Dietet. Assoc.* 89(2):259–60.

Chapter 20

Evaluating Clinical Nutrition Services

Although clinical dietetic managers continuously monitor activities of their staffs, occasionally they need to conduct an in-depth review and evaluation of programs and services. This chapter offers a conceptual framework to illustrate the relationship among monitoring, departmental evaluation, quality assurance, and administrative control. Guidelines are given for both the development of evaluation tools and the implementation of a departmental evaluation.

DEFINITIONS

Several concepts associated with evaluation seem to have similar meanings. To avoid confusion the meaning of these is clarified below.

- To conduct an *assessment* is to determine the status quo or appraise the current situation. In management, feasibility studies and market research are often used to assess the demand for certain programs, such as modified diet cooking classes. An assessment often precedes development of a business or marketing plan for new services.

- An *audit* is a formal examination of events to verify the accuracy of a report or classify information for detailed analysis. The *management audit* is a technique used for departmental evaluation or a formal review of management functions.

- *Control* is a major function of management and is a corollary to planning as described in Chapter 1. The control function typically encompasses development of plans, measurement of results, determination and explanation of degrees of success, and recommendations for appropriate action in view of the variance between predetermined objectives and actual results (Levey and Loomba 1984).

307

- *Evaluation* is the systematic use of organized data to make judgments. The process consists of obtaining and interpreting information; it is a tool for examining critical issues and making better decisions (Clemenhagan and Champagne 1986). In nutrition services, evaluation may be defined generally as a set of procedures to appraise the overall merit of programs and to provide information about goals, activities, services, outcomes, impact, and justification of costs.
- *Management review* is a structured process to access compliance with established standards and norms. The American Hospital Association offers a management review program for food service departments (1988).
- To *monitor* is to keep a watchful eye on designated key indicators that have a marked impact on overall performance. Monitoring is a continuous process of data gathering (Donabedian 1988). It provides ongoing information and allows disciplined adjustments to ensure compliance with standards or ultimate goal achievement. Monitoring is an essential component of control because it helps identify deviations before the situation gets out of control. Immediate steps can be taken to bring activities in line with desired outcomes. For example, quality monitors mandated by the Joint Commission ensure the sustained delivery of high-quality of care.
- *Program evaluation* can be applied to any hospital service, activity, or intervention that has objectives, resources, services, and effects (Clemenhagen and Champagne 1986). As such, they lend themselves to evaluative scrutiny as a ''program.''

ESSENCE OF EVALUATION

Evaluation is the beginning and the end of a manager's job. Only through rigorous assessment, innovative planning, and thorough evaluation can nutrition services move from the back seat of crisis care to the forefront of comprehensive health care. The central thrust of evaluation is not so much to look back, but to look around and to look ahead.

Inquiry (looking and asking) is at the heart of evaluation. Commitment to evaluation prompts the manager to ask the right questions of the right people (Bennett 1987). Doing so requires critical thinking, as well as fortitude and courage. The questions may be hard and the answers not always pleasing. Inquiry may reveal deep-seated problems that need to be addressed. If one listens closely, the answers often call for major changes in operations or programs, perhaps involving great risk to the operation of present systems.

The full power of evaluation is released only when results are analyzed and used to forge change. Allied Stores Corporation reinforces this point on its company letterhead:

> To *look* is one thing.
> To *see* what you look at is another.
> To *understand* what you see is a third.
> To *learn* from what you understand is still something else.
> But to *act* on what you learn is all that really matters (Bennett 1987).

The value of evaluation, then, is the key role it plays in shaping the future. Without honest and thorough evaluation, stagnation sets in. Only through evaluation can a unit move from ordinary performance and perhaps inadequate services to extraordinary performance and outstanding achievements. For those already at the leading edge, evaluation can fuel staff enthusiasm and intensify the quest for excellence.

Benefits

The energizing quest for information and the stimulation of pursuing intellectual curiosity often bring personal satisfaction to those who engage in evaluation. However, the organizational benefits of evaluation result primarily from changes brought about by program assessment or a management audit. These benefits may be either (1) measurable and open to quantification, or (2) intangible and unmeasurable but still enhancing enthusiasm, morale, and commitment (Bennett 1987).

Some measurable benefits of evaluation cited by Bennett include

- dollar savings
- better utilization of labor and other resources
- improved productivity
- quality enhancement
- increasing innovation
- greater operational efficiency
- improved communication and coordination
- supervisory and professional skill building
- greater staff participation
- successful cost-containment efforts
- more problems solved, and at the right level

Intangible benefits of evaluation include (Bennett 1987):

• stimulation of departmental improvement activities
• enhanced care and delivery of services
• better utilization of human talents and skills
• improved employee morale and job satisfaction
• positive channeling of creative energies and fuller accommodation of creative people

In addition to these generic benefits, evaluation can benefit nutrition service units in some specific ways, such as

• expanded level of activity for professional staff
• greater response to institutional or community needs
• improved role differentiation for professional and support personnel
• revenue generation and contributions to improved financial status of the institution
• contributions to the educational and research missions of the institution or the dietetic profession
• improved image for the profession, as well as for individual dietitians

EVALUATION AND PLANNING

The relationship between the food service department and nutrition services must be clarified before responsibilities for evaluation and control can be established. Throughout this book the authors have asserted that every aspect of nutrition for optimal health is within the purview of the clinical dietetic manager. Thus, even when nutrition services are organizationally subsumed under the food service department, the clinical dietetic manager should have full authority for the planning, implementation, and evaluation of programs and activities associated with its delivery. Therefore, the clinical dietetic manager provides leadership for nutrition services sponsored by the institution. The clinical dietetic manager works closely with the director of food services and other department heads to ensure the integration of nutrition objectives with the overall goals of the department and the institution as a whole.

Evaluation begins with program planning. The model shown in Figure 20-1 illustrates that evaluation can easily be applied to all programs and activities in the department. All facets of departmental operation (problems, objectives, resources, services, impact) come under managerial influence—

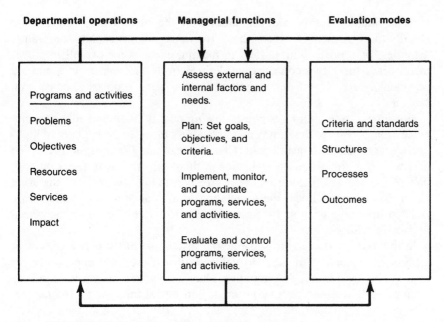

Figure 20-1 Model for Evaluation of Departmental Operations

assessment, planning, implementation, coordination, evaluation, and control—shown as influencing both departmental operations and evaluation modes. Each dimension of departmental operation can furthermore be evaluated using criteria to examine structures, processes or outcomes. Evaluation, in turn, affects managerial functions.

In a managerial capacity, the clinical dietetic manager interprets both the external and organizational environment, asserts a vision, and formulates goals that, when achieved, will bring the vision to reality. With involvement of dietetic personnel, objectives are delineated and performance criteria established. Both continuing activities and new programs are monitored during implementation and modified as necessary to meet established goals, norms, and standards. The process leads to a formal evaluation using specified criteria that may address structures, processes or outcomes. Finally, the cycle begins again when evaluation results are used to determine the need for program changes or new goals and objectives.

EVALUATION AND QUALITY ASSURANCE

Quality assurance has traditionally referred to medical audits using objective criteria to measure either the processes or outcomes of care for specific clinical situations. Program evaluation, on the other hand, refers more broadly to assessments used as a basis for value judgments about programs, activities, or services with a view to making changes for overall improvement. Since these two concepts are derived from different sources and are commonly used for different purposes, they are ordinarily considered separately.

However, some authors suggest viewing quality assurance and program evaluation as parts of the same entity to address the ultimate concern of high-quality, cost-effective health care (Clemenhagan and Champagne 1986). To deal with one dimension of evaluation without the other is to focus on only half of the clinical dietetic manager's responsibility. Because of the Joint Commission's guidelines, the temptation is to evaluate direct patient care isolated from organizational structures and processes that have a pronounced impact on quality care.

In this text we decided to separate the discussion of these two important aspects of evaluation in order to delineate procedures and approaches for both quality assurance and program evaluation, without confusing either by attempting to integrate both into a single conceptual framework. In practice, both quality assurance and program evaluation can merge and coincide with the management control function.

EVALUATION PROCESS

The steps in departmental or program evaluation are similar to those used in quality assurance (Exhibit 20-1). Before the process can begin structural or

---

Exhibit 20-1 Steps in Nutrition Services Evaluation

1. Affirm or establish structural components for a model nutrition service unit (see Exhibit 20-2).
2. Set goals and objectives congruent with departmental or institutional missions, goals, and objectives.
3. Establish measures of performance and monitoring markers for each of the structural components and/or objectives.
4. Plan new programs or operational changes as appropriate.
5. Implement new programs or changes in procedures as planned.
6. Monitor activities; adjust procedures as needed.
7. Develop evaluation tools and use to collect data consistent with established measures of performance.
8. Analyze and interpret results.
9. Determine and explain the degree of success.
10. Recommend appropriate actions in light of any variance between predetermined objectives or norms and actual results.

organizational standards must be developed. These standards should spell out specific criteria for nutrition services and may be derived from role delineation studies and recent research in the field.

If no recent evaluation of the overall clinical nutrition services has been conducted, it would be well to do one in addition to the annual evaluation of departmental goals, objectives, and activities. Nutrition service evaluations should be conducted as a part of departmental preparation for accreditation site visits.

Most clinical dietetic managers are accustomed to evaluating individual programs or services in the department, such as group classes, quality assurance programs, professional education, enteral feeding protocols, etc. The development of an integrated system of evaluation allows managers to target and review all activities formally within their scope of responsibility.

Evaluation may be undertaken for a variety of purposes (Rossi and Freeman 1982):

- to judge the value of ongoing activities and programs and to estimate the usefulness of attempts to improve them
- to assess the utility and feasibility of innovative programs and initiatives
- to increase the effectiveness of unit or program management and administration
- to meet various accountability requirements

Clinical dietetic managers need to conduct periodic reviews to assure quality performance, assess the outcomes of planned change, and to generate momentum toward improvements in the way things are done. A departmental evaluation, using a checklist similar to the one provided in Exhibit 20-2, will support and enhance the appraisal of nutrition services.

Exhibit 20-2 Criteria for a Model Nutrition Service Unit

	Yes	No	NA*
I. Structure			
A. A registered dietitian has authority over nutrition services	____	____	____
1. Written job description outlines management responsibilities	____	____	____
2. Qualifications include advanced education, clinical experience, and management training	____	____	____
3. RD devotes time to management responsibilities	____	____	____

Exhibit 20-2 continued

   B. Functions and objectives of nutrition services are outlined in writing . . . .   ____ ____ ____
      1. Mission is identified . . . .   ____ ____ ____
      2. Goals and objectives are reviewed periodically . . . .   ____ ____ ____
      3. Goals and objectives are integrated with departmental and institutional goals . . . .   ____ ____ ____
   C. Registered dietitians are employed to deliver nutrition services . . . .   ____ ____ ____
      1. Number is sufficient to provide optimal service . . . .   ____ ____ ____
      2. Education, competence, and skills are congruent with job expectations . . . .   ____ ____ ____
      3. Specialization is encouraged; certification is valued and pursued where appropriate . . . . .   ____ ____ ____
      4. Career, professional, and personal development are supported . . . .   ____ ____ ____
   D. Supportive personnel are employed to assist in delivery of nutrition services . . . .   ____ ____ ____
      1. Dietetic technicians assume responsibilities appropriate to their level of training . . . .   ____ ____ ____
      2. Supervisory personnel, clerks, and diet aides assist with clerical duties and patient services . . . .   ____ ____ ____
   E. Standards of Care
      1. Defined in writing . . . .   ____ ____ ____
      2. Individualized for major disease conditions seen in the institution . . . .   ____ ____ ____
   F. The Quality Assurance Program is effectively used for problem solving . . . .   ____ ____ ____
      1. Quality assurance criteria have been established for major aspects of care . . . .   ____ ____ ____
      2. A system of monitoring quality care has been established . . . .   ____ ____ ____
      3. Audits are regularly completed, including plans for follow-up and re-evaluation . . . . . .   ____ ____ ____
      4. All professional personnel are aware of quality assurance activities . . . .   ____ ____ ____
      5. Outcome indicators are monitored . . . .   ____ ____ ____
      6. All mixtures of volume, quality, and appropriateness indicators are monitored . . . .   ____ ____ ____
   G. Appropriate technology is used in the unit . . . . . .   ____ ____ ____
      1. Computers are available for menus, calorie counts, and other management activities . . .   ____ ____ ____
      2. Tools are available for nutritional assessment . . . .   ____ ____ ____
      3. Programmable calculators (hand-held) are available for use by dietitians . . . .   ____ ____ ____

Exhibit 20-2 continued

    4. Audiovisual equipment is available for
       teaching patients and professional groups .. ____ ____ ____
    5. System is established for review of tech-
       nology .... ____ ____ ____
H. Productivity standards are established .... ____ ____ ____
    1. Standards are congruent with patient mix
       and with job expectations .... ____ ____ ____
    2. Productivity is monitored and results used in
       administrative reports .... ____ ____ ____
I. The Nutrition Service unit is established as a cost
   center or evaluates self as a cost center .... ____ ____ ____
    1. A schedule of charges has been set for nutri-
       tion services, such as nutritional assess-
       ments, diet counseling, group classes,
       nutrient analysis .... ____ ____ ____
    2. Dietitians accept fiscal responsibility for nu-
       trition services .... ____ ____ ____
    3. Fiscal goals have been established for the
       Nutrition Services Unit .... ____ ____ ____
    4. Budgets are planned at least 1 year in ad-
       vance .... ____ ____ ____
J. A program of marketing is established to pro-
   mote both the professional staff and the services
   provided .... ____ ____ ____
K. Dietitians participate in research studies related
   to clinical nutrition and dietetics .... ____ ____ ____
L. Inservice and continuing education programs are
   provided .... ____ ____ ____
M. Clinical dietitians participate in institutional
   committees, including quality assurance, ethics,
   and patient care committees .... ____ ____ ____
N. There is an institutional nutrition committee .... ____ ____ ____
O. A policy on patient discharge planning is in ef-
   fect .... ____ ____ ____
P. Systems of evaluation and control have been established as a means of monitoring and achieving
   predetermined objectives .... ____ ____ ____
Q. Accountability of the Nutrition Services Unit has
   been established .... ____ ____ ____
    1. The clinical nutrition manager is account-
       able to a designated administrator .... ____ ____ ____
    2. Appropriate responsibilities have been del-
       egated to the clinical nutrition manager in-
       cluding
       • education of patients, students, and health
         care professionals .... ____ ____ ____
       • patient nutritional care .... ____ ____ ____
       • nutrition standards .... ____ ____ ____

Exhibit 20-2 continued

> - therapeutic diets ....   ____ ____ ____
> - marketing nutrition services ....   ____ ____ ____
> - clinical nutrition research ....   ____ ____ ____
> - evaluation of nutrition services ....   ____ ____ ____
> 3. Reporting mechanisms utilize input from the
>   nutrition services unit ....   ____ ____ ____
> R. There are effective communication channels and
>   systems for
>   1. Diet ordering and changes ....   ____ ____ ____
>   2. Medical record documentation ....   ____ ____ ____
>   3. Coordination and continuity of patient care ..   ____ ____ ____
>   4. Administrative reporting ....   ____ ____ ____
> S. Procedures are established for dietitian involve-
>   ment in
>   1. Planning therapeutic diets ....   ____ ____ ____
>   2. Cost-containment efforts ....   ____ ____ ____
>   3. Health care team activities ....   ____ ____ ____
>   4. Nutritional adequacy of menus ....   ____ ____ ____
>   5. Selection of special dietary products ......   ____ ____ ____
>   6. Selection of education materials ....   ____ ____ ____
>   7. Guidelines for preparing foods for modified
>   diets ....   ____ ____ ____
>   8. Guidelines for serving food ....   ____ ____ ____
>   9. Health care facility policies related to clini-
>   cal dietetic activities and personnel ....   ____ ____ ____
>   10. Policies and procedures for nutritional care
>   of individual patients ....   ____ ____ ____
> T. Dietitians set standards and procedures for pre-
>   paring enteral nutrient solutions and supplemen-
>   tal nutrient products for modified diets ....   ____ ____ ____
> U. Dietitians participate in parenteral and enteral
>   product selection ....   ____ ____ ____
> V. Effective procedures for outpatient referral are in
>   use ....   ____ ____ ____
> W. Clinical dietitians manage clinical dietetic sup-
>   port personnel
>   1. Develop and implement orientation and in-
>   service programs for clinical dietetic support
>   personnel ....   ____ ____ ____
>   2. Supervise clinical dietetic personnel ....   ____ ____ ____
>   3. Evaluate performance of clinical dietetic
>   personnel ....   ____ ____ ____
> X. Clinical dietitians integrate political, legal, and
>   fiscal factors into the nutritional care system ....   ____ ____ ____
> Y. Policies and procedures for sanitation and safety
>   are rigorously upheld in areas under the direction
>   of clinical dietitians ....   ____ ____ ____

Exhibit 20-2 continued

AA. Laws, standards, and regulations are observed carefully:
    1. Local laws, standards, regulations . . . .
    2. State laws, standards, regulations . . . .
    3. Federal laws, standards, regulations . . . . . .
BB. Each dietitian has a written plan to advance his or her competence as a practitioner; the plan is implemented and evaluated periodically . . . .
CC. There is a program of staff development
    1. For dietitians . . . .
    2. For dietetic technicians . . . .
DD. Nutrition education programs are available to meet the needs of target populations . . . .
EE. Nutrition education resources are available as appropriate for the scope of programs offered . . . . .
FF. Ongoing studies are conducted for effectiveness of nutritional care; results are shared for incorporation into Nutrition Services Payment Systems programs . . . .
GG. Professional resources are available for use by dietitians and clinical support personnel: continuing education, books, journals, reports, etc. . . . .
HH. A strategic plan has been developed to address future changes . . . .
II. Professional service is regularly given by
    1. Clinical dietetic manager . . . .
    2. Clinical dietetic specialist . . . .
    3. Clinical dietitians . . . .
    4. Dietetic dietitians . . . .
JJ. Hiring practices meet all codes and regulations . .

II. Process
A. There is a system of screening patients for nutritional risk . . . .
B. Patients with special nutritional needs are identified within the total client population . . . .
C. Nutritional assessments are conducted and results interpreted and documented for patients who meet predetermined screening criteria . . . .
D. Nutritional care plans are developed and documented as indicated in institutional policy . . . . . .
    1. Level of risk is identified . . . .
    2. Desired outcomes are identified . . . .
    3. Energy and nutrient needs are specified . . . .
    4. Feeding modalities are recommended . . . . .
    5. Food sources, special products, and nutrient solutions are determined . . . .

Exhibit 20-2 continued

6. Diet prescriptions are recommended for individual patients ....

7. Policies for follow-up care, including implementation and evaluation, are established ..

E. Clinical dietitians communicate nutrition care plans to
1. Patients and significant others ....
2. Health care team members ....
3. Clinical dietetic support personnel ....

F. Clinical dietitians document nutritional care of individuals ....

G. Clinical dietitians monitor nutritional care, evaluate its effectiveness for individual patients, and revise care plans as needed ....

H. Individual patients and their families/significant others receive individual and/or group diet counseling as appropriate ....

I. Individual patients and their families/significant others receive individual nutrition education opportunities ....

J. Group nutrition education is available through the nutrition services unit ....

K. Diet counseling and nutrition education for individual patients are documented ....

L. Follow-up and continuity of care are arranged through the Nutrition Services Unit ....

M. Diet counseling and nutrition education programs are offered on an outpatient basis ....

N. The Nutrition Services Unit offers a structured program of nutrition education for ....
1. Patients ....
2. Health care professionals ....
3. The general public ....

O. Patient counseling and education materials are reviewed annually for currency ....

P. Dietetic staff assignments and job responsibilities are based on levels of care within the institution

Q. Nutrition is integrated with the total health care process ....

R. Dietitians attend medical rounds, team conferences, and discharge planning meetings ....

S. The "Art of Dietetics" is regularly practiced by clinical dietetic personnel: amenities, confidentiality, attentiveness to patient rights, etc. ......

T. Codes of ethics are maintained ....

U. Patient satisfaction is included in routine evaluation studies of nutrition services ....

Exhibit 20-2 continued

	V.	Current research findings are applied to daily activities and incorporated into policies and procedures as appropriate	____	____	____
	W.	Each program within the department is subject to formal scrutiny, including its goals, activities, outcomes, impacts, and costs	____	____	____
III.		Outcomes			
	A.	Predetermined standards are maintained	____	____	____
	B.	The Nutrition Services Unit is in full compliance with local, state, and federal laws, standards, and regulations	____	____	____
	C.	Goals and objectives of the Nutrition Services Unit are achieved	____	____	____
	D.	Goals and objectives for individual patient nutritional care are achieved	____	____	____
	E.	Patient satisfaction is at an acceptable level	____	____	____
	F.	Costs and income are in line with predetermined figures	____	____	____
	G.	Job satisfaction is high	____	____	____
	H.	Clinical dietitians and support staff maintain expected levels of certification, competence, and continuing education	____	____	____
	I.	Accountability is maintained	____	____	____
	J.	Data are collected on outcomes of patient care, such as weight control attained and number of diet changes recommended/actualized	____	____	____
	K.	Patient outcomes are documented in the medical record	____	____	____
	L.	Research data are disseminated at professional meetings and/or published in professional journals	____	____	____

*Not Applicable

REFERENCES

American Society for Hospital Food Service Administrators of the American Hospital Association. 1988. *Hospital food service management review*. Chicago: American Hospital Association.

Bennett, Addison C. 1987. The imperative of assessment. *Health Care Sup.* 5(2):1–10.

Clemenhagen, Carol, and Francois Champagne. 1986. Quality assurance as part of program evaluation: Guidelines for managers and clinical department heads. *Qual. Rev. Bull.* 12(11):383–87.

Donabedian, Avedis. 1988. Monitoring: The eyes and ears of healthcare. *Health Prog.* 69(9):38–43.

Levey, Samuel, and N. Paul Loomba. 1984. *Health care administration: A managerial perspective.* Philadelphia: J. B. Lippincott, Co.

Rossi, Peter H., and Howard E. Freeman. 1982. *Evaluation: A systematic approach.* 2d ed. Beverly Hills: Sage Publications.

SUGGESTED READINGS

Allensworth, Diane, and Cynthia Luther. 1986. Evaluating printed materials. *Nurse Educ.* 11(2):18–22.

American Dietetic Association. 1984. *Role delineation and verification for entry level positions in clinical dietetics.* Chicago: American Dietetic Association.

American Dietetic Association. 1990. *Role delineation for registered dietitians and entry-level dietetic technicians.* Chicago: American Dietetic Association.

Elbeck, Matt. 1987. An approach to client satisfaction measurement as an attribute of health service quality. *Health Care Man. Rev.* 12(3):47–52.

McConnell, Charles R. 1988. *The effective health care supervisor.* 2d ed. Gaithersburg, Md.: Aspen Publishers, Inc.

Verhey, Shirley, and Beth Upton. 1988. Evaluation system assesses rehabilitation. *Health Prog.* 69(9):48–51.

Vuori, Hannu. 1987. Patient satisfaction—an attribute or indicator of the quality of care? *Qual. Rev. Bull.* 13(3):106–08.

Wakim, Judith. 1986. Developing evaluation tools. *Nurse Educator* 11(4):26–30.

Chapter 21

Moving toward the Future: Strategic Planning

In 1935 Charles Kettering said, "My interest is in the future because I shall spend the rest of my life there" (Cornish 1977). Planning for the future is a constant process. Strategic or future planning is based on the premise that, through deliberation and forecasting, the future can be molded. Planning encourages the monitoring of change, even gradual change, and assumes that even a wrong forecast is better than no forecast at all.

The process of strategic planning involves setting a realistic plan and monitoring progress toward predetermined goals. Strategic planning is done through systematic development of ideas that consider the past, present, and future. Forecasts are made through the analysis of trends and patterns, and using creative thinking. The forecast identifies possible goals. Finally a plan, including allocation of resources to achieve the goals, is established.

This chapter briefly reviews the history of dietetic practice, examines the current nutritional care environmental influences, and then identifies possible future directions for dietetics.

HISTORY OF DIETETIC PRACTICE

The dietetic practitioner reached professional stature with the emergence of scientific nutrition knowledge and development of a national organization in the early part of the twentieth century. The American Dietetic Association (ADA) was founded in 1917 to advance both the science of nutrition and the art of feeding people. From its inception, the ADA was concerned with the nutritional needs of individuals and how best to satisfy these needs through daily dietary practices (Barber 1959). It also served as a unifying body to clarify and affirm the purposes of dietitians (Hallahan 1974).

By 1936 the Bureau of Vocational Information had distinguished the classifications of administrative and therapeutic dietitians and listed responsibilities that conformed to standards established by the American College of Surgeons. The *Dictionary of Occupational Titles* listed increasingly specific definitions for "dietitian" with each edition. In the early editions of the dictionary from 1939 to 1949, a single general definition for dietitian was given. In the 1949 edition the definition read:

> Applies the principles of nutrition to the feeding of individuals and groups: plans menus and special diets with proper nutritional value for a hospital, institution, school, restaurant, or hotel. Determines dietetic value of food and food products. Purchases food, equipment, and supplies. Supervises chefs and other food service employees. Maintains sanitary conditions. Prepares educational nutrition materials (United States Department of Labor 1949, 202).

In the supplement to the second edition published 6 years later, classifications for therapeutic and administrative dietitians were differentiated. The 1977 edition of the *Dictionary of Occupational Titles* offered a greater number of definitions to reflect the expanded roles within the profession. Titles included "research," "chief," "community," "clinical," "consultant," and "teaching dietitians," as well as "dietetic intern" and "dietetic technician." These definitions clearly illustrate an interdependence among the roles, linking the various classifications of dietitians and emphasizing involvement on the health care team (United States Department of Labor 1977).

The 1988–89 edition of the *Dictionary of Occupational Titles* describes dietitians as professionals who counsel individuals and groups, establish and supervise food service systems in institutions, and promote sound eating habits through education and research. Specialty areas described are clinical and community dietetics, administration, and research. Clinical specialties are mentioned in eight areas: obesity, critical care, diabetes, kidney disease, cancer, heart disease, pediatrics, and gerontology. The role of the clinical dietetic manager is alluded to in one statement: "Aside from assessing nutritional needs and developing a plan of treatment for individual patients, clinical dietitians may also have administrative and managerial duties" (U.S. Department of Labor 1990, 150).

Practice reflects that component of a professional's activities seen as "obligation for service to the client" beyond just a job; professional practice is often viewed by society as service that overrides personal considerations. The Standards of Practice (1985) are statements of the dietetic practitioners' responsibilities for providing quality nutritional care. After 4 years of development they were approved in 1984 by the ADA House of Delegates to provide the individual practitioner with a systematic plan to implement, evaluate, and adjust performance in any area of practice. The standards include two on self-assessment, one to practice based on consumer needs and current knowledge and experience, and one to collaborate with others and communicate sound principles of nutritional care. Based on a need for continuing competence as a professional, another standard is lifelong self-development to improve knowledge and skills. A final standard is to generate, interpret, and use research to enhance dietetic practice. Continuing education should be goal-directed for each individual.

EVOLUTION OF HOSPITAL DIETETICS

In 1924 the American Hospital Association published a report stating that more than half of the hospitals surveyed admitted that their food services were not satisfactory. Concern for adequate, competent staffing was voiced by many hospital administrators, and systematic recruitment of dietitians was begun. As hospital administrations became aware that the area of food service, on which one third of its total budget was spent, deserved more recognition and support, the dietary department gained a place among the major services provided in the hospital (MacEachern 1949). As the science of nutrition developed into a field requiring technical and professional skills, hospital dietitians were hired as managers and assumed roles as directors of dietary departments. These dietitians were given authority over semiskilled and unskilled dietary workers. These departments encompassed an ever-increasing sphere of responsibilities (Burling, et al. 1959).

By the 1930s and 1940s, hospitals that had predominantly employed dietitians as nursing instructors or food service administrators began to employ clinical dietitians. In the 1950s, the role of clinical dietitians changed to have a greater emphasis on patient education, especially for clients with diabetes. Education and counseling were greatly enhanced by an important teaching tool, the 1950 American Diabetic Association Diabetes Exchange Lists. In the 1960s, other modified diets became popular, especially the low cholesterol diets and low protein renal diets.

Over the last 30 years, responsibilities of the clinical dietitian have evolved in response to new metabolic discoveries, tools for nutrition counseling, and greater use of diets as an adjunct to medical treatments. To be effective in this milieu, practitioners need to

- increase their breadth of knowledge
- increase their depth of knowledge
- focus on the needs of the client
- concentrate on both food and nutrients
- recommend new modes of feeding

- document in the medical record
- become team-centered

Clinical dietetic management developed in response to the need for effective administration of human potential and the material resources of nutrition care. Managerial skills were emphasized in the definition of dietetic practice in the conceptual framework for the profession. Parks and Kris-Etherton (1982) found the two most essential competencies for dietitians entering the profession in the 1980s were (1) an understanding of the management processes of planning, organizing, leading, evaluating, and controlling and (2) an understanding of the interrelationships among the management of human, material, and financial resources. Others advocated a need to improve managerial effectiveness and called for greater competency in management as an essential element for a strong dietetics profession (Hoover 1983). Katz and Kahn (1978, 187) observed that "technological advancements in management theory caused specialization of tasks, uniform role performance, standardized practice, and avoidance of duplicated functions." Some of these factors are evident in dietetics, which has recognized 24 special interest groups or dietetic practice groups since 1975.

Specialization of duties began to appear within the profession by 1971. In that year the ADA defined four specialty groups: the general practitioner, the administrator of dietetic services, the clinical nutrition specialist, and the nutrition educator. The Profession of Dietetics Report (American Dietetic Association 1972) postulated that the future of dietetic practice would be altered by increased differentiation in roles and functions, more specialization, new and additional competencies, increased delegation of tasks and duties to other less highly trained workers, and more practice in association with other professionals. Since the early 1970s a trend of specialization, delegation of duties, dietetic teamwork, and professional registration has indeed emerged and flourished.

The Council on Practice of the American Dietetic Association was established in 1977, and 12 dietetic practice groups were organized immediately. A practice group for clinical nutrition managers was not formalized until 1983 because there was a moratorium on new practice groups. Finally, with the support of over 50 petitions and the resolve to focus on reimbursement for clinical services and clinical productivity, the Council on Practice approved the formation of a dietetic practice group in Clinical Nutrition Management. From its first business meeting with 80 attendees, the practice group has grown to over 1400 members in 1990. According to its newsletter,

> The practice of Clinical Nutrition Management is founded on the skills of the clinical practitioner who has expanded into the field of

management while maintaining a clinical perspective. The unique position emphasizes legal, fiscal, and systems management of clinical nutrition services in a health care setting. The clinical nutrition practitioners are registered dietitians who vary in educational background, expertise, and depth of management application. All bring to their positions the desire to apply sound management principles to the clinical arena by effectively promoting programs, research, and quality assurance systems; developing policies and procedures related to clinical practice; developing methods of measuring standards of practice, productivity, and cost benefit of nutrition services; and pursuing issues related to third-party reimbursement. Effective intradepartmental communication and cooperation are emphasized as is cooperation with educational institutions dedicated to the broad training of dietitians through exposure to such areas of unique practice (Gobberdiel 1988).

In 1984, a study commission recommended that ADA broaden into new areas of practice, evaluate its educational preparation, advance education into specialty training, formally recognize specialities, conduct cost-benefit studies, utilize dietetic practice personnel more, and develop a realistic licensure act (ADA 1985). In terms of inpatient acute care, the Study Commission on Dietetics also recommended broad specialties as the starting point for recognition of advanced-level practitioners in clinical dietetics (ADA 1985).

In 1989 the ADA funded role studies to examine current dietetic practice from technical to advanced levels. Three specialties are under rigorous scrutiny: metabolic nutrition care, pediatrics, and renal nutrition. Disagreement surrounds the issue of whether the market demands a broad advanced-level professional or a clinical dietitian who practices in narrow specialties or even whether any formal specialties are needed in the profession. The involvement by dietitians in dietetic practice groups and specialty organizations such as the Council on Renal Nutrition, suggests that they have a sustained interest in specialty practice. The existence and need for clinical dietetic specialists must be assessed in the strategic plan developed by each clinical dietetic manager.

STRATEGIC PLANNING

Adequate preparation for the future of clinical dietetics requires strategic planning with input from all members of the professional staff. The plan is a process of evaluation that answers the following questions:

• Appraisal of the external environment: What factors are influencing health care delivery? What are the anticipated trends?

- Internal evaluation: What are the mission and philosophy of the organization? What is the dietetic staff doing currently? What are the goals of the institution and its employees?
- What alternatives are possible, including how are other departments handling the situation and adapting to environmental changes?
- What is the primary focus of the department, based on what it was, is now, and could become?
- What strategies can be adopted to accomplish the goals of the department, and what is the timeline?
- Finally, what is the employee level of commitment to the organization and the plan?

Environmental assessment addresses technological trends, demographic issues, and health care issues. Trends in technology affect dietetic practice. The ability to feed enterally or parenterally most individuals has resulted in many ethical dilemmas. Health care cost containment has shifted the emphasis from quality of care alone to cost evaluation in relation to outcomes. The increased number of aged are placing growing demands on the health care system. The decreasing number of young people suggests greater competition for recruits to the profession and shortages of both professional and support staff in the future.

Trend analysis also examines the potential result of insufficient clinical dietetic intervention. Will the result be

- regulatory noncompliance?
- disease acceleration?
- late identification of malnutrition?
- inability to assess intake?
- decreased chance of client lifestyle change?

The next question is "so what?" Will the lack of dietetic intervention jeopardize funding, accreditation, or the achievement of institutional goals? The more significant the impact of insufficient intervention, the more important the function.

In addition, mandates and recommendations from outside organizations should be reviewed. Do federal, state, or local regulations or private guidelines, such as those of the Joint Commission, govern care?

Techniques for Preparing a Strategic Plan

A number of techniques are appropriate for developing a strategic plan, including scenario generation, Delphi technique, and nominal group method.

Scenario generation is a trend analysis technique. Both the Delphi and nominal group techniques utilize a primary researcher or planner who drafts a basic questionnaire based on the purpose of the plan and the knowledge of internal and external factors influencing the group.

Scenario generation enables the analysis of the effect of competing trends. Rather than one forecast of future needs, two, three, or more alternative scenarios can be developed. For example, the trend under examination could be the effect of hiring (1) advanced-level clinical practitioners; (2) narrow specialists, such as in renal or nutrition support; or (3) no specialist at all. After an historical overview of clinical dietetic specialties and an analysis of trends in health care and credentialing, several scenarios would be developed, with emphasis on the opportunities and obstacles of each one. The particular scenario that the institution finds most reasonable and desirable is then selected. Scenarios focusing on trends in health care are particularly useful. What will the hospital of the future look like? Who will the patient population be? How will costs and reimbursement change? What will the major diagnoses of the next century be?

The Delphi process, a second useful technique for strategic planning, has four major components (see Figure 21-1):

1. Experts are questioned individually by a leader using a structured questionnaire.
2. A series of rounds occur with the collective answers shared and the questions repeated. The answers are generally subsumed under the major answers and mailed to the experts. All of the experts prioritize their answers, adjust their answers, and return the second round of information to the leader.
3. The leader of the group again decides what information to share with the experts and summarizes the next round of questions.
4. The process continues in rounds until consensus occurs.

An advantage of the Delphi technique is that each expert has an equal voice in the response to the questions; no individual overpowers or intimidates anyone. Unique creative ideas can be suggested without the fear of ridicule. The method can be used for the strategic plan of dietetic departments. One person serves as the leader, drafting the original document and coordinating the distribution and consolidation of comments until consensus is reached.

A third strategy is the nominal group method. In this method experts are brought together, rather than responding independently. Again, the goal is to obtain independent opinions. The experts are asked to present their ideas on a topic. The group continues around the circle until all ideas are stated. A

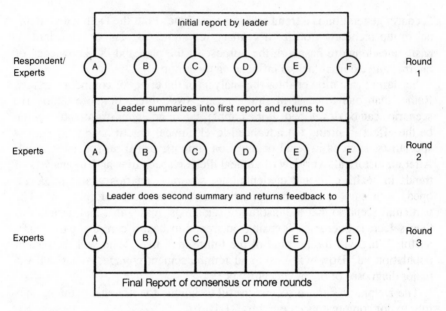

Figure 21-1 Helmer and Dalkey: Delphi Technique

---

composite list is then generated. Ideas are clarified, discussed, and then ranked by the individual members of the group. Discussion ensues until consensus is reached or deemed impossible (Fink et al. 1984).

ISSUES OF THE COMING DECADES IN DIETETICS

Exhibit 21-1 lists some anticipated shifts in dietetic practice in the next two decades.

Emergence of Advanced-Level Practice

One key factor in the future of dietetics is the emergence of advanced-level practice. A 1971 ADA position paper stated, "Career advancement will be to the level of the specialist through in-depth study leading to an advanced degree in a defined specialty area" (ADA 1971, 372). The ADA position paper defined the clinical nutrition specialist as follows:

A clinical nutrition specialist: (is) a person with expertise in nutritional treatment. One who can evaluate the nutritional status of a

Exhibit 21-1 Possible Trends Affecting Dietetics Practice in the 1990s and 2000s

NUTRIENTS

Emphasis on components of macronutrients
More precise information on micronutrients
Alternations in vitamin/mineral content of foods

EATING HABITS

More ethnic variations
Snacking replacing large meals
More pre-prepared meals
More healthy food choices

STANDARDS OF CARE

Defined by diagnosis and nutritional risk
Drug-nutrient interactions more complex
Diet manipulation for many disorders
Measurable outcomes of care
Documentation of the implementation and evaluation of care
Intervention standards
Routine use of enteral/parenteral feeding
Individualized counseling
Better referral mechanisms
Routine computer use for diagnosis, education, and management

RESPONSIBILITY

Diet prescription to be written by dietitians or specialists in certain settings
Increased legal responsibility
Active ethical role
Increased quantity and quality of research
Expanded titles within organizations
Reimbursement a reality

person, plan his nutritional care, and direct implementation of the plan. Such a specialist would work with other members of the health care team, but would accept responsibility for the diet prescription and the patient's nutritional care (ADA 1971, 372).

There are diverse opinions of what dietitians actually do and what they perceive as their desired role. Gaare et al. (1990) found that dietitians in nutrition support wanted more decision-making responsibility than they have and perceived themselves as having more responsibility than appropriated to them by physicians. Physicians were willing to have more dietitian input on diet prescriptions, but wanted the burden of responsibility to be their own. A study by Spangler (1974) found similar results: the physicians in Michigan perceived that they should be the prime decision makers, whereas the dietitians wanted more decision-making authority. Schiller and Vivian (1974) found that dietitians theoretically subscribed to high levels of decision making, but showed less consensus on assuming specific tasks. The physicians surveyed by Schiller did not perceive the dietitian as playing a key role in the decision-making process. King (1984) found the same results among renal physicians and dietitians 10 years later.

The level of dietitian responsibility in relation to physician responsibility is an essential component of the departmental plan. If the goal is more high-level decision making, clinical dietetic specialists may be needed to provide this care. Increased autonomy for dietitians may be expedited by initially achieving this autonomy for clinical dietetic specialists and then determining the appropriate role for the clinical dietitian. This goal of increased autonomy can be achieved through promotion of institutional changes and legislative reforms in licensure, health care financing, and regulatory codes.

OTHER HEALTH CARE TRENDS

The role of the physician is changing as the twenty-first century approaches. Two trends are occurring simultaneously: the physician market is becoming saturated, and more care is being delegated to physician extenders. The growth in the number of physicians is forcing physicians to expand the number of direct services provided by physicians and delegate less responsibility to other health professionals. Simultaneously, other forces are limiting the physician's role. Trust in the physician model is eroding, which is limiting the doctor's authority (Stuart 1981). Clients are better-educated consumers who weigh alternatives and want options in health care (Pellegrino 1983). Many health care decisions are shifting from the provider to the consumer, thereby changing the physician-patient relationship (Annison 1986).

The definition of health care itself is expanding. The incorporation of wellness into health care is projected to continue, with preventive medicine as an important component. "Well care" and "managed care" are replacing the classical medical model. Holistic concerns, related to the expanding knowledge of the connection between the mind and body, is altering medical care delivery (Annison 1986). Diagnoses based on noninvasive therapies are decreasing the use of hospitals for diagnostic workups.

Ethical dilemmas on the extent and amount of care to be provided are becoming the norm. Criteria for withholding care will be established in the coming decade. These criteria may include age, financial ability, likelihood of successful intervention, previous medical treatments, or other factors. The conflict between social responsibility and individual rights will surely lead to complex disagreements, confrontation, legislation, and litigation (Callahan 1987).

Geriatric health care must expand greatly to keep pace with demographic changes. Services for elderly adults can best be provided by allied health care personnel both from an economic standpoint and because these professionals have developed interpersonal skills that seem to best suit the needs of geriatric patients.

PLANNING OUTCOMES

Strategic planning provides a systematic method for innovative and opportunistic action. Outcomes may include creative ways of financing nutrition services, a plan to sell nutrient-specific meals to clients, the development of large-print instructional materials or new cooking techniques to meet the needs of the visually impaired aged, and discount meal purchases for outpatients. Negative trends in health care provide opportunities that await solutions. For example, the trend of an increased clinical dietitian turnover rate could possibly be altered by incentives based on length of employment. Effective planning requires constant watching, especially of successful competitors. What are they doing and how can we do it better? Would flex time better meet staffing needs? Would part-time or shared positions help solve staff shortages?

Clinical dietetic managers play a major role in strategic planning. They hold the key to progress in the delivery of nutritional care services. Through their ability to identify opportunities and develop bold new programs to address health care trends, the profession will move forward. Various strategies, skills, and techniques addressed in this book can be used to facilitate both personal satisfaction and advancement of dietetics into the next century.

REFERENCES

American Dietetic Association. 1971. Position paper on education for the profession of dietetics. *J. Am. Dietet. Assoc.* 59(4):372-73.

American Dietetic Association. 1972. *The Profession of dietetics: The report of the Study Commission on Dietetics.* Chicago: American Dietetic Association.

American Dietetic Association. 1985. *A new look at the profession of dietetics: A report of the 1984 Study Commission on dietetics.* Chicago: American Dietetic Association.

Annison, Michael H. 1986. It's bigger than the both of us. Health Care Forum (March–April):23-25.

Barber, Mary I. ed. 1959. *History of the American Dietetic Association.* Philadelphia: J.B. Lippincott Co.

Burling, Temple, Edith M. Lentz, and Robert N. Wilson. 1959. *The give and take in hospitals.* New York: G.P. Putman's Sons.

Callahan, D. 1987. Setting limits: *Medical goals in an aging society.* New York: Simmon and Schuster, Inc.

Cornish, Edward. 1977. *The study of the future: An introduction to the art and science of understanding and shaping tomorrow's world.* Bethesda, Md.: World Future Society.

Fink, Arlene et al. 1984. Consensus methods: Characteristics and guidelines for use. *Am. J. Public Health* 74(9):979-83.

Gaare, Judith, et al. 1990. Perceptions of clinical decision making by dietitians and physicians. *J. Am. Dietet. Assoc.* 90(1):54-58.

Gobberdiel, Linda. 1988. CNM—A five year retrospective. *Clin. Nutr. Manage.* 6(3):5.

Hallahan, Isabelle A. 1974. The American Dietetic Association—pacesetter for the profession. *J. Am. Dietet. Assoc.* 64(6):603-07.

Hoover, Loretta. 1983. Enhancing managerial effectiveness in dietetics. *J. Am. Dietet. Assoc.* 82(1):58-61.

Katz, Daniel, and Robert L. Kahn. 1978. *The social psychology of organizations.* 2d ed. New York: John Wiley and Sons, Inc.

King, Dorothy Gatt. 1984. Diet prescription decision autonomy and perceptions of legal responsibility of New York State end-stage renal-disease clinical dietitians. Ph.D.Diss., New York University.

MacEachern, Malcolm T. 1949. Advances in dietetics from the hospital viewpoint. *J. Am. Dietet. Assoc.* 25(6):494-99.

Parks, Sara C., and P.M. Kris-Etherton. 1982. Practitioners view dietetic roles of the 1980s. *J. Am. Dietet. Assoc.* 80(6):574-76.

Pellegrino, E.D. 1983. What is a profession? *J. Allied Health* 12(3):168-76.

Schiller, Mary Rosita, and Virginia Vivian. 1974. Role of the clinical dietitian. *J. Am. Dietet. Assoc.* 65(3):284-87.

Spangler, Alice A. 1974. Physicians' attitudes on dietitians' contributions to health care. *J. Am. Dietet. Assoc.* 65(6):646-50.

Standards of Practice for the profession of dietetics. 1985. *J. Am. Dietet. Assoc.* 85(6):723-26.

Stuart, G. W. 1981. How professionalized is nursing? *Image* 13(1):18-23.

U.S. Department of Labor, Bureau of Labor Statistics. 1990. *Occupational Outlook Handbook.* 1990-91 ed. Bulletin 2350:150-52.

United States Department of Labor, Manpower Administration. 1949. *Dictionary of Occupational Titles.* 2d ed. Vol. 2. Washington DC: US Government Printing Office, I, 202.

United States Department of Labor, Manpower Administration. 1977. *Dictionary of Occupational Titles.* 4th ed. Vol. 2. Washington DC: US Government Printing Office, I, 60–61.

SUGGESTED READINGS

Ad Hoc Committee on Specialization. 1990. *Report of the Ad Hoc Specialization Committee submitted to the 1990 Midyear House of Delegates of the American Dietetic Association.*

Cassell, JoAnne. 1990. *Carry the Flame: The History of the American Dietetic Association.* Chicago: The American Dietetic Association.

Cornish, Edward. 1985. Outlook '86—and beyond. *The Futurist* (December):51–60.

Lanz, Sally J. 1983. *Introduction to the profession of dietetics.* Philadelphia: Lea and Febiger.

Lowry, Stephen F. 1989. Nutrition support and the wave of the future. *Nutr. Clin. Pract.* 4(3):93–94.

New Jersey Hospital Association. 1985. *Health care now and beyond: Strategies for the future.* Princeton, N.J.: NJHA.

South, Mary Lou. 1981. The President's Page. *J. Am. Dietet. Assoc.* 79:66–67.

Waitley, Denis, and Robert Tucker. 1987. How to think like an innovator. *The Futurist* (May–June):9–15.

Ward, Lane. 1982. Eight steps to strategic planning for training managers. *Training/HDR* (November):22–25, 29.

Job Descriptions

Exhibit A-1 Clinical Dietitian

Job Title: Clinical Dietitian

Dept. Name: Clinical Dietetics

Prepared by: _____

Admin. approval: Director Food Service   Date: _____

Date of original or previous revision: _____

Personnel: _____ Date: _____

Exempt: _____   Non-exempt: _____

Reports to: Chief Clinical Dietitian

                 Title of Immediate Supervisor

MAIN FUNCTION (Summarize Responsibilities in 1–2 Sentences).

Provides optimum nutritional care to the patients through assessing nutritional needs; developing, implementing, and re-evaluating nutritional care plans; and educating patients and families

DUTIES AND RESPONSIBILITIES

Performs nutritional assessment on high-risk patients hospitalized over 48 hours to determine nutritional status and level of care needed

Develops and implements needed care plans based on established standards of practice for patients at high nutritional risk

Communicates pertinent nutritional data through established written record systems in established format

Provides follow-up nutritional assessments and updates care plans as needed

Collaborates in establishing standards of practice on nutritional care and in the development of educational material, clinical procedures, and clinical records

---

Exhibit A-1 continued

Participates in health team conferences and serves as the consultant on nutritional care conferences, including medical rounds, grand rounds, nutritional meetings, and food service meetings

Confers with members of the health care team about patient needs and problems

Individualizes patient meal patterns and menus to comply with the diet prescriptions and patient preferences in conjunction with the technician

Compiles and utilizes pertinent productivity and outcome data to assure provision of quality nutritional care

Supervises dietetic technicians and dietetic assistants assigned to floor to optimize nutritional care of all patients

Confers with dietary assistants and technicians on the status of patients

Enforces established policies and procedures of the department to ensure continuity in operations

Participates with Assistant Chief Clinical Dietitian in performance evaluation of dietary assistants

Interprets, evaluates, and utilizes pertinent current research related to nutritional care

Participates in workshops, seminars, and meetings to update nutritional knowledge

Participates in inter- and intradepartmental research protocols

Provides nutrition education/training/inservices to interns, students, and other professionals

Provides group education to patients when appropriate

Performs other related duties as required

KNOWLEDGE REQUIRED (Minimum education or equivalent experiences; licensure)

Must be a registered dietitian (RD)
(If RD Eligible, must submit proof of registration within 1 year of employment or services will be terminated.)

Source: Courtesy of Memorial Sloan-Kettering Cancer Center, New York, NY.

Exhibit A-2 Dietetic Technician

POSITION TITLE:	**DIETETIC TECHNICIAN**
FUNCTION:	Functions as a member of the nutritional team, obtains diet histories from patients, collects assessment data, assists patients with their menu selection according to diet prescription, provides dietetic in-

Exhibit A-2 continued

formation to assigned individuals in uncomplicated situations, calculates nutrient intakes, reports findings to dietitians, assists in the supervision of food service

REPORTS TO: Clinical dietetic manager

DUTIES: Assesses the nutritional needs of patients on regular diets and deemed at low nutritional risk based on established criteria. Monitors the status of the patient while hospitalized and evaluates effectiveness of nutritional intervention

Provides basic education to patients and families on nutritional principles, food selection and economics, and meal planning for patients on regular diets

Plans menus for patients on special diets based on established guidelines, individualizing menus as needed

Monitors food intake on patients through periodic meal rounds

Obtains diet histories and analyzes nutrient intakes from patients when assigned

Communicates appropriate dietary information in the medical chart and to the dietitians

Maintains Kardex of all patients and their diet prescriptions

Prepares, organizes and correlates with the dietary assistants the organization of menus and premeal service

Confers with clinical dietetic manager or dietitians on problems related to dietary service and distribution of food to assigned patients

Monitors the quality of care given by Dietary on the floors; includes distribution and collection of selective menus, proper distribution of trays, accurate reliable delivery of prescribed diets, collection of information concerning plate waste, and surveys of patient intake and opinions about the food

Collects data to aid in assessing quality of food service and nutritional care

Follows procedures given by dietitians to implement designed plans of dietetic service

Remains current in therapeutic dietetics

Attends ongoing inservice education of employees

Trains dietetic students in technical functions

Participates as part of the health care team

Performs other duties as requested by the clinical dietitian and clinical dietetic manager

Exhibit A-3 Dietary Assistant

Date effective: _____
Facility: _____

FOOD SERVICES

Functions as a member of the nutritional team providing services to Level 1 care clients, collecting quality assessment data, and supporting diet office duties

- Interviews clients to obtain diet histories, food preferences, and makes referrals to the dietetic technician or dietitian
- Conducts meal rounds
- Communicates appropriate dietary information in the medical chart and to dietitians
- Collects data to aid in assessing quality of food service and nutritional care
- Collects and modifies weekly menus from renal dialysis
- Surveys diet transmission accuracy
- Plans menus for clients on regular and modified diets, individualizing menu as specified
- Assists in collating weekly and monthly operating reports for the clinical unit
- Performs other duties as required

REQUIREMENTS

High school diploma or equivalent plus two (2) years experience as a Diet Assistant and successful completion of a certified dietetic assistant course within one (1) year of date of hire

Source: Courtesy of Memorial Sloan-Kettering Cancer Center, New York, NY.

Types of Evaluations

Exhibit B-1 Criteria-Based Performance Standards

Title: Clinical Dietitian   Code: 1001
Department: Food & Nutrition   Grade: 0
Section: Revision No: 0
Unit: Support Services
Reports To: Support Services

Summary: Assesses and intervenes clients for nutritional risk. Plans treatment and evaluates client's response and program.

	Weight	Perf. Level	Total Points Possible
1. Assesses and triages clients	____		8
a. Completes 100% of all nutritional assessments within 72 hours of admission as indicated by medical chart reviews		1 2	
b. Completes Nutritional Assessment Data Base within policy guidelines as indicated by medical chart reviews		1 2 3	
c. Triages clients into level of care required as indicated by medical chart reviews		1 2 3	

Comments: _____

	Weight	Perf. Level	Total Points Possible
2. Evaluates client's progress	____		9
a. Monitors patient's response to treatment and modifies intervention to maximize therapy as indicated by quality assessment reports		1 2 3	
b. Complies with follow-up standard of care as indicated by medical chart reviews		1 2 3	

Exhibit B-1 continued

   c. Completes all forms to support clinical data on
current patient status as indicated through tubefeeding records and quality assessment tracking   1 2 3

Comments: _____

	Weight	Perf. Level	Total Points Possible
3. Demonstrates current knowledge of trends and developments in the field	____		9
a. Demonstrates competent practices in nutritional care as indicated by medical chart reviews		1 2 3	
b. Provides one clinical update per year to coworkers		1 2 3	
c. Maintains 15 CEUs per year as indicated by ADA records		1 2 3	

Comments: _____

	Weight	Perf. Level	Total Points Possible
4. Counsels clients and significant others on nutritional requirements and therapy	____		6
a. Develops instructional materials to support patient learning as observed through education resources utilized		1 2 3	
b. Educates patients and significant others with skills to promote learning as indicated by post-test results		1 2 3	

Comments: _____

	Weight	Perf. Level	Total Points Possible
5. Maintains accurate nutritional care records	____		8
a. Maintains clear, accurate Kardex information on menu modifications as indicated by monthly Kardexes inspection		1 2 3	
b. Maintains current worksheet on all clients currently admitted as indicated by quarterly reviews		1 2 3	
c. Completes monthly reports with 100% accuracy and submits them by the third of the month as indicated by record review		1 2	

Exhibit B-1 continued

Comments: _____

_____

6. Provides nutrition education to employees and
   community groups and patient   _____   <u>3</u>

   a. Provides a minimum of 12 group teaching ses-
      sions to designated groups per year as indicated
      by monthly reports.   1 2 3

Comments: _____

_____

	Weight	Perf. Level	Total Points Possible
7. Promotes departmental goals and objectives	_____		6
a. Develops primary unit goals and reports prog-ress on a monthly basis as indicated by reports submitted to department director		1 2 3	
b. Participates in departmental projects to advance the marketing of nutrition to targeted groups as indicated by committee and goals accomplish-ments		1 2 3	

Comments: _____

_____

8. Serves as preceptor to dietetic interns   _____   9

   a. Provides interns with direction of rotation as
      monitored by the interns' progress reports   1 2 3
   b. Provides positive role model as indicated by pre-
      ceptor's evaluations   1 2 3
   c. Provides minimum of one didactic training ses-
      sion to interns per year as observed by super-
      visor   1 2 3

Comments: _____

_____

Suggested Terminology for Nutrition Services

The terminology presented here includes the detailed nomenclature presented in the 1984 *Nutrition Services Payment System* manual and the more general nomenclature developed for submission to Health Care Financing Administration (HCFA) for inclusion in Health Care Procedural Coding System (HCPCS). These terms are only *suggested* terms for describing nutrition services and should be modified as necessary to describe individual services rendered.

Nomenclature

COMPREHENSIVE: NUTRITION ASSESSMENT

*Nutrition assessment to define nutrition status

†Consultation and reassessment of nutrition status and disease management

†Comprehensive consultation with complex disease and diagnostic nutrition assessment

†Nutrient intake analysis: comprehensive

Definition of Service

Includes the recording/interpretation of anthropometric measurements, clinical and biochemical findings, nutrient and drug interactions, medical, psychological, socioeconomic and diet histories; and determination of nutrient requirements and/or outcome of nutrition intervention.

Reassessment of the patient/client with a specific disease or multiple diseases or requiring diagnostic nutrition assessment.

The comprehensive nutrition consultation with a new patient/client having a specific disease or multiple diseases or requiring diagnostic nutrition assessment. Includes assessment and recommendation for treatment program. For example:

Specific disease nutrition assessment: Evaluation of a specific health condition, including history and examination, review of medical management, evaluation of appropriate diagnostic tests and procedures, and recommendations for the adjustment of therapeutic management.

Multiple disease nutrition assessment: Evaluation of a patient/client with multiple system problems or a problem complicated with a new diagnosis or medical problem. It is necessary to obtain evaluation of pertinent history and diagnostic tests and procedures and to make recommendation as to appropriate therapeutic management.

Diagnostic nutrition assessment: Evaluation of a patient/client with protein and/or calorie malnutrition. This service requires a complete evaluation of medical data and recording of personal history, anthropometric evaluation, and results of appropriate diagnostic tests and procedures and may also include a limited physical examination. This service includes formulation of a nutrition diagnosis and recommendation of appropriate nutritional intervention.

Detailed calculation or extensive computerized nutrient/energy analysis for treatment or to confirm a diagnosis.

LIMITED: NUTRITION ASSESSMENT

* Nutrition assessment to define nutrition status

Includes the recording/interpretation of anthropometric measurements, clinical and biochemical findings, nutrient and drug interactions, medical, psychological, socioeconomic and diet histories; and determination of nutrient requirements and/or outcome of nutrition intervention.

† Nutrient intake analysis: limited

Calculation of selected nutrient/energy intake, such as carbohydrate, protein, fat, and kilocalories.

† Screening assessment to rule out malnutrition

Detection of nutritional depletion or risk of malnutrition, which may include patient/client's present height and weight, usual weight, history of appetite and food intake changes, serum albumin, CBC, or routinely available laboratory data. Includes recommendations for nutrition management to physicians.

† Initial screening with limited assessment

Initial visit to assess individual group member for eligibility in preparation for admittance to special programs.

COMPREHENSIVE: NUTRITION CONSULTATION

* Nutrition consultation

The recommendation of appropriate nutrition intervention based on the assessment of nutrition status.

† Consultation with initial history of current lifestyle, habits of nutrition, environment, exercise, and stress

Consultation with new patient/client to determine nutrition status through initial history of current lifestyle habits, including nutrition, environment, exercise, and stress. Includes recommendation of treatment program.

† Comprehensive consultation with complex disease and diagnostic nutrition assessment

The comprehensive nutrition consultation with a new patient/client having a specific disease or multiple diseases or requiring diagnostic nutrition assessment. Includes assessment and recommendation for treatment program. For example:

Specific disease nutrition assessment: Evaluation of a specific health condition, including history and examination, review of medical management, evaluation of appropriate diagnostic tests and procedures, and recommendations for the adjustment of therapeutic management.

Multiple disease nutrition assessment: Evaluation of a patient/client with multiple system problems or a problem complicated with a new diagnosis or medical problem. It is necessary to obtain evaluation of pertinent history and diagnostic tests and procedures and to make recommendations for appropriate therapeutic management.

Diagnostic nutrition assessment: Evaluation of a patient/client with protein and/or calorie malnutrition. This service requires a complete evaluation of medical data and recording of personal history, anthropometric evaluation, and results of appropriate diagnostic tests and procedures and may also include a limited physical examination. This service includes formulation of a nutrition diagnosis and recommendation of appropriate nutritional intervention.

LIMITED: NUTRITION CONSULTATION

*Nutrition consultation

The recommendation of appropriate nutrition intervention based on the assessment of nutrition status.

†Patient-related team conference

Participation on treatment team for the purpose of delineation, implementation, and evaluation of nutrition management.

†Follow-up evaluation

Limited instruction or guidance following initial visit.

†Crisis intervention/emergency phone consultation

Emergency phone consults of a critical nature with severe physiological or psychological ramifications.

COMPREHENSIVE: NUTRITION COUNSELING

*Nutrition counseling

The provision of advice and services to individuals and groups to meet goals of nutrition intervention for disease management and/or prevention.

†Behavioral/psychosocial counseling (individual, family, group)

Psychosocial counseling for an individual, family, or group, with emphasis on nutrition intervention; may include behavior modification. Analysis of reasons for behavior with psychological emphasis and determination of objectives for behavior change. This is an ongoing process.

†Structural health management (individual, group)

Structured health care program for an extended period of time for individuals with conditions such as diabetes, hypertension, post-MI, depression, or hypometabolic states. May include wellness and fitness program.

LIMITED: NUTRITION COUNSELING

*Nutrition counseling

The provision of advice and services to individuals and groups to meet goals of nutrition intervention for disease management and/or prevention.

†Behavioral/psychosocial counseling (individual, family, group)

Psychosocial counseling for an individual, family, or group, with emphasis on nutrition intervention; may include behavior modification. Analysis of reasons for behavior with psychological emphasis and determination of objectives for behavior change. This is an ongoing process.

UNLISTED NUTRITION SERVICE

†Prescription and formulation of enteral nutrition product

Determination of appropriate oral or tubefeeding formula to meet specific nutrient requirements. Requires calculation of specific formula composed of at least two components.

†Preparation and/or dispensing of proprietary supplements and defined formula diets

Preparation and/or dispensing of proprietary supplements and defined formula diets. Application may be provided by support personnel under the direct supervision of a registered dietitian.

†Dispensing pharmaceutical products and administration of supplies and equipment — Pharmaceutical product prescribed by physicians as part of the nutrition prescription. Documents product name, manufacturer, and dosage. Feeding tubes, bags, pumps, and so forth may be charged here.

†Special reports — Includes legal, workers' compensation, and insurance company inquiries. Appropriate fees may be charged for completion of the requested reports.

†Education materials — Publications, books, manuals, pamphlets, or menus charged at cost plus handling.

†Telephone conference — Provision of information to enhance program management.

†Miscellaneous

Note: Following terms are defined as:
Comprehensive: a level of service requiring in-depth data and evaluation for complex nutrition management.
Limited: a level of service requiring standard data and evaluation for uncomplicated nutrition management.
Home Visit: initial and/or follow-up visit conducted in the home of the patient/client.
Hospital Visit: initial and/or follow-up visit conducted in the hospital.
Office Visit: initial and/or follow-up visit conducted in the office of the dietitian, whether private or within a clinic, hospital, or physician's office.
* Terms submitted to Health Care Financing Administration (HCFA).
† Terms included in the 1984 *Nutrition Services Payment System* manual.

Source: © 1985, The American Dietetic Association. *NSPS: Nutrition Services Patient System Guidelines for Implementation.* Used by permission.

Nutrition-Related
ICD-9-CM Codes

CODES QUALIFYING AS A SUBSTANTIAL COMORBIDITY OR COMPLICATION

260   *Kwashiorkor:* nutritional edema with dyspigmentation of skin and hair.

261   *Nutritional marasmus:* nutritional atrophy, severe calorie deficiency, severe malnutrition NOS.*

262   *Other severe protein-calorie malnutrition:* malnutrition of third degree according to Gomez classification (weight for age <60% of standard), nutritional edema without mention of dyspigmentation of skin and hair.

263.0   *Malnutrition of moderate degree:* malnutrition of second degree according to Gomez classification (weight for age 60% to <75% of standard).

263.1   *Malnutrition of mild degree:*

*NOS = not otherwise specified.

malnutrition of first degree according to Gomez classification (weight for age 75% to <90% of standard).

263.2   *Arrested development following protein-calorie malnutrition:* nutritional dwarfism, physical retardation due to malnutrition.

263.8   *Other protein-calorie malnutrition.*

263.9   *Unspecified protein-calorie malnutrition:* dystrophy due to malnutrition, malnutrition (calorie) NOS. Excludes: nutritional deficiency NOS (269.9).

269.0   *Deficiency of vitamin K.* Excludes deficiency of coagulation factor due to vitamin K deficiency (286.7) and vitamin K deficiency of newborn (776.0).

276.0   *Hyperosmolality and/or hypernatremia:* sodium excess, sodium overload.

276.1   *Hypo-osmolality and/or hyponatremia:* sodium deficiency.

276.2   *Acidosis:* acidosis NOS, lactic, metabolic, respiratory. Excludes: diabetic acidosis (250.1).

276.3   *Alkalosis:* alkalosis NOS, metabolic, respiratory.

276.4   *Mixed acid-base balance disorder:* hypercapnia with mixed acid-base disorder.

276.5   *Volume depletion:* dehydration, depletion of volume of plasma or extracellular fluid, hypovolemia.

276.6   *Fluid overload:* fluid retention. Excludes: ascites (789.5), localized edema (782.3).

276.7   *Hyperpotassemia:* hyperkalemia, potassium excess, intoxication or overload.

276.8   *Hypopotassemia:* hypokalemia, potassium deficiency.

276.9   *Electrolyte and fluid disorder not elsewhere classified:* electrolyte imbalance, hypo- or hyperchloremia.

277.00 *Cystic fibrosis:* fibrocystic disease of pancreas, mucoviscidosis, without mention of meconium ileus.

277.01 *Cystic fibrosis:* with meconium ileus.

279.10 *Deficiency of cell-mediated immunity with predominant T cell defect, unspecified.*

279.3   *Unspecified immunity defect.*

279.9   *Unspecified disorder of immune mechanism.*

280.0   *Iron-deficiency anemia secondary to blood loss (chronic).* Excludes: acute posthemorrhagic anemia (285.1).

281.4   *Protein-deficiency anemia:* amino-acid-deficiency anemia.

281.8   *Anemia associated with other specified nutritional deficiency:* scorbutic anemia.

285.1   *Acute posthemorrhagic anemia:* anemia due to acute blood loss.

286.7   *Other and unspecified coagulation defects.*

305.00 *Alcohol abuse, unspecified.*

305.01 *Alcohol abuse, continuous.*

305.02 *Alcohol abuse, episodic.*

307.1   *Anorexia nervosa.*

425.7   *Nutritional and metabolic cardiomyopathy:* code also underlying disease as beriberi (265.0), amyloidosis (277.3), etc.

536.0   *Achlorhydria.*

536.1   *Acute dilation of stomach:* acute distention of stomach.

564.3   *Vomiting following gastrointestinal surgery:* vomiting (bilious) following gastrointestinal surgery.

579.3   *Other and nonspecified postsurgical nonabsorption:* hypoglycemia or malnutrition following gastrointestinal surgery.

CODES NOT QUALIFYING AS A SUBSTANTIAL COMORBIDITY OR COMPLICATION

536.2   *Persistent vomiting:* habit vomiting, uncontrollable vomiting.

783.0   *Anorexia.*

783.1   *Obesity.*

783.2   *Abnormal loss of weight.*

783.3   *Feeding difficulties or mismanagement:* elderly or infant.

783.4   *Lack of expected normal physiological development.* Failure to gain weight, failure to thrive, lack of growth, physical retardation, short stature.

783.5   *Polydipsia.*

783.9   *Other symptoms concerning nutrition, metabolism, and development.*

988   *Toxic effects of noxious substance eaten as food.*

990   *Effects of radiation, unspecified:* complication of radiation therapy.

994.2   *Effects of hunger:* deprivation of food, starvation.

994.3   *Effects of thirst:* deprivation of water.

Source: Reprinted with permission of Ross Laboratories, Columbus, Ohio 43216, from *The Cost Effectiveness of Nutrition Support,* © 1985 Ross Laboratories.

Index

A

Academic preparation. *See* Education
Accreditation. 29, 38
Acknowledgements (research projects),
  289
Action plans, 120
Activity coordination, 11
Adams, Simone O., 227
Administration, ethical issues and, 143
ADVANCE concept, management and,
  12–14, 62
Advance directives, 135–36
Advanced–level practice, 328–30
Advertising, 231
Age Discrimination Act, 88
Alford, Betty J., 217
Alldredge, Everett O., 217
Allen, Bruce H., 24
Ambulatory care, 244–48
American College of Surgeons, 322
American Diabetic Association, 323
American Dietetic Association, 17, 174,
  187, 231
  career advancement and, 328
  dietetic management and, 324, 325
  education and, 294, 299

ethics and, 132
founding of, 321
manual of, 267
professional activities and, 322
research and, 277
role delineation and, 45, 78, 163, 299
SOP of, 38
terminally ill patients and, 137
American Hospital Association, 308, 323
American Medical Association, 199
American Society of Clinical Nutrition, 39
American Society of Parenteral and
  Enteral Nutrition, 38–39, 250
Anderson, Gary R., 133
Anderson, Sara L., 134
Annison, Michael H., 331
Approved preprofessional practice
  program (AP4), 295
Arnold, Susan E., 250
Assessment (defined), 307. *See also*
  Evaluation
Assessment procedures (basic), 162
Audiocassettes, 213
Audit (defined), 307
Audits (quality assurance), 150–51, *152,
  156–57*
Austin, Nancy K., 62

Note: *Italicized* page numbers indicate entries found in figures, tables, or exhibits.

Autonomy, 131
Avard, D., 137

B

Baird, S. C., 48
Barber, Mary I., 321
Barsky, Arthur J., 31
Bartley, Katharine Curry, 143
Bassett, Laurence C., 62
Bell, Donna M., 242
Bell, Eunice, 109
Bell, Stacey J., 132
Beneficence, 131–32
Benefits of Nutritional Care, 177
Bennett, Addison C., 308, 309, 310
Bennis, Warren, 20
Bergstrom, Nancy, 284
Berryman-Fink, Cynthia, 262, 265
Berry, Michelle W., 277, 278, 280
Bezold, Clement, 30
Binder, Clifford, 30
Birge, Kistine R., 250
Blackburn, Sara A., 29
Blackley, Joanne, 94
Blanchard, Kenneth, 129, 141
Blomberg, Robert, 116
Boisaubin, Eugene, 134, 137
Bonner J. L., 48, 277
Brannon, Diane, 54
Brower, Terri H., 287
Brown, Montague, 30, 61
Budget, 7, 174
    financial management and, 185, 186,
        190–95
Bunjes, M, 126, 304
Bunting, Sheila, 133
Bureau of Vocational Information, 321
Burling, Temple, 323
Business letters, 269–70
Buzby, Karen, 181

C

Calbeck, Doris C., 97

Califano, Joseph A., 228
Callahan, D., 331
Calorie counts, computer use and, 201
Calvert, Susan, 53, 70. *See also* Finn,
    Susan Calvert
Canizaro, Vincent J., Jr., 293
Canter, D., 126, 304
Career advancement, 328–30
Career planning (professional
    development), 103
Case studies, ethical issues, 139–40, *141*
Census data, 207
Champagne, Francois, 308, 312
Chance, Helen C., 285
Change, 122–23, research utilization and,
    286
Charold, L., 278
Chernoff, Ronni, 142
Childress, James F., 137
Civil Rights Act, 88
Clemenhagan, Carol, 308, 312
Cleveland Metropolitan General Hospital,
    242
Clinical dietetic management
    ADVANCE concept and, 12–14
    defining, 3–4
    development of, 324
    directing, 9–11
    ethical issues and, 133–38
    evaluation and control and, 11
    function of, 8–11
    internal and external influence on
        departmental
            individual employees and,
                19–21
            labor relations and, 21
            unit organization and, 21–23
    institutional
        corporate culture and, 24
        financial expectations and, 25
        impact of, 23–24
        interdepartmental relationships and,
            26–27
        organizational growth phase and, 28
        patient mix and, 25–26

resource allocation and, 26
size and, 24
technological advances and, 24
management milieu diagram and,
31–32
overview of, 17–18
regulatory
hospital accreditation and, 29
legislation and, 29–30
prospective payment systems
and, 28–29
societal, 30–31
new trends and, 7
nutritional care and, 5–6
organizing, 8–9, 39, 40–47
physical resources and, 7
planning and, 8
scope of, 5–7
staff and, 6
styles of, 12, *13*
Clinical dietetic manager
advanced education (graduate studies)
and, 55
as change agent, 61
defined, 4
employment interview and, 86–89
ethical issues and, 138–43
experience (life and work) and,
54–55
external regulations and, 37–38
generic and specific standards of
practice and, 39–40
health promotion and, 229
Joint Commission and, 38
leadership and, 10, 24, 56, 61–62
management skills and, 56–63
mission statement and, 35–36
organizational design and, 40–47
organization of serivces and, 39
personal background and attributes
and, 51–56
problem solving and, 56–61
professional development and,
105, 109
professional organizations and, 38–39

research role of
changing current practices
(research utilization) and, 286
cost effectiveness and, 285–86
creating environment for, 279–80
daily practice and, 280–82
departmental research and, 284–85
developing projects for, 282–84
role requirements and, 278–79
roles and responsibilities of, 47–49
self-evaluation and, 56
self-perception and, 53–54
skills summary and, 62–63
strategic planning and, 331
Clinical nutrition care audits, 150–51, *152,
156–57*
Clinical Nutrition Management Group of
Greater New York, 70, 116
Clinical nutrition services evaluation.
See Nutrition services evaluation
Code of Ethics, 130. *See also* Ethical
issues
Codes
establishing policy and procedure and,
37–40
nutrition-related ICD-9-CM, 349–51
Collaboration. *See also* Team building
research and, 283–84, 289
teamwork and, 119, 122, 123
Communication, 297
diet and nutrition manuals and, 266–67
employee selection and, 86
interdepartmental, 26
medical records and, 272–74
meeting management and, 262–65
memos and letters and, 267–70
menus and, 271–72
oral, 261–62
policy and procedure manuals and,
265–66
public relations and, 231
reports and proposals and, 270–71
supervision and importance of, 10
Computers
administrative decisions and, 26

advantages of, 24
manuals and, 265
patient care process and, 71
patient population profiles and, 25
selection of, 201–207
Conklin, Martha T., 175, 177
Consumers, 31
Continuity of care concept, 6
Continuity of care programs
ambulatory care
establishing outpatient services
and, 245
reimbursement for, 245–48
setting for, 244–45
developing
advantages of proposed services
and, 254–55
competition and, 254
current services description and,
252–53
financial aspects of, 256
market analysis and, 253–54
marketing strategy and, 255
plan overview and, 252
structure of (managment and
organization), 255
timeline and, 255–56
discharge planning and, 237–44
Continuity of care programs
home care
benefits of, 248–49
home delivered meals and, 251
hospice care and, 251–52
nutrition support team and, 251
HMOs and 244, 248
Contractors (outside), 23
Control (defined), 307
Control of established nutrition service
standards. See Standards
Copyright ownership, 217–18
Cornish, Edward, 321
Corporate culture, 24
Cost-benefit analysis (CBA), 176–81, 185
Cost containment, 78, 80, 194
cost-benefit analysis and, 176–81

cost effectiveness of nutritional
support and, 181
expenditure goals and caps and,
174–75
patient education and, 210
staff needs justification and, 175–76
Cost effectiveness, 29, 181
evaluation and, 309, 312
Cost-effectiveness analysis (CEA),
177, 185
Cotner, C., 151
Cox, Barbara G., 210
Crissey, Janice, 97, 162
Crist, Mary Ann, 287
Cronewett, Linda R., 285
Cronin, Thomas E., 61
Crouch, Jean Baker, 288
Cruzan, case, 136
Cultural attitudes, 31
CUTS (cost containment acronym),
161–62

D

Data
computers and dietary census, 207
ownership of research, 284
quality assurance and, 149, 154–59
requests for research, 280
DATA (job function analysis), 78, 79
Deane, Barbara, 267
Decision-making capacity, 78
ethical issues and, 132–33
DeHoog, S., 161
Delegation, 123–24
Dellinger, Susan, 267
Delphi surveys, 287, 326–27
Denial of nutritional support, 134–35,
136–37
Departmental management
directing daily activities and, 9–11
employees and, 19–21
interdepartmental relationships and,
26–27
labor relations and, 21

needs assessment and, 109–10
productivity and, 168–74
research and, 284–85
systems identification and, 68–70
unit organization and, 21–23
Development. *See* Professional
development
Dewey, John, 293
Diagnosis, 331
Diagnostic-related groups (DRGs), 28, 29,
175, 176, 181
Dictionary of Occupational Titles,
322
Dietary census data, 207
Dietetic management. *See* Clinical dietetic
management
Dietetic manager. *See* Clinical dietetic
manager
Dietetic marketing. *See* Marketing plans
Dietetics
advanced-level practice and,
328–30
evolution of hospital, 323–25
historical overview of, 321–23
new trends in, 7
Dietitian (defining), 322
Diet manuals, 266–67
Directing of department's daily activities,
9–11
Discharge planning, 39
Discharge plans (for patient), 237–44
Discharging employee, 96
Disciplinary actions, 10–11, 143
performance discrepancies and,
94–96
Discrimination, employment and, 88
Disease prevention, 227–28
Documentation, 71, 134, *135,* 166, 272
Donabedian, Avedis, 308
Donato, Donna, 227
Doty, Donald, 62
Douglas, Priscilla D., 228
Dowling, Rebecca A., 151
Dresser, Rebecca, 134
Drucker, Peter, 3–4

E

East, Dorothy, 26
Edmundson, R. William, 176
Education. *See also* Nutrition education
advanced (training and graduate), 55
annual plan and continuing, 295
costs of continuing, 112–16
current challenges and continuing, 30
department needs and continuing, 109,
110
employee inservice training and, 21
enhancing skills and continuing, 11
ethical issues and, 143
job function concurrence and, 162–63
patient, 39
professional
components of
defined, 293
factors in today's, 293–94
maintaining certification and,
295–96
standards in, 294–95
framework for, 296–97
performance assessment, 299–304
teaching role and, 297–99
teaching of other health
professionals (by RD), 304
professional development and, 99–100,
110–12
specialization and, 48–49
Egan, Mary C., 230
Eisenberg, Joni G., 230
Elbert, Norbert F., 109
Emerson, Ralph Waldo, 293
Employee mix, 20. *See also* Staff
Enteral nutrition, 38–39
equipment, 200–201
formulas for, 198–99, *200*
Environmental assessment, 326
Equal Employment Opportunity
Commission (EEOC), 88
Equipment, 68. *See also* Computers
clinical dietetic manager and, 7
enteral nutrition, 200–201

Ethical issues
  ADA's code and, 38
  advance directives and, 135–36
  clinical applications and, 133–38
  clinical dietetic manager and, 138–43
  codes of ethics and, 130
  concepts in, 129–32
  decision-making and, 132–33
  economic considerations and, 137
  ethical power and, 141–42
  first-time managers and, 20–21
  hospital committees and, 137–38
  institutional operations and, 142–43
  morality and, 130–31
  nutritional support denial and, 134–35,
    136–37
  principles of, 131–32
  research and education and, 143,
    288–89
  trends in, 331
Evaluation. *See also* Nutrition services
  evaluation; Performance analysis
  (employee); Performance appraisal
  (employee); Performance
  assessment (professional
  education); Performance
  disrepancies (employee);
  Quality evaluations; self-evaluation
  defined, 308
  forms for types of, 339–41
Evaluation errors (performance appraisal),
  92
Experience (life and work), 54–55

F

Facilities, ethical issues and, 143
Fairchild, Michele, 181
Fargen, D., 54
Fee-for-service (financial management
  analysis), 187–90
Feitelson, Marion, 150
Financial analysis (continuing care), 256
Financial expectations, 25
Financial management

  budget and, 185, 186, 190–95
  evaluating cost of services and, 190
  fee-for-service and, 187–90
  financial plan as important dietetic
    service tool, 185–87
Fink, Arlene, 328
Finn, Susan Calvert, 53, 62
Firing a subordinate, 96
Flow charts, 71
Foltz, Mary Beth, 22
Food service, 22, 323
  budget and, 186
  ethical issues and, 142
  evaluation and, 310
  management review and, 308
  relationship with, 36
Ford, Margaret, 207
Formulas (enteral), 198–99, *200*
Freeman, Howard E., 313
Friedrich, Otto, 136
Frongillo, Edward A., 251
Fry, Edward, 217

G

Gaare, Judith, 330
Gaffney, Joan T., 249
Geriatric health care, 331
Gibbs, Nancy, 31
Glantz, Leonard H., 134
Glesnes-Anderson, Valerie A., 133
Goals
  mission statement and, 35–36
  personal career, 54–55
Goddard, Robert, 138
Gobberdiel, Linda, 325
Goodhue, Phyllis J., 249
Grady, Ann P., 278
Greenhouse, Linda, 136
Green, Karen, 227
Green, Richard A., 134
Grieco, Anthony J., 248
Groner, Pat N., 62
Gross, Neal, 40
Group dynamics, 21

Gussler, Judith D., 53

H

Hallahan, Isabelle A., 321
Harger, Virginia P., 26
Harrington, K., 48
Harris, Louis, 20
Hartshorn, Jeanette, 250
Health maintenance organizations
 (HMOs), 244, 248
Health Objectives for the Nation
 (Sorenson, Kavel, and Stephenson), 228
Health promotion
 defining, 228–29
 dietitian and, 229
Healthy People (U. S. Health and Human
 Services, 1979), 228
Hendricks, Suzanne, 278
Hergert, L., 122
Hess, Mary Abbott, 217
Hestwood, Thomas M., 265
Hickman, Susan P., 29
Hinshaw, Ada Sue, 280, 285
Hinton, Agnes W., 248, 251
Holistic care, 331
Home care, 248–52
Home-delivered meals, 251
Hoover, Loretta, 324
Hospice care, 251–52
Hospital dietetics (evolution of), 323–25.
 See also Dietetics
Hospital ethics committees, 137–38, 140
Hopital nutrition service units,
 organizational framework for, 5–6
Hospital Research and Development
 Institute, 62
Hutchins, E. D., 48
Huyck, Norma, 168, 181, 297

I

Indianapolis Veterans Hospital, 250
Information analysis (performance
 appraisal), 91–92

Informed consent, 131
Innovation, 122
Inservice programs, 109, 110, *111*
Institutional management influences
 corporate culture and, 24
 financial expectations and, 25
 impact of, 23–24
 interdepartmental relationships and,
 26–27
 organizational growth phase and, 28
 patient mix and, 25–26
 resource allocation and, 26
 size and, 24
 technological advances and, 24
Interdepartmental relationships, 26–27
International Committee of Medical
 Journal Editors, 289
Interview (personnel), 86–89
 ethical issues and, 142
Interviews (patient education), 210, 211

J

Jago, leadership analysis and, 61
Jargon, 272
Jasmund, Joanne M., 150
Job analysis, 70
 level of performance and, 78
Job applicant interview, 86–89
Job descriptions, 9
 clinical manager, 51, *52–53*
 form for, 335–38
 performance appraisal and, 90–91
 role delineation and, 47
 self-evaluation and, 56
Job function, educational background
 concurrance and, 162–63
Job satisfaction, 86, 97
Jont Commission on Accreditation of
 Healthcare Organizations
 accreditations and, 29, 38
 monitoring and, 308, 312
 quality assurance and, 149, 152
Jolowsky, Christine M., 199
Jones, M. G., 48, 277

Journal of the American Dietetic Association, 295
Journal clubs, 110, *113, 114*
  research and, 286
Journal reviews, 110, *114–15*

K

Kahn, Robert L., 324
Kane, Michael, 45, 78
Kardex system, 71
Katz, Daniel, 324
Kaufman, Mildred, 230
Kellerman, Barbara, 62
Kettering, Charles, 321
King, Dorothy-Gatt, 330
Kositsky, Ann M., 287
Koteski, Dorothy R., 249
Kotler, Philip, 230
Kris-Etherton, Penny, 48, 324

L

Labor relations, 21
Laws, 29–30
  ethics and, 132, 142
Leadership, 10, 24, 56, 61–62, 104, 124–26
LeBouef, Michael, 54
Legal issues
  ethics and, 132
  job applicant interview and, 88
  medical records and, 272
Legislation, 29–30
Length of stay (LOS), 29
  average (ALOS), 181
Lenz, Elizabeth R., 284, 285
Letters, 269–70
Level of performance analysis. *See* Performance analysis (employee)
Levey, Samuel, 307
Lewandowski, Linda A., 287
Licensure, role delineation and, 47
Lifestyle, illness and, 227, 228, 229
Life and work experience, 54–55

Lindeman, Carol A., 287
Lintzenich, Joanne, 149
Living wills, 136
Loacker Georgine, 299
Loomba, N. Paul, 307
Loucks-Horsley, S., 122
Luce, John M., 132
Lutton, Sarah E., 6
Lynn, Joanne, 137

M

McCabe, Beverly, J., 211, 217
McConnell, Charles R., 269
McCool, Barbara P., 61
McCormick, E. J., 78
McEachern, Alexander, 40
McEachern, Malcolm T., 26, 323
McEwan, Celine W., 161
McInerny, William, 130
McKinney, Shortie, 249
McLeod, Don, 136
McManis, Gerald L., 30
McMillin, Bonnie A., 150
McNamara, Patricia, 168
MacStravic, Robin Scott, 231
Magee, J. F., 94
Major, Victoria H., 133
"Making Your Reports More Meaningful" (Roswell), 270
Malloy, Cathrine, 250
Malnutrition, 181
Management. *See* Clinical dietetic management
Management milieu diagram, 31–32
Management review, 308
Management skills
  change and, 61
  leadership and, 10, 24, 56, 61–62
  problem solving, 56–61
Manager. *See* Clinical dietetic manager
Manuals
  diet and nutrition, 266–67
  policy and procedure, 9, 265–66

Marketing analysis (continuing care),
253–54, 255
Marketing plans
analysis of, 230–31, *231–34*
defined, 229–30
publicizing the department, 231
Marram, Gwen, 286
Marris, P., 122
Martin, Deborah A., 116
Matejski, Myrtle, 131
Maxwell, Douglas R., 250
Mayo Clinic Diet Manual, 267
May, William W., 137
Meals delivered to home, 251
Media (patient education), 213–14
Medicaid, 249
Medical records, 272–74
Medicare, 28, 249
Meetings (management of), 262–65
Memorial Sloan-Kettering Cancer Center,
71
Memos, 267–69
Mentoring, 126, 304
Menus, 271–72
Messersmith, Ann, 161
Metzger, Norman, 62
Mishkin, Barbara, 135, 136
Mission statement, 35–36
Monitoring, 308
Moody, Debra L., 7, 230
Morale, 11, 21
Morality, 130–31
Motivation (employee), 20, 86, 94
Muller, Andreas, 54
Munn, Harry E., Jr., 20
Murray, Nancy, 29

N

Nanus, Burt, 20
Nauright, Lynda, 92
Nestle, Marion, 48
Networking, 119
Neville, Janice, 142
Newsletters, 218

1990s Objectives for the Nation, 228
Noland, Marion S., 166
Nominal group strategy, 327–28
Nordstrom, Richard D., 24
Nutritional care mix, 40
Nutritional support denial, 134–35, 136–37
Nutrition care audits, 150–51, *152, 156–57*
Nutrition counseling, 26, 29
Nutrition education, 248. *See also*
Education
development of
approvals and, 214
assessing needs and, 210–22
evaluation and, 214–16
material selection and, 212–14
priority setting and budget
decisions and, 211–12
timelines and, 214
focus of, 209
nutrition service organization
framework and, 6
patient and, 39
as career goal, 55
printed material preparation and,
216–18
visuals development and, 218–24
Nutrition manuals, 266–67
Nutrition rounds, 110, *115*
Nutrition services evaluation
benefits from, 309–10
defining terms used in, 307–308,
343–48
planning and, 310–11
process of (steps in), 312–19
quality assurance and, 311–12
value and thrust of, 308–309
Nutrition services management. *See*
Clinical dietetic management
Nutrition service personnal. *See* Staff

O

Oberst, Marilyn T., 278
O'Donnell, Michael P., 229
Orentlicher, David, 135

Organization design, 40–47
    staff needs and, 67–68
Organizational growth phase, 28
Organizing, 8–9
Orientation, 89
Ostling, Richard N., 133
O'Sullivan Maillet, Julie, 22, 48, 272
Ott, Dana B., 251
Outreach programs, 29
Outside contractors, 23
Owen, Anita L., 30

P

Palmisano, Donald, 134
Parks, Sara C., 7, 48, 230, 324
Partlow, Charles G., 116
Patient care levels analysis, 79–83
Patient care process, 70–77
Patient-dietitian time ratio, 70
Patient food service, 22. *See also* Food
    Services
    relationship with, 36
Patient mix, 25–26
Patient nutrition education. *See* Nutrition
    education
Patient services, 39
    staffing needs and, 77
Peale, Norman Vincent, 129, 141
Pellegrino, E. D., 331
PEOPLE (job function analysis), 78, 79
Performance analysis (employee), 78–79
Performance appraisal (employee), 89–96
Performance assessment (professional
    education), 299–304
Performance discrepancies (employee), 94
Permissions
    research project acknowledgements
        and, 289
    for use of published printed materials,
        217–18
Personal background and attributes
    (manager)
    life and work experience and, 54–55
    self-perception and, 53–54

successful career and, 51–53
Personnel. *See* Staff
Personnel interview, 86–89
    ethical issues and, 142
Petroglia, Maria, 61
Physical facilities, ethical issues and, 143
Physical resources, clinical dietetic
    management and, 7
Physicians, 22, 330
Pictographs, 220
Plan, Intervention, Evaluation (PIE)
    system (progress notes), 272
Planning
    evaluation and, 310–11
    organizational, 67–68
    strategic, 321, 325–28
    outcomes and, 331
Policy and procedure manual, 9
    communication and, 265–66
Poster sessions, 218, *219*
The Power of Ethical Management
    (Blanchard and Peale), 129, 141
Pownall, Mark, 137
Prevention, 227–28
Printed materials (patient education),
    216–18
Problem solving, 56–61, 119–20
Procedure defined, 37
Productivity
    components of, 161–62
    departmental, 168–74
    educational background and job
        function congruence and, 162–63
    fee-for-service and productive time
        and, 187
    time utilization review and, 163–72
Productivity studies, 80
Professional development
    career planning and, 103
    clinical dietetic manager and, 105
    continuing education and, 99–100,
        110–16
    patterns of, 101–105
    purpose of, 100–101
    role models and, 103

staff development needs assessment
  departmental, 109–10
  for individuals, 105–106
  terms associated with, 99, *100*
Professional organizations, 38–39, 113–16.
  See also American Dietetic Association
Program planning, evaluation and, 310–11
  See also Planning
Proposals, 270–71
Prospective payment systems, 28–29, 175
Protocol defined, 37
Public relations, 231

Q

Quality assurance
  audits and, 150–51, *152, 156–57*
  defining, 49
  evaluation and, 311–12
  problem identification and, 149
  process of, 152–60
  productivity and, 174
  quality indicators and, 150
Quality evaluations, 92–94
Questionnaires (patient education), 210–11
Quinn, Eileen, 199

R

Raatz, Susan, 199
Raygor, Alton, 217
Referral, 39, 237, 242–44
Regulations
  codes and standards, 37–40
  continuing case program and, 254
  hospital accreditation and, 29
  legislation and, 29–30
  prospective payment systems and,
    28–29
Rehabilitation Act, 88
Reilly, James J., 29
Reimbursement
  continuity of care and, 245–48
  home care and, 249, 251
  job descriptions and, 47

malnutrition and, 181
  prospective payment and, 28–29, 175
Religious attitudes, 31
Reports, 270–71
Research, 7, 24
  audits as quality assurance, 150–51,
    152, 156–57
  as "backbone" of profession, 277–78
  current status of dietetic, 277
  dietetic management and, 278–86
  ethical issues and, 143, 288–89
  nutritional care and LOS and, 29
  resources for, 288
  topics for clinical, 286–88
Resource allocation, 26
Responsibility
  delineation of, 123
  physician-dietitian, 330
  power sharing and, 124
Retrospective studies, 155
Revenue generation, 24, 29, 177
  ethics and 142–43
Rinke, Wolf J., 55, 277, 278, 280
Rizzuto, Carmela, 116
Robinson, Georgia, 29
Role delineation, 40–47, 78, 163, 299
Role models, 103
Rose, James, 280
Rosoff, Arnold, 132
Rossi, Peter H., 313
Ross Laboratories, 119, 126, 162
Roswell, C. G., 270
Ryan, Alan S., 22, 53

S

Salaries, 53–54, 187, 190, *192,* 194
Sandrick, J. G., 48
Sanger, Monica T., 109
Scenario generation, 327
Schaffarzick, Ralph W., 197, 198
Schantz, Donna, 287
Schiller, M. Rosita, 53, 143, 277, 284, 288,
  298, 330
Shuster, Karolyn, 62

Schwartz, Denise, 48
Screening data evaluation, 71
Screening procedures, 162
Screening tests, health programs and,
    227–28
Self-evaluation, 56, *57–60*
Self-perception, 53–54
Services
    evaluating cost of, 190
    terminology for, 174
Sharp, Marsha, 278
Sheridan, John F., 70
Shortliffe, Edward, 201
Shovic, Anne C., 244
Siegrist, Linda M., 272
Signore, Juliette, 267
Singer, Gloria R., 249
Skipper, Annalynn, 262, 272
Slide presentations, 213, 220–24
Sloan-Kettering Cancer Center, 71
Smelter, Carolyn H., 280
Smith, Alice, 29
Smitherman, Alice L., 277
Smith, Howard, 109
Smith, Phillip, 29
Smith, Suzanne B., 217
Societal management influences
    consumers and, 31
    megatrends and trends in health care
        and, 30
Society for Nutrition Education, 231
Society for the Right to Die, 136
Sorenson, Ann W., 228
Sovie, Margaret, 101
Space needs, 7
Spangler, Alice A., 330
Spears, Marian C., 142
Specialization, 48–49
Spencer, Robin, 133
Sprung, Charles L., 136
Staff. *See also* Team building
    clinical dietetic management and, 6
    cost containment and, 78
    decision-making capacity and, 78
    departmental influences and, 19–23

determining needs of
    organizational plans and, 67–68
    system identification and, 68–70
    development of, 96
    health promotion program and, 231
    job candidate interivew and, 86–89
    as "knowledge workers," 3–4
    level of performance analysis and,
        78–79
    organizational design and, 40
    organizing function of management
        and, 9
    orientation and, 89
    patient care level analysis and, 79–83
    patient care process and, 70–77
    performance appraisal and, 89–96
    power sharing and, 124
    retention of, 97–98
    role delineation and, 40–47
    selection of, 85–89
    services to patients and, 77
Staffing needs justification (cost
    containment), 175–76
Standards
    dietetic practice and 322–23
    establishing policy and procedures and,
        37–40
    evaluation and control and, 11
    management review and 308
    research and, 278
Steinbaugh, M., 270
Steinberg, Ruth, 166
Stetler, Cheryl, 286
"Sticker notes," 71–77
Stitt, Kathleen R., 48, 277
Stokes, Judy, 175
Stone, P. K., 97
Strategic planning. *See* Planning
Strong, Carson, 136
Stuart, G. W., 331
Sullivan, C., 124
Supervision (directing), 9–11
Surveys (patient education), 210–11
Systems identification (departmental),
    68–70

T

Teaching. *See also* Education
  of dietitians, 297–99
  of health professionals, 304
Team building. *See also* Staff
  action plans and, 120
  change and innovation and, 122–23
  collaboration and networking and, 119
  delegation and, 123–24
  leadership and, 124–26
  mentoring and, 126
  problem solving and, 119–20
  responsibilities and rewards and, 123
Technology. *See also* Computers
  advances in, 24, 197
  assessment of, 198
  enteral nutrition and, 198–201
  use of appropriate, 197
Television, 207
Terminally ill, 131, 135, 137
Termination, 96
THINGS (job function analysis), 78, 79
Thomasma, David, 131
Thompson, John D., 28
Time studies, 80, 82
Time utilization review, 163–68
Touger-Decker, Riva, 166
Training (defined), 293
Trend analysis, 326
Trends
  dietetic new, 7
  in health care, 30, 330–31
  megatrends, 30
Tubefeeding. *See* Enteral nutrition
Turnover, 9, 21

U

Unions, 21, 131
  team building and, 120
Unit organization (departmental), 21–23

V

Vaden, Allene, 142
Vance, Connie N., 126
Veatch, Robert, 137
Vegetative states, 136, 137
Vendors, ethics and, 142
Ventura, Marlene R., 287
Verbal communication, 261–62. *See also*
  Communication
Videotapes, 213
Vitali, James, 54
Vivian, Virginia, 330

W

Wagstaff, Margene A., 298
Waligora-Serfin, Barbara, 287
Wallis, Claudia, 136
Walters, Farah M., 242
Walters, Le Roy, 137
Webb, Adele, 133
Wegman, Judith A., 248
Wellness, 228
*Worksite Nutrition: A Decision-Making
  Guide,* 231
"Writing Technical Reports" (Steinbaugh),
  270
Wyse, Bonita W., 277, 287

About the Authors

M. Rosita Schiller, RSM, PhD, RD, LD, is Professor and Director of the Medical Dietetics Division, School of Allied Medical Professions in the College of Medicine, the Ohio State University in Columbus, Ohio. Previously, Dr. Schiller was director of the Career Mobility Program in Dietetics at Mercy College of Detroit. She spent 6 years in dietetic practice and management at Manistee Community Hospital, Manistee, Michigan and at St. Lawrence Hospital, Lansing, Michigan.

Dr. Schiller earned her PhD in Foods and Nutrition at Ohio State and her MA in Institutional Management from Michigan State University in East Lansing. She completed her undergraduate work at Mercy College in Detroit, Michigan and received her dietetic internship at Henry Ford Hospital, also in Detroit.

Dr. Schiller is known among dietetic circles for her work in role delineation, quality practice, leadership, and dietetic education. She has written numerous articles and facilitated several workshops on these subjects in the United States, Germany, and South Africa. Dr. Schiller is active in the American Dietetic Association, the American Society for Enteral and Parenteral Nutrition, and the American Society for Allied Health Professions. She is a former member and chair of the ADA Commission on Accreditation and is an ADA delegate from Ohio.

Judith A. Gilbride, PhD, RD, is associate professor in the Department of Nutrition, Food, and Hotel Management, New York University. She is director of the undergraduate and graduate nutrition programs and oversees the supervised practice program. Before entering the education arena, Dr. Gilbride was a dietitian in the clinical research center at Mount Sinai Hospital in New York City.

Dr. Gilbride received her PhD in nutrition and her MA in Food, Nutrition and Dietetics at New York University. She received her BS in Dietetics and Home Economics Education at Framingham State College. She completed her dietetic internship at Bronx Veteran Administration Medical Center.

Dr. Gilbride has been involved in dietetic association activities at the local, state, and national level, including being a delegate from New York; a member of the 1989 Role Delineation Study, the Commission on Dietetic Registration, and the Council on Education; and president of the Greater New York Dietetic Association. She is also active with the American Heart Association. She has published articles on geriatric nutrition and dietitian roles in long-term care and is an author of *Nutrition Assessment: A Comprehensive Guide for Planning Intervention* with Margaret Simko and Catherine Cowell. Dr. Gilbride recently became Associate Editor of *Topics in Clinical Nutrition.*

Julie O'Sullivan Maillet, PhD, RD, is associate professor and director of the dietetic internship at the University of Medicine and Dentistry of New Jersey (UMDNJ): School of Health Related Professions. She is also chairman of the Department of Primary Care. Before entering the education arena, Dr. O'Sullivan Maillet was a clinical dietetic manager at Memorial Sloan-Kettering Cancer Center, New York City and at UMDNJ: University Hospital, Newark, for a total of 8 years.

Dr. O'Sullivan Maillet received her PhD in nutrition, her MA in Nutrition and Higher Education, and her BS in Home Economics and Nutrition at New York University. She completed her dietetic internship at UMDNJ.

Dr. O'Sullivan Maillet has been involved in dietetic association activities at the local, state, and national level, including being a member of the Commission on Dietetic Registration, delegate from New Jersey, a member of the Advanced Level Practice Committee, a geographic area representative for Council on Education, chairman of Dietetians in Nutrition Support in the mid-1980s, state president for New Jersey, and state legislative chairman. She has published articles and book chapters on ethics, cancer, surgery, and dietitians' responsibility in decision making.